BLACK AND GREEN REVIEW
NO 3, SPRING 2016

Photo by York

BLACK AND GREEN REVIEW
NO 3, SPRING 2016

CONTENTS

Cover photo by Sofia Yu.
Layout and design by KT.
Printed in Canada on recycled paper.

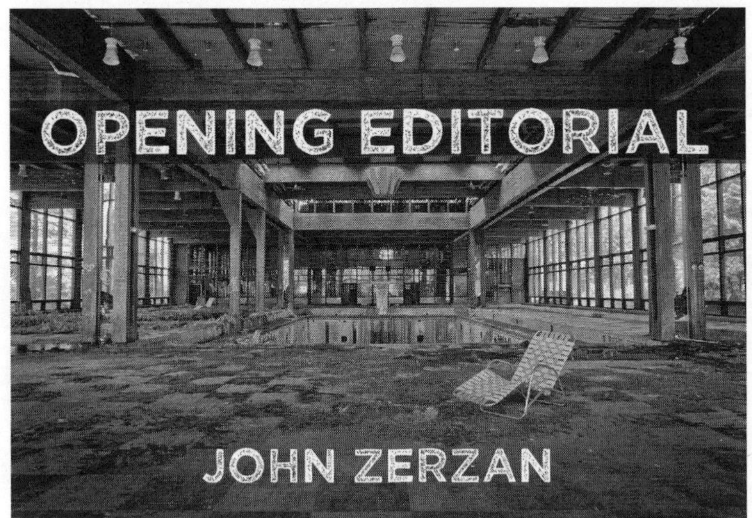

Inaugurated only last year, the focus of *BAGR* seems already in need of adjustment. Kevin Tucker's "Opening Editorial" announced that the *Review* would emphasize the promotion of critique and discussion within the anarchist milieu. That milieu, sadly enough, now appears undeserving of much attention.

A few years back, around Occupy time, 2011-2012, various voices proclaimed the ascendancy of anarchism. Its time has come, now is the opening to anarchism, etc. This has not blossomed into anything, and Occupy is one place to explore this failure.

The spontaneous outburst of Occupy energy was aimed at the excesses of capitalism. Even when militant, which was rare, it only amounted to more leftism. Occupy Oakland was its high point and anarchists were quite active there, but, fatally it seems, failed to add content to the Occupy energy. Supposedly post-Left and even anti-civilization, Bay Area anarchists apparently provided no voices along these lines.

A potential turning point of Occupy would have been, for starters, to rechristen it De-Occupy. But that would have constituted an actual turn away from the Left, in favor of waking up to the indigenous dimension, and how very much could be found there. Anarchists largely voted with the (rest of) the Left to reject such a proposed name change, having been easily fronted off by a few identity politics thugs who wanted to be in charge of the De-Occupy (or "De-Colonize") position. Our post-Left anarchists gave no voice to that outlook overall and when Occupy fizzled out were left with the hangover of their non-presence. Even now, it seems, little insight and even less energy can be seen. A persisting postmodern haze prevails, where egoists and nihilists compete to now even deny that reality is knowable. How this is anarchist at all escapes me. It more resembles the insular scenes of cynical hipsters, offering no analysis, no inspiration.

The very ambitious To Change Everything tour in fall 2015 was a Crimethinc. production, involving speakers from various continents. Civilization, domestication, mass society, industrialism, and other institutions foundational to our immiseration and the systematic environmental devastation were never mentioned.

On the other hand, there certainly are those who confront the nature of things, how we got here. And put such concerns into practice, such as anarchists in British Columbia and Arizona who've striven to be "accomplices not allies" to Native people whose ties to the land have not been broken after all they've had to endure, who still resist. The DOA (Dine-O'odham-Anarchist) black bloc, Phoenix 2010, was one instance among many of collaboration in Arizona. Others find a helpful challenge in anarcho-primitivist ideas in lots of places, a phenomenon that seems to be steadily gaining ground. An indirect testimony along these lines is the *Black Seed* zine, which feels the need to call itself the successor to *Green Anarchy*, even though its overall agenda is egoist-nihilist-postmodern.

Many things are at a low ebb these days and we don't have a real clear picture of where the anarchist milieu is at. It is clear that everything's at stake and that we are not interested in in-group parlor games. Anarchy seemed promising pretty recently, but lately too much of it has almost no bearing on what is going down, little interest in that, and not much relevant to offer. The conversation about technology, for example, is apparently ignored by anarchism. We are anarchists and in no way are we shutting the door on anarchists. But a mammoth challenge faces us all, so we haven't time to waste.

Black and Green Review is a publication of Black and Green Press.
Editors: Kevin Tucker, John Zerzan, Evan Cestari, Yank, Cliff Hayes, Ian Smith, and Lilia.

Black and Green Review
PO Box 832
Ephrata, PA 17522
blackandgreenreview@gmail.com
http://www.blackandgreenreview.org

ESSAYS

Bison. Photo by Yank.

Bison. Photo by Four Legged Human.

> *I wondered: how free were we if we'd become so dependent on the comforts produced by industry that we couldn't do without them? How free was I, that the first thing I wanted and had been craving for weeks was a sweet and fizzy caramel-colored beverage that came in a bottle with a scarlet label and passed itself off as the Real Thing? May the Arrow People never come to know it. As long as they had streams unsullied by mercury and sprawling woodlands rich with animals, they could remain beyond our reach, beyond the swirling vortex of consumer society and the machinery that manufactures our wants, creates our needs....May they never come to know the squalor of their brethren...who have been sucked in, then spat out and left to wander dusty frontier streets or the hopeless, crack-infested subdivisions on the rez, filthy and destitute, the objects of scorn and derision. What they had could never be measured in dollars...they could never be adequately compensated if they were to ever lose their freedom. The Unconquered*[1]

A Middle Finger Extended Stiff and Pointed at the Civilized Masses

The wind roars ferociously. Cold rain pelts down. The walls shake. Caribou sheds stacked along the outside wall collapse in a crash. A piece of whale baleen, tacked to the door, shoots across the sky and into the adjacent brush, like a giant leaf, dark black foliage. The stack of spruce poles leaning up against an old tree, the ones I use for a hide stretching rack, fall over. A fish spear propped up against the other wall lands with a thud, its prongs impaling the dirt. "Good thing I decided not to go fishing tonight", I tell myself.

The phone rings. "You should go running" she says. "You've got to run up the mountain, it doesn't work if it's flat".

"Why? It's too windy and did you see how hard it's raining?"

"When it rains hard and the wind blows it only makes me want to run more"

For the last several months she's been sleeping on a hard floor. She says it's better for her bones, her muscles, her blood.

She lives on a mountain. She stays there, almost always. A part of that mountain. Sometimes I try to call her at night and there will be no answer. "Where were you"? I ask. "Outside looking at the sky". She'd rather be out even when the temperatures drop below zero than inside under artificial light. "I love being out in the dark" she says. Sometimes she stays out all night, under the stars, with Aurora as her light. She is going feral.

A few years ago, when I was living in a cabin alone, the spirits put one of my arrows through the heart of a moose – a magic Osage bow. I take no responsibility other than some idea of rewilding I had by which my wanderings brought me the gift. But a man without community alone with a moose brought despair, the loneliest I've ever been. Now when my wanderings gift me flesh, fur, fat, bones I share. Wildness is sharing rather than hoarding.

I bring her something. She tells me there is nothing she would rather do than carefully dissect a wild being – a feral connection to her ancient woman genes. When I kill I find myself thinking of her, bringing her the meat, the heart, the bones, the skin. I brought her a caribou. She tried to resist. Perhaps because she thought acceptance would mean a contract, an obligation, so used to men trying to manipulate her in the past she was afraid to trust. But I had to share, my spirit, my wildness urges to me to give what I hunt to a strong hearted woman and to others. None of this matters without others. We hung the caribou legs in a tree on the side of her mountain…

One late October I brought her a bear – fat from a fall spent high in the mountains living on blueberries – brown fur, with a tongue dyed blue. She rendered piles of bear fat that we trimmed and fleshed from the skin. We made medicine. Some of the old people say that a woman should never look at a bear, let alone use her knife to cut into a bear's flesh. I knew it would be powerful medicine but my path to wildness and her feral spirit threw caution aside. We are so far domesticated and wanted to be within wildness so bad, we took the risk. We wanted to make a bearskin robe. She wanted to skin out the skull from the bear, but her knife slipped on the skull. Resistance - a protest from the bear spirit? Or a gift? A lesson? "I think I'm going to faint" she said softly as she clutched her finger and the blood dripped.

"Oh Fuck" I let slip, because it looked bad. "I think it's really deep" she said. Her middle finger cut to the bone, barely hanging on. "I need you to stitch it for me". "I don't think I can" I replied, "I'm taking you to the hospital". "No". She hates the system, industry, synthetic places and synthetic drugs. She desperately does not want to leave her mountain. But I could not do it. Could not stomach sewing up her raw skin with a sewing needle and thread. She tried her best to insist. I insisted we drive to civilization, an emergency room door on a Saturday night. Victims of alcohol related accidents from the city streets and one woman there because of her being overruled by the spirit of the skull of a bear. The doctors sewed her up and gave her some drugs. Severed tendons and heavy nerve damage was the diagnosis. The function of the finger may never return they told her. For the last year sweet bear fat has been one of her staple foods, and everywhere she goes her middle finger has been stuck in one place; elongated, unbendable, and straight…

The Process of Hominid Domestication

We stopped to visit some ruins of the Hohokam, the ruins of a long defunct civilization based upon irrigation agriculture. Upon approach I tried to envision what might have went on in the minds of the Hohokam, what motivated them to embark on such a path of attempted ecological control, and what kept them desperately clinging to the system they had initiated, despite its obviously diminishing material, social, and spiritual returns. I entered a brick-walled shelter of over a thousand years in age, I sat down inside, the coolness of the shaded sandstone comforting and relieving from the one hundred-degree desert sun. I pondered the structure, the masonry of the ancients; their presence once here in the place I sit, I look to the stone lined food storage pit to my left and wonder about the socioeconomic situations that were spawned from that storage pit; the sharing? The conflict? The hierarchy that evolved as a result of the necessary control of food and nature. The abandonment and the collapse, the disbursement into smaller semi-nomadic bands, the return to living as gatherer hunters and small scale horticulturists, as the Hohokam system of irrigation and production agriculture failed. The realization that the experiment had failed and that it most likely had taken willing individuals to make the choice to break free from the pack and abandon it, rather than continue to be coopted by its grip. Journal Entry, Band Tour, 2007

Domestication is a particularly contagious disease. Fire and Ice [2]

Domestication is a far-reaching topic. Most broadly discussed in relation to the anthropogenic control of non-human flora and fauna, here we speak instead of human domestication, particularly its breaking of an original place-rooted human wildness and liberty, and the resulting material and psychological condition which now holds us captive[3].

The influence of human domestication on world history has been profound and reveals a reality that the vast majority of once land-based, self-sufficient indigenous peoples have been coopted into mass dependence on power relationships oriented to production and wealth growing psychoses.[4] Whether culturally self-inflicted or conquered via enculturation, human domestication particularly tends to progressively annihilate a peoples capacity to effectively resist its all-engulfing, tyrannically debilitating forces, including alienation from nature and community, the division of labor, feudalism, militarism[5], technology, and global capitalism: the overall totality of civilization.

At the non-colonial, and thus indigenous level we witness the process of self-domestication occurring among the more sedentary and high-density resource oriented wild food foraging peoples, often those who specialize in fish and/or marine resources, and/or those who domesticate animals and plants, in their employment of wealth generating control of surplus, hereditary nobility, and slavery[6]. Here, not only do oppressive sociopolitical environments result, increasing population densities generally lead to inevitable ecological complications and social conflicts, further increasing a need for societal control and military adventures, thus continually enhancing and reinforcing both ecological and cultural domestication. From here we move towards production agriculture and even deeper and insidious levels of culturally-induced domestication, an example being the Hohokam (cited above), among countless others which have been heavily documented and discussed by scholars of various backgrounds[7]

In general, once settlement and bondage to elite classes occurs, in order to stay alive, domesticated life for the non-elite masses is essentially one of either slavery or indebtedness and payments of tribute and taxes to the rich. So disempowered and separated from a free life within intact social and ecological communities, the domesticated mind often can no longer envision life outside the shackles of the totality. By about 2,000 years ago this was the predicament for the vast majority of humans in all of the civilized regions of the world. For example, for the Ch'in Dynasty peasantry in 1st century AD China:

> *Livelihood came from farming their individual plots and they could not afford to leave them for more than a short period of time... those who stayed on their land might dream of a better world, without toil, hardship and famine. But they depended on the state administrators when it came to irrigation and flood control, the provision of iron tools, and access to the goods which they could not grow themselves. They could conceive of a world in which the administrators behaved better and the landowners did not squeeze them. But they could not conceive of a completely different society run by themselves.*[8]

This total loss of self-reliance and the concomitant failure to conceive of any alternative is a highly accurate description of the conditions of human domestication within the totality of civilization, not only for the poor but also for the elite programmers of civilization themselves. Enslavement was, in many cases, a necessity for the surplus production which fed the elites. For example, in 5th century BC Athens the only value of the peasantry for the elites was in "how important they were to producing the surplus, for without this there could be no life of idleness for the ruling class...the ruling class owed its position to the control of land cultivated mainly by slaves, to such an extent that the classic Greek writers and philosophers saw the ownership of slaves as essential to civilised life."[9]

Within civilization, survival for the ultra-alienated lifeways of the controllers and programmers depends entirely upon a deliberately developed hierarchy and a continuously self-reinforced domestication. During the 10th century, for example, so enslaved by such arrangements were the citizens of the Byzantium Empire that tax collectors travelled the countryside accompanied by soldiers. Those who could not pay were jailed or tortured, and in some cases had hungry dogs sent on them.[10] During the 2nd millennium AD, the arrangements of European feudalism, which ultimately spawned global colonialism and industrialism, were essentially the same – as domesticated dependents there was no freedom for a commoner to leave the farm, the village, or the authority of the lords. The domesticated lords could do nothing on their own, and were dependent on the peasants they held in bondage for food and on middle-tier specialists for wine, silk, spices, and iron weapons and tools.[11]

In Western Europe, 1000-1300 AD, the production of excess surplus, and growth in trade with the Far-East, in tandem with the lords' increasing need for trade goods allowed some from the lower rungs to break-free from the destitution of the fields and establish themselves as middle-class traders. In order to facilitate this, these merchants relocated to settlements, initiating a further domestication of the populace as increasing numbers of people became oriented to life inside of cities.[12] In this manner "the humble bagman could transform himself into a respectable trader, and the respectable trader into a wealthy merchant".[13]

As the colonial activities of kings and empires expanded and the kings and lords became more and more dependent upon the merchants for goods, the merchants became increasingly wealthy. All the while, "to obtain money to buy luxuries and arms, lords [needed to] encourage serfs to produce cash crops".[14] With the establishment of these arrangements arose the increasing emphasis on international trade which fueled European colonialism for centuries.

Throughout this time, as more and more markets emerged, the demand for labor in the non-agricultural sectors continued to grow thus further transforming, across many parts of the world, once self-sufficient land based peoples into members of a new working class who increasingly immigrated to cities.[15] The dream for a new life has always remained elusive for many of these emigrants. Vagabondage emerged early-on among city dwellers who could not obtain employment. In 1570s Britain, King Henry VIII made the persecution of vagabonds' official policy, whipping and imprisoning them due to their being viewed as a threat to order.

All-in-all, mercantilism and its resulting middle-class consciousness spawned the so-called economically independent, free-willed average-joe capitalist trader attitudes and arrangements which have shaped much of how the domesticated masses perceive and live in the world today.

Expanding globalization is often portrayed as solely originating in the west, neglecting the significance of the rise and influence of non-globalist indigenous capitalists around the world as colonial capitalism spread. Countless populations of 3rd world poor peoples have been victimized by clever and manipulative members of their own cultures who learned how to play the games of domestication, exploitation, and overall tyranny.

Throughout this history and continuing into this century, wild and free peoples were crudely subjugated via their initial experiences with wealth and modern technology, marking "the beginning of a gradual seduction, a growing dependence on the manufactured goods that invariably bedazzle technologically primitive aboriginals".[16] For example, the Huitoto Indians of the Putumayo River region of the Amazon "[who] initially venerated steel axes as divine objects that conferred fertility and abundance", once entranced and dependent, "willingly swapped orphans or low-status members of their clans to obtain the goods from slave traders".[17] Another example comes from Australia, where "the introduction of steel axes by missionaries among Yir Yoront aborigines led to the complete collapse of their ancient culture within a generation. Trade relations disrupted, taboos violated, myths shattered, age and gender roles overturned".[18]

As a means to conquer and subjugate the remaining wild peoples in the Amazon jungles "the allure of…magical objects – mirrors, machetes, phonographs, cameras – lay at the strategic core of campaigns waged over decades to attract countless tribes…from the bush….by [government agencies], missionaries, oil companies, road builders, adventurers".[19]In some cases, such as with the Yanomami groups of the Orinoco River region in Venezuela, this led to relocating themselves away from their traditional homes in the highlands to mission posts along the rivers in the lowlands simply to obtain access to trade goods. In other cases, the results were even more deleterious, such as with "some isolated tribesmen [who] were…known to launch attacks to gain access to manufactured goods [which] they…developed a taste for but could acquire by no other means".[20] In Brazil this included the Kayapo, who "raided settlers time and time again during the 1950s with the express purpose of taking their guns and ammunition, which they used in turn to gain an upper hand on their traditional tribal enemies", and also the…

> *Arara and the Parintintin who made off with knives, machetes, and axes from the tapiri de brindis[21] [having] no idea what taking the bait would immediately lead to. Epidemics were just the beginning. Once they were crippled by demographic shock, their lands were easily overrun. They often lacked the will or the strength even to feed themselves, let alone resist. The survivors were soon corralled on marginal parcels, bereft of the traditions and know-how that*

> *had sustained them for thousands of years, despised by the society that hoodwinked them with a boundless flow of gifts and promises of a better life.*[22]

There were also the Kanamari, who "reduced to utter dependence on [government agency] paternalism for manufactured necessities, such as shotguns and shells" ended up "caught between the ancient ways they were forgetting and a world of fast-moving boats, planes, and commerce that was passing them by [and thus] no longer knew how to hunt with bow and arrow, much less to make them."[23] For the Marubo "only the...elders still knew how to make the stiff but supple long bow and the fletched cane arrows tribesmen had hunted with for eons" and shotgun shells thus became a commodity essential to a Marubo man's ability to provide for his family.[24]

All of the above represent examples of an essentially global event throughout history since the beginnings of domestication, as virtually all land based peoples have become dependent upon the world system, leading generally to the enhancement of ever more hideous levels of human domestication. In their manifesto, Marx and Engels summarized the societal shifts associated with global capitalism as leading to the masses becoming merely "a class of labourers who live only so long as they can find work".[25] Certainly, for the vast majority of humanity, survival is now entirely dependent upon involvement with the forces of technology and production, and along with that, survival is now dependent upon furthering our alienation from the natural world and maintaining our own state of domestication – this is the ruling paradigm. Self-domestication continues to reign over us all as most of the lower and middle classes the world over, rather than reject the growth of markets, urge them on, further domesticating themselves, separating communities, driving thousands of wild species to extinction, and deepening overall human estrangement from direct relations with the real world. Furthering these processes offers no semblance of a way out, and any modicum of a future socioecological restoration and sustainability continues to be utterly annihilated.

Domestication: The Culprit in a Persistently Failed Leftist Resistance

> *The sense of shock had gone by the 20th century. People could still be amazed by individual innovations, like the motorcar or electric light. But they were not shocked any more by a society built on competition, timekeeping and greed. Capitalist society was all that people knew. Its characteristic forms of behavior seemed to be 'human*

> *nature'. People no longer realised how bizarre their behavior would have seemed to their forebears. A People's History of the World* [26]

> *I've wasted too much time being motivated by shame and guilt. I know now who my enemy is...it's not the cops, not the feds, not the president, not corporate CEOs, though I'm not trying to say they aren't worth pushing off a cliff. My enemy is civilization and the collective insanity it stems from. My enemy is domestication. Fire and Ice* [27]

At all costs, the vast majority of us seem to be highly contented with a continuation of the domestication process. Those who question domestication are often labeled as radicals and activists of all stripes seems to have great difficulty in coming to terms with the fact that, when compared to the vast majority of human history lived in wildness, it is domestication which is actually "bizarre" and "radical". Yet the long history of failed attempts at resistance and defeat by the totality, the failure to change our circumstances any decisive degree, has resulted to a large magnitude from living within a state of both physical and psychological domestication[28].

World history, since the dawn of civilization, can be characterized as both continuous bondage and continuous class struggle against resource theft and hierarchical power, which, over the course of time, not one entity has ever successfully risen to overthrow. Nowhere on the planet today does the totality not exist. Its overall long-term trajectory continues and propagates daily largely because our domestication amounts to physical and psychological dependency. World history shows that the maintenance of the totality requires that the common masses are continuously swindled into becoming dependent on landowners, successful traders, religious elites, and the state. Moreover the role of the middle-class, including those who identify as anti-capitalist pro-environment leftists, has been fundamental in the effort to maintain domestication in the form of privileged lifestyles associated with progress, industry, and overall techno industrial expansion. Civilized humans, both Left and Right, will do just about anything to maintain their domestication.

Domestication is so immensely powerful it has kept billions of humans timid and enslaved throughout known history. Local, small-scale native people are not exempt as they have often proven just as gullible in their desires for wealth[29]. At whatever cultural scale, wealth has always been generated by, an often willing, mass of commoners in service to an elite. Depraved and shameless, capitalism is essentially a deception of the masses into a reified need for a product or a service that can be extracted or produced by one group and sold back to another group by the trading and owner classes who benefit. Once obtained, the benefactors have always viewed the preservation of their privilege and profit as primary; no matter how compassionate, caring, and liberal, whenever they are backed against a wall they have chosen to side with domestication.

A review of all the great revolts against tyranny in history reveals either movements which were crushed by the more powerful, or victorious ones which promised a new society but simply ended up reproducing all of the destructive tendencies and oppressions of civilization[30]. This trend will continue, no matter how hard those who resist fight back, as long as the wealth and power of the elitist domesticators and programmers depends entirely on our direct compulsion in the game of wage slavery, production, commodification, mercantilism, and technology.

The risks involved with authentically breaking this pattern and thus doing away with our domestication run deep. Civilizations have a long history of using strong handed tactics, including police and military violence, against those who threaten mass compulsion in their domestication scheme. And ever since the programmers of surplus production coaxed us away from dependence on immediate return wildness, the domesticated elitists have generally always controlled the food, albeit in an acknowledged state of paranoia and vulnerability.

With the almost total dependence on mass produced cereal grains for survival, both elites and commoners became keenly aware that any social or ecological glitch which caused a substantial harvest failure would equal starvation[31]. For this reason European feudal kings were constantly worried about peasant revolt or any rejection of exploitation by the masses of common farmers – not only did their power, but also their lives, depended on peasants playing the game. They capitalized on the fact that the poor masses were domesticated, unable to fend for themselves, and chained to the fields and used this bondage to redirect any despair, anger, and revolt. For instance, in 12th century Constantinople, the rulers of the Byzantium Empire, "afraid of any class emerging whose closeness to production might lead to it diverting some of the surplus into its own pockets"[32] found security in the fact that "lacking an independent base, the poor could not act as an independent force. They could cause brief mayhem by rioting.

But even their bitterness was all too easily manipulated…utilised by aristocratic forces"[33]. Throughout history, in their own self-imposed desperation, constantly terrified of any unrest which might result in forcing them down into destitution, mid-level aristocrats have always played along.

Moreover, in order to oppose any radical shifts which might undermine their positions on the ladder, the propertied liberal classes have always, when then the system is faced with any threat, tended to unite with fascistic right-wing forces.

Typical of the fantasies and psychoses of middle-class liberals everywhere today, was the cowardice of the liberal bourgeois social democrat leaders of pre-WWII Nazi Germany, whose ultra-domesticated fear of economic collapse contributed greatly to the rise of Adolf Hitler. "Nazisim…was the product of an already mature industrial capitalism. The German ruling class saw the only way to escape from a deep economic crisis was to hand political power to a totalitarian movement based on the irrational fantasies of a middle class driven mad by the crisis"[34]. The evolved comfortable dependence of the liberal bourgeois on the domesticated order has always meant that they shall never put their careers at risk, even if, thoroughly enlightened of the actual problems via their privileged educations.

As a result of their own enslavement to the arrangements of production and their personal comforts resulting from their position within the totality, middle class intellectuals, including university professors and civil servants of all stripes, even if keenly aware of these patterns in history, generally always seem more than willing to toe the line for the totality. The contemporary postmodernist surrender of left wing intellectuals is entirely rooted in their own domestication and fear of breaking free of it. It should be clear, at this stage, that allowing the forces of passive and comfortable bourgeois liberalism to be a guide in any manner means certain defeat for humanity and for the planet.

For their part, the lower-level urban working classes are almost equal enemies to planetary ecology, wildness, and self-reliant indigenous lifeways. As the blue collars struggle for their piece of the pie, and thereby internalize the struggle for income equality and 'economic justice' as a priori, they position themselves as willing exploiters and decimators of both ecosystems and non-capitalistic land-based lifeways[35]. Particularly disheartening is the witness of increasing numbers of indigenous peoples with the most direct connections to free and wild ancestors of any populace on the planet willing to sell away everything while claiming allegiance to an indigenous culture, in an effort to somehow separate themselves from the overall imperial ideology, a measure to comfort them in their cognitive dissonance and overall psychological despair[36].

For the domesticated, rather than step away from the totality and attempt a return to a stable social and ecological lifeway, belief in a better future via technology and shifting societal consciousness becomes a fundamental guiding force. The idealization of progress has always been fundamental to leftist thinking – 'some day we can get there, we just need to keep pushing on and the dreams of advancement for all can finally be fulfilled'. Total faith in science and reason continues as a product of all this, as most, rather than come to terms with the reality of human domestication, cling to faith in the future as if it were a god, marching onward down the pavement staring into and poking away at their screens passively chanting 'the future can only ever be better than the present – modernity can only mean improvement'.

The entire notion of a progressive movement to a finally just world has been a massive failure for all of its believers, but has worked well as another scheme of the cunning for growing their wealth and power – from the long ago incubation of the first indigenous civilizations through till now. This forward march to progress has given rise to all the devastation which has occurred, and thus, now, any true resistance movement must first and foremost reject solutions that involve 'progress' in any shape or form[37].

Through its history of fits and starts over the last few millennia's, the momentum of leftist oriented resistance is picking up in this second decade of the 21st century: Occupy, Black Lives Matter, Climate Change, Anti-fracking, Anti-Pipeline– yet none of this is fundamentally different than left style resistance of past centuries[38]. In fact, by necessity against the most powerful state paramilitary police forces in known history, it is fundamentally more passive than any of the more forthright armed leftist revolutions of the past. Ultimately, hemmed in by domestication - dependency on the industrial supply chain, digital communication, and corporate health care - none of what is occurring now will bring us or the planet out of annihilation by the totality, as long as the primary agitation in such activism is a fight to be more of an equal part of the system rather than a call for the disenfranchised to voluntarily cease acting out their traditional roles as surplus producers for the domesticators. As time plays out, the revolts of the 21st century will continue and even expand, but as the historical track record shows, such movements will always be co-opted unless those revolting choose to abandon the industrial system itself and develop a new world of actualized community self-reliance[39].

Do they owe us a living? Why keep producing for them? What compels it? Domestication.

What if rather than fighting for equal treatment, just wages, and better working conditions the producers instead just stopped playing the game? Is it really a matter of survival? Or is it actually a matter of reified dependencies?

One of the fundamentals of liberal intellectual theory regarding the obviously approaching dark times for modern civilization is the notion that it is the poor who will continue to suffer and the rich who will prosper and survive. For all classes who rely on producing inputs for the global machine this will certainly be a reality, yet the impotence of the ultra-domesticated who now live the most privileged lifestyles should not be underestimated.

As the belt on the dominant economy and culture continues to tighten and the numbers of disenfranchised grow, the elite shall find themselves at their most vulnerable. In the face of their frantic paranoia and their access to police and military enforcers our challenges will remain extremely formidable, no doubt. But there is a fighting chance if rather than remaining in bondage to technology and capital we can build self-reliance while simultaneously resisting and attacking these supposedly inviolable institutions.

During the 1930s when the US stock market collapsed, igniting the Great Depression, the implications were felt worldwide. US and European banks collapsed and world industrial output fell almost by half, devastating 3rd world countries and peasants across the planet "whose economies had been tailored to produce food and raw materials" for the colonial world markets:

> *Suddenly there was no market for their output. People only recently pulled into the world of money were deprived of access to it, yet they no longer had any other means of obtaining a livelihood…those who were least 'advanced' in capitalist terms – subsistence farmers still barely integrated into the cash economy – survived best. Those who relied on selling their labor power had nothing to fall back on.*[40]

Obliterating our dependency on selling our labor power, whatever it is we produce, is an absolutely key element in resistance.

Civilization is life lived off the production of otherness – as long as we remain domesticated we all ultimately live off the backs of otherness –this is where your smartphone comes from. The history of civilization is not simply class struggle; it is essentially the sapping of communal self-sufficiency by self-domesticated elitists and, in many cases, the simultaneous surrender of communal self-sufficiency by commoners who end up in a state of desire for their own piece of the pie. This is the actual dialectic – surrender of our wildness and liberty in exchange for dependency on reified needs and desires represents the opposing forces annihilating us through time via self-domestication. As a first step a once primal wild and free peoples fell prey to the promise of an easier life via surplus production – an initially innocent human impulse that has ultimately become the undoing of our species and the global ecology which supports us.

Taken as a whole, and in proper temporal context, the 21st century can be described as an episode of impending confusion and socio-ecological destruction resulting from the continuing surge of mass capitalism, colonialism, and industrial technology with the masses generally following along and/or coming up with untenable solutions as result of their own domestication . We witness the momentum of this psychology today, but confidence is waning and the ridiculousness of the proposed solutions is apparent as time and space for their implementation quickly runs out.

All of the upheavals of socialist oriented rebellion across Europe, Asia, and Latin America during both the 19th and 20th centuries are representative of the same very confused attempt to make correct what went so wrong. Both then and now the ideologies which drive most efforts of resistance have been without the necessary historical, anthropological, ecological, and psychological context – self-domestication so deeply entrenched that all of this effort at resistance and revolt has simply been banging fruitlessly on an impenetrable wall – billions of people dying all in desperation to find security in industry, technology, government, military force, agriculture, economics – in sum – to find security in our domestication.

The only hope forward is feral, a return from our captivity to a state of wildness – the middle-ground compromises of past and present resistors take us nowhere but further into enslavement and ecological despair – further into domestication. Rewilding is the antithesis. Only a feral return to self-reliant non-technological community will be adequate. The crucial calling is for the masses is to discontinue producing, stop trading, to band together on land and as a communities, Occupy farms and forests – not city streets: to grow[41], steal, scavenge, forage and procure the necessities, begin to unhinge domestication, to stop playing the game[42].

Photo by Four Legged Human.

Indigenous Wildness, Self-Reliance, and Resistance

> *I shared the evening campfire with men who in this lifetime had believed jet aircraft to be supernatural beings. But they had evolved a way of life perfectly suited to this harsh realm. They'd known how to survive in it, even to thrive in it, with nothing of our complicated technology. Every one of them at one point or another had stood face-to-face with a jaguar in the forest, armed with only an arrow or a stick, and come out on top. Did the bearer of a SAM-7 missile, who with a squeeze of a finger could shoot one of those ancestral spirits out of the sky, possess any greater intelligence than a flecheiro who knew how to stalk prey silently in the forests and whose people had managed to arrive at the third millennium still free from civilization's relentless efforts to subjugate them, dispossess them, and have at their resources? The Unconquered* [43]

> *They are a reminder that it's possible to live another way. They are the last free people on this planet. Brazillian National Indian Foundation agent Jose' Carlos Meirelles to a BBC journalist on being shot at in an airplane with a fusillade of arrows from the bows of the Indios Bravos when flying low over an encampment in 2008.*

Recognizing the reality of our debilitating domestication requires that we now must define its opposing condition; a feral world of wildness and self-reliance, inspired by examples of actualized wild liberty and resistance.

It has been estimated that today in the last primal vestiges of the Brazilian Amazon exist up to 43 uncontacted indigenous tribes, *Indios Bravos* or The Arrow People. Often characterized as 'uncontacted', the more likely reality is that these Amazonian bands consciously choose to live in isolation and evade interaction precisely due to a deep intergenerational knowledge of the calamitous consequences associated with their ancestors and their neighboring indigenous brethren becoming domesticated and civilized:

> *Willful determination, or rather self-determination...seems to attend all the isolated tribes still roaming the forests of the Amazon... Indigenous groups living in isolation are isolated because they choose to be. It's not for complete lack of contact, but precisely because previous experiences of contact with the outside world proved so negative.*[44]

Not only have The Arrow People been refugees fleeing from the violence and conquest of European and mestico colonialism and the associated global economy for 500 years, many of them likely originate from small scale cultures which were effectively evading the evolving tyranny of South American indigenous groups which began to settle and domesticate the region around 2,000 years ago[45]. As these indigenous empires and foreign resource extractors invaded further and further into the depths of the Amazon, The Arrow People developed a successful lifeway which incorporated continuous evasion from the turmoil of civilization, effectively keeping their cultures and their wildness intact up until today[46]. They have voluntarily isolated themselves and "developed a heightened resistance to contact – refusing all gifts, spurning all overtures, fleeing deeper and deeper into the jungle"[47]. With a legacy of two millennia's of successful resistance against the forces of domestication and five centuries of successful resistance against enslavement by the modern industrial world, "everything they [do suggests] a deliberate decision, an act of self-determination, to shut themselves off from the rest of us."[48]

There are many other examples of such attempts at resistance and evasion by indigenous nomads, hunters, and foragers across the world, but it seems that none have held on to the degree The Arrow People have. One of the deepest and most enduring examples of tremendous persistence in fighting the dominant order is the fact that, for entire decades during the European conquest of the American West in the nineteenth century, groups such as the Apache, Cheyenne, and Lakota were defeating the US Army day-in-day-out in various battles and skirmishes while simultaneously continuing to feed themselves and their children via wild food hunting and gathering. This capability is an immense testament to the strength and resilience of such people, whose enemies were meanwhile being fed, sheltered, clothed, and armed primarily through organized supply chains. With some access to firearms, these near victors of the Indian Wars also continued to maintain heavy reliance on primitive technology, annihilating hundreds of cavalrymen with handmade bows and arrows, among other traditional weaponry. The only way these groups were defeated was through the implementation of a military strategy to destroy their food-base and by hemming them in on limited parcels of land. Perhaps, in the face of such a powerful leviathan, defeat was sadly inevitable. Nonetheless our current cultures of resistance should draw on this history for inspiration.

Through this we should also continue to make note of the destructive consequences for the indigenous groups who have initially welcomed domestication and then continued to blindly make concessions to it, effectively allowing themselves to become dependents of the industrial system as a result.[49] For example, in contemporary Alaska many native people continue to survive to a large degree by hunting, fishing, and gathering but only accomplish this with modern technology and fossil energy. So much direct knowledge of ancient skills has been lost that any long-term glitch in the long supply chain which impedes receipt of now necessary goods and services into remote Alaska would likely become a humanitarian crisis. This situation can be contrasted with the far greater level of self-reliance and traditional skills retained by some Siberian indigenous peoples whom have had much less opportunity to tinker with industrial consumption and technology over the course of both Soviet and Russian Federation history. Compared to the Alaskans, the Siberians are well-posed to endure upcoming supply chain collapses.

None of this is to be taken lightly however. Primitive survival in Artic and Subarctic environs presents formidable challenges which few of the domesticated masses would ever be willing to confront. Although, examples throughout the ethnographic record do inform us what our species is capable of, especially in cases where we are born and raised outside of domestication. For instance, at the tip of the Southern Hemisphere in Tierra Del Fuego, in a much harsher climate than exists in today's last stronghold of wild indigenousness in the Amazon, the Yahghan people lived for thousands of years "practically naked" without shoes in the winter snows[50]. They were expert swimmers in the cold waters of the southern Pacific near Cape Horn. Further into the interior existed the Ona who, rather than having the woven grass skirts occasionally worn by the Yaghan, survived the mountain winters clothed by a one-piece un-tanned guanaco skin robe. "Ona men cared nothing for being clothed". Their single sheet guanaco skin was not sewn and was "never fastened in any way, but was held in a position with the left hand in which the hunter also carried his bow and quiver" [51]. Once in range of game, or in preparation to encounter an enemy, "the hunter discarded his robe before using his bow and arrows"[52]. The legacy of these bands of Tierra Tel Fuego Indians is one of hardness and resilience for multiple thousands of years. Today, as a result of the effects of European colonization, they are extinct. Not a single language speaker or full-blooded Yaghan or Ona remains. In the necessity to procure food, their attempts to resist the colonization of their lands proved futile. "These unfortunate natives, though, as a rule, vastly superior physically…to their enemies, were hopelessly handicapped by having to provide for their numerous families"[53].

This is the unfortunate story for thousands of wild cultures who have become victimized by the onslaught of domestication and civilization across the globe over the course of the last two thousand years. Yet The Arrow People have maintained their wildness and capacity to endure and they provide all of us and the planet with a sliver of hope.

Nevertheless, in face of this grand reality, the domesticated cry out "it is hopeless!" And why? Because the picture is clear. In order for The Arrow People to accomplish wildness and true liberty continuously over the course of at least five centuries they have needed to maintain an extremely high threshold for psychical discomfort[54]. Yet they are humans just as we are and they had the resilience of our forebears deep inside their minds and bodies. Not only this, they also had to maintain a great capacity for mobility and it is surmised that the ancestors of some of these bands were also once sedentary farmers but that "to stay a step ahead of the invaders, they abandoned their crops and villages to forage in the forest"[55].

This is what victory looked like: The Arrow People, holding forth in the Parallel Realm. Uncontacted. Untamed. Unconquered.[56]

For us, is it hopeless? In the face of overwhelming odds (*too many people, not enough land, mass extinction* – are all common reproaches) it very well may be. But we have no choice. The only way forward is to somehow develop a capacity not to be dependent on the Leviathan. Unhinge our domestication. The task before us is immense. It is undoubtedly multigenerational, yet not unreachable and not pushing forward with it means failure for all that is decent about humanity and means utter destruction for the ecology of this sacred wild planet.

Forward into Rewilding Realities: Risk, Hardship, Humility, Community

> *Out of these [21st century] struggles will emerge new attempts to remould society around the values of solidarity, mutual support, egalitarianism, collective cooperation and a democratically planned use of resources. The ruling classes of the world, like their predecessors for 5,000 years, will do their utmost to thwart these attempts and will, if necessary, unleash endless barbarities so as to hang on to what they regard as their sacred right to power and to property. They will defend the existing capitalist order to the end – even if it is the end of organized human life. A Peoples History of the World* [57]

> *I just know I want out. And I don't know what my limitations are, but I'm ready to find out. The Black Wolf Woman –Anonymous Alaskan Rewilder*

> *Every day is a physical toil, but never before have I felt such undaunted enthusiasm for my scope and freedom. On the Run in Siberia* [58]

We have clearly established that a rewilding component is a necessary foundation for any effective and enduring resistance against, and liberation from, the shackles of civilizational tyranny. This is not meant to discredit the efforts of others or to disrespect or reduce the value of the countless acts of self-sacrifice in the long history of action and resistance against the totality, in one form or another, around the world. Rather, the point is to identify the critical missing element – a concurrent pathway to undomesticate and rewild. For any suite of actions to have long-term beneficial outcomes for humans and the planet, this is mandatory. It is the only way forward; action without wildness as a foundation can only result in domestication, no matter what victory comes of it. Any modicum of authentic resistance now depends on shedding domestication[59].

Those of us involved in the many forms of resistance occurring today, especially those of us who were born and now reside in the westernized regions of the world, including many of us who have come to reject civilization, have been raised as humans in the most comfortable conditions ever know to our species. We are domesticated. This provides us perspective on both the advantages and limitations of domesticated lifeways which those 'less fortunate' do not have. But since our domestication tends to be our primary foundational life experience, we are left at a great disadvantage in gaining the capability to disembark from the complex systems which now prop us up.

If there was to be a great victory over the totality what would we be left with, without the physical and psychological ability to exist outside of its grip? We would be left with little ground to stand on and the situation would turn back to tyranny, unless rewilding occurs within our every physical, mental, emotional, sensory, and social faculty. Without this there is nothing. Yet the challenges to shift are immense. We need an authentically feral resistance but to go feral we need to cross boundaries, both physical and spiritual, throw caution to the wind, and embark full-throttle into wildness.

When the topic of physical discomfort and toil comes up, and when some primitivists and rewilders such as I promote embracing these things as virtuous, we are often accused of being arrogant and macho. We make no romanticized attempts at machismo associated with the trials and errors involved with our attempts to endure inside of wildness. Arrogance is our enemy. It is civilization talking. Above all else, rewilding shall teach us a humility which the civilized lack and which we must embrace wholeheartedly. An atmosphere of tougher-man, smarter-man arrogance is countered when a person with real on-the-ground experience displays some personal humility in regards to the situation[60]. And when it comes to gender, I am continuously humbled by the women I have spent time with in pursuit of rewilding.

Let us also, once and for all, set straight the notion that anarcho-primitivists romanticize, and thus do not take seriously, the realities of dispensing with civilization. We fully recognize the complete package of consequence involved with doing away with civilization and make no attempt to avoid the harsh physical and psychological realities which accompanies a feral return; hard work, discomfort, pain, danger, risk, lack of outside support to fall back on[61]. I hold no illusions regarding what befalls us and I say this all with a deep humility based on my own feeble attempts at rewilding, experiences which have often left me retreating back into the comforts of civilization. Again, in the face of all this, constant humility is the overarching perspective and state of being. The reality is that going feral requires physical and mental toughness. This is not a macho thing. It is a human thing. Domestication has softened us immensely. And thus we also need to be realistic about the overall legitimacy of training and physical fitness – swimming, climbing, jumping, running, travelling long distances on foot, carrying heavy weight, self-defense – and cast-off any labeling of physical fitness activities as macho or militarist by lethargic anarchists and passive leftist activists. There is no easy way out – domestication debilitates physically into decrepitude and it has evolved our necessity for civilized comforts which ultimately destroy wildness and annihilate the planet. The overall physical alienation and feebleness of the most powerful elitist programmers, technologists, domesticators, and capitalists is perhaps one of the primary weaknesses in the totality that we ourselves should be capitalizing on. Even the hardiest of them ends up worthless without technology, motors, grocery stores, and guns.

I witness each day the end result of this alienation, insistence upon the virtues of domestication by the vast majority of humans around me. A fear of the natural world, a fear of the dark, the cold, of being dirty, of being outdoors, of being human, of being an animal, and the natural world continues to suffer concomitantly. Feral pathways inevitably come with personal risks and require a mental, and often physical, crossing of the threshold of domestication. As a Tanana Athabascan activist once told me, "well-being was widespread before contact, but we cannot romanticize it, being hungry, which the elders have caught a glimpse of". Danger certainly lurks here. I am aware of the risk. And in situations without civilized control I am not without fear.

We have always heard from the domesticated the inaccurate assessment that life for primitive people was "nasty, brutish, and short". Life expectancy at birth for hunting and gathering peoples was lower than in modernity not because no one survived into old age but because less children survived in proportion to the population as a whole. Healthy seventy-plus year old elders from hunting and gathering cultures have been well documented in the anthropological record[62]. If a person survived to adulthood, mortality was related mostly to accidents and violence. In the case of an accident there was no modern medicine, surgery, or life-support. This is perhaps one of the most difficult realities for us to face. It certainly was for me when I cut myself deep while butchering a deer while in a very remote camp on an island for several weeks and became paranoid that I was getting an infection. This humble reality became even more critical for me when I stared directly at my friend's finger hanging lopsided and barely attached to the bone while she begged me to sew it for her so that she could *avoid* going to a hospital. And these little incidents are relatively minor in comparison to the medical situations we will inevitably face one day no longer linked to the matrix, in full reliance only on one and other, in wildness, where anything can happen[63].

As domesticates we often find ourselves distressed by elements of unpredictability, accident, and chance, yet an embrace of these is one important element which builds the adaptability and resilience of the feral, wild and free human. Our domestication of animals and plants was essentially an unprecedented psychological transition "from unpredictability to reliability".[64] Yet, dependence upon "reliability" ultimately initiates a psychological dependence on control, and thus a control logic which originates from a fear of uncertainty.[65] I get frustrated with uncertainty personally, and I can see how a culture would make efforts to reduce it via domestication. As such it may be that this psychology has played a massive role in our own domestication and its comprehensive impacts to wildness and the planet. The unpredictability of wildness offers both risk and award. Some who have found boundless healing, meaning, purpose, hope and spiritual solace in rewilding have disappeared on vision quests into wildness, as a result of chance or simple mistakes, or both, never to be seen again. I do not valorize this.

Prior to domestication, if a lone hunter crashed through the ice and could not start a fire then there was no cell-phone to call in a heli-vac, there was no airplane to search for them when family became concerned. Thus, there must have been a much greater acceptance of death in those wild cultures than we have in ours. Such are the risks that we take, especially when we travel solo in remote locations. We are realistic about the risks and we strive to develop the courage and honor to accept our predicaments and their consequences. In those cases, we should prefer to become a bear or part of a river, rather to go on with civilization. This would be more along the lines of the spirituality of the old hunters where humans and wildness are one and where the spirits of people do not die but instead only change forms. Better to die in the wild than in car wreck, better to eat the dirt than to eat the pavement, better to be eaten by a beautiful wild creature than to be shot apart by bullets and thus eaten away for nothing by a domesticated and lost predator in our nation's ongoing epidemic of mass-murder public shootings (a perfect example of the ever escalating civilized psychosis occurring in our obviously crumbling society).

There exists a fine line between just wanting out of the system, or the ability to survive the collapse, and an actualized feral anarchy movement. Anarcho-primitivists do not attempt to go feral and re-wild just because we want out – we do so because we see it as a vital component in the package of resistance actually necessary to bring the totality crashing down.

Rewilding is not a survival course and any machismo survivalist cultural baggage that people incite regarding it should be done away with. Survivalists see wildness as an enemy which they must over-come to survive. Rewilding requires an in-depth focus on rethinking our ways of being and our ways of perceiving ourselves as human beings on planet earth. It is the learning of LIVING skills, both the material and the psychological. Authentic rewilding requires just as much focus on healthy social skills, community building, and mental awareness as it does on the practical elements needed for the establishment of small-scale, localized, self-reliant, primitive-technology based societies. Rewilding goes beyond survival, and into deep relationship with the ecology of the planet and thereby fosters long-term resilience, deep personal character, and community self-reliance: developing a new sense of what it means to be a successful human being on planet earth based upon the actual 2 million year evolutionary legacy of ecologically adapted human lifeways and psychologies.

Practical skills are critical not because they are needed to "survive" in the here-and-now but because practicing them develops mental awareness and strength of character; these skills build a foundation for dismantling our domestication by teaching the essence of self-reliance within an ecosystem through intimately knowing that ecosystem with no technological mediation. All of this is easily romanticized on paper and we should not underestimate its complexity and challenges while nonetheless not losing sight of the fact that it is all necessary to an actualized resistance against civilization, and a future without it.

The challenges and complexity mean that what needs to be accomplished cannot be accomplished entirely by any group of us any time soon and not likely within our own lifetimes. By necessity the pathway needs to be multigenerational and anyone who embarks upon it should have as a priority passing on the spirit of rewilding to children.

Prior to global industrialism people were generally only a step or two away from a return to wildness – yet today domestication runs so deep that several steps are likely required for our return . We need to come to terms with the fact that no one can do it all and release our-selves from the politically correct guilty burdens which cause so many of us hopeless despair. Reality means certain levels of compromise with domestication, but settling at these stages certainly means failure. In this sense, rewilding can realistically be viewed as occurring across tiers. Any small step away from domestication has merit and value in the spectrum of resistance but each step should take us further and deeper into wildness and not domestication. Leftist strides for better or equal treatment from within the totality do not fall into this category. This has become highly apparent to me in my work with disenfranchised indigenous peoples whom have lost their wildness and self-sufficiency as a result of being coopted into dependence on the totality. For instance, a Suqpiaq elder recently said to me:

> *As long as the government is giving away free money, Medicaid, and food stamps, and other welfare checks its gonna keep going like we see it here in the villages, no matter what the prices are like. Gas has been going up. Its way over $6 a gallon but these kids and people, they can afford it and we wonder where they are getting all that money? It's easy to figure that out. It's good old government money. Too much handouts. So if that stops, that might take care of everything, we might go back to our own tradition.*

This is just one of dozens of comments I have from interviews with indigenous elders on how dependency destroys self-sufficient land-based cultures. What these elders have witnessed constantly makes clear to me that as long as we remain dependent upon the totality for survival we will increasingly revert to collaboration with it. Moreover, because evolved dependence on technology and the need to pay for it represents for these elders a primary driver of the problem, the situation also makes clear to me that viewing technology as liberatory or neutral is a critical mistake, and not in any way a solution. This reality should cause those who claim to be anti-civilization or pro-indigenous but who are simultaneously uncritical of the contemporary obsession/addiction to digital technology to think more critically about their stances on the matter.

Today we have the historical and anthropological knowledge to lead us out of the despair created by 10,000 years of domestication. It is not the time for a 'sit-in', it is the time to stand up and walk into the forest, leaving behind all of our domesticated baggage. We must now ultimately become The Arrow People. A feral future represents our only pathway forward. I posit that the resilient feralist rewilders will be the last one's standing after the massive upheavals to come, able to do so purely because of the strides made on a multigenerational level to undomesticate. I envision the formation of tight-knit feral bands (bandits!) not chained by circumstance but instead fleet-footed occupiers of forests, mountains, and brush impenetrable by the domestic – inhabitants of our own 'grizzly maze' in which the domesticated dare not enter[66]. Not only this, but bandits also effective at striking the infrastructure of civilization, doing irreparable damage, and readily disappearing into the shadows only to emerge to strike again and again.

Photo by Four Legged Human.

...and through her the bear's spirit of wild resistance lives on.

Sometimes, when she drives a car through town, random paranoid ego and violence obsessed people catch a glimpse of her middle finger stretched straight over the top of the steering wheel –pointed directly at them and their way of life. They have trouble understanding what they have done to deserve such a greeting from such a seemingly innocent young woman. But somehow, in their hearts, they know it. Her presence there on the road is a reminder to their souls that this way of life is failing, a reminder of its destruction and hopelessness. "I sorta see it as a mirror pointed directly back at them" she says.

In their frustration they react. Some just return the gesture and peel out. Others have tried to chase her down, screaming and yelling obscenities, flashing their guns. She just keeps driving slow and waves that finger with a smile. Stumped and confused the perpetrators thus far have all eventually just put the pedal to the metal and sped onward down their roadways to nowhere. Her middle finger will not bend. Neither will her spirit. Her wildness just grows.

She tells me she that she often gets messages from birds, from eagles, from mountain sheep, and continuing messages from bears, messages of encouragement to never give in and to continue spreading to any human who will listen the spirit of feral wildness and unrelenting resistance to civilization. Perhaps some of those people who catch a glimpse of that middle finger stuck straight will get the message and rather than attack and threaten her will become infected with her mother bear spirit, as have I.

In order to grow into wildness we must release ourselves into constant opportunity to experience all that is wild within us and around us and forgo dogmatic, elitist etiquette and politeness to the domesticators, and their reified notions of what it means to be human. I must admit that sometimes going feral seems like a hopeless cause, but no matter how hard I get my ass kicked every single hopeless, painful, and depressing moment has ended up paying off for me psychically, mentally, socially, and in strengthening my understanding of what it will actually take for humans to stop civilization. As long as we stay domesticated in mind, body, and culture we will never be free, the earth will suffer, and the takers will win. Like her, it is time to use every fragment of spirit we have to overturn this predicament.

This essay has made an attempt to say much within little space. Readers will undoubtedly be left with questions and critique. How is it even possible? What should I do? What are the steps? In BAGR #4 I will attempt to answer some of those questions by providing some detailed and specific Feral Prescriptions and Pathways for moving forward. Stay tuned.

Endnotes

1 S. Wallace, *The unconquered: in search of the Amazon's last uncontacted tribes.* Crown Publishers, 2011. Pg. 391

2 L. Luddite and M. Skunkly, *Fire and ice: disturbing the comfortable and comforting the disturbed while tracking our wildest dreams.* Apeshit Press. 2004. Pg. 31

3 There are biological aspects to domestication, easily discernable in domesticated species of flora and fauna. Views of any mutation in human biology resulting from our domestication are conflicted. A complex discussion/argument can be had regarding the possible long-range effects of human domestication on certain aspects of our biology. For example, does not a few thousand more years of daily life engaged in digital technology present the potential to initiate mutations in our eyes, hands, and brains? This article is not the place for such a discussion. The sole focus here is on the material and psychological aspects of our domestication.

4 Here 'indigenous' is used and defined as all local once self-sufficient land based peoples and includes not only groups that todays civilized masses would consider indigenous but

also the forbears of those civilized masses themselves. There was a time when all of our ancestors were land-based, self-sufficient and not dominated by division of labor, production for trade, a time when we were not domesticated.

5 A category which rightly should include the conquest and domination of other species, in many cases leading to their extinction.

6 E.A. Smith et al., Wealth Transmission and Inequality among Hunter-Gatherers. *Current Anthropology.* Volume 51, Number 1, February 2010.

7 In BAGR issues 1 and 2 I have previously written about other aspects of what I see as the process of our domestication. This essay is a necessary further elaboration. See The commodification of wildness and its consequences in *Black and Green Review,* Issue #1, Spring 2015 and Written in stone: maladaptive symbolic alienation vs. functional liberty and temporal continuity in stone tool design in *Black and Green Review,* Issue #2, Fall 2015. There are dozens of references on this topic. For example see P. Shepard, *Coming Home to the Pleistocene.* Island Press: Washington DC, 1998., P. Shepard. *The tender carnivore and the sacred game.* Scribners, New York, 1973. P. Shepard, *Nature and madness.* University of Georgia Press, Athens, 1998, J. Zerzan, *Origins: a John Zerzan reader.* FC Press/Black and Green Press, Milwaukee and Greensburg. 2010, K. Tucker, *For wildness and anarchy.* FC Press/Black and Green Press, Milwaukee and Greensburg. 2010. For a non-technical story book narrative which aptly describes much about the process and consequences of human domestication see D. Quinn, *Ishmael: an adventure of the mind and spirit.* Penguin Random House, 1995. For the story of the Hohokam see Crown, P.L. and J.W. Judge, eds. *Chaco and Hohokam: prehistoric regional systems in the American Southwest.* School of American Research Press, Santa Fe, New Mexico, 1991.

8 C. Harman, *A people's history of the world: from the Stone Age to the new millennium.* Verso, London and New York, 2008, Pg. 61.

9 Ibid, Pg. 65. Also see To produce or not to produce? (Pg. 179-185) and Revolution and/or insurrection (Pg. 186-200) in Tucker, 2010.

10 Harman, 2008

11 Ibid

12 Ibid. The emergence of Islam in 7th century Mecca resulted from nomadic herding families who began to settle as they acquired wealth through trading. Trading seems to be a major impetus for all former nomads who have chosen to settle and organized religion an associated manipulation tool used by the elite classes for social control. For further analysis on the necessity of organized religion and priests in maintaining these arrangements see To produce or not to produce? (Pg. 179-185) in Tucker, 2010.

13 Harman 2008, Pg. 144

14 Ibid, Pg. 144

15 As continues around the world today.

16 Wallace, 2011, Pg. 226

17 Ibid, Pg. 226-227. Also see C.M. Mann, *1491: New revelations of the Americas before Columbus.* Vintage Books. 2006 who notes that when missionaries and anthropologists provided steel tools violence increased amongst Amazonian tribes. Prior to steel axes many forest dwelling Amazonian groups did not bother to clear forest and plants gardens because it was impractical to cut down large trees with stone tools. For these groups steel axes allowed agriculture and they became highly prized by those groups who desired to settle. Some became warlike in order to obtain these axes. Also see endnote 46.

18 Wallace, 2011, Pg. 252

19 Ibid, Pg. 226

20 Ibid, Pg. 232

21 Rubber tappers

22 Wallace, 2011, Pg. 299

23 Ibid, Pg. 337

24 Ibid, Pg. 363

25 K. Marx and F. Engels, *Manifest der Kommunistschen Partei.* London, 1848.
26 Harman, 2008, Pg. 384
27 Luddite and Skunkly, 2004.
28 Some of the BAGR editors were recently accused of being "anti-action". We take none of this lightly. Each and every detailed analysis the BAGR editors embark upon and relay has a core purpose of cultivating and maintaining effective cultures of resistance against civilization with the long term stability of resilient AP communities in mind. We ask our accusers to communicate more clearly and specifically the level of analysis and action they are embarked on, so that we might better understand our supposed shortcomings.
29 This is not to deny whatsoever the fact that domestication has been forced and not voluntary for thousands of indigenous cultures. But a major problem is that once the process sets in, all of us, no matter what our backgrounds, seem to end up more than willing to surrender to it and help it along in our daily decisions.
30 I'm not going to take space up going through the litany of examples here. Review Harman 2008 for a very clear picture of this reality. Also see To produce or not to produce (Pg. 179-185) and The failure of revolution (Pg. 201-210) in Tucker, 2010.
31 For more on the consequences of dependency on storehouses see To produce or not to produce?, Tucker, 2010.
32 Harman, 2008, Pg. 121
33 Ibid, Pg. 212
34 Ibid, Pg. 511. Reference to the global economic crisis of the 1930s. A similar situation is faced in the US today as the number of right wing militias grows, right wing illusions regarding the actual causes of impending collapse remain prolific, and right wing 2nd Amerikkkan Revolution fantasies are leading to fascistic political candidacies with totalitarian mindsets. Take heed of the looming threat of enhanced totalitarianism in the 21st century.
35 See Class struggle, commodification, and modernized society (Pg. 166-178) in Tucker, 2010 for more in-depth analysis on class-struggle ideologies being barriers to actual resistance.
36 This observation is by no means meant to overlook the role that colonialism, governments, and corporations have played in these events, nor is it meant to discount indigenous efforts at resistance. The point here is to focus on how we self-domesticate and how this softens us and thwarts effective resistance. I do not include mention of the indigenous role here lightly. My position stems from years of on-the-ground observation in some of these cultures. The main point here is that, at this stage, very few of us are exempt from the process and that activists need to dig deeper and stop blaming only the western empires ect. for the problem and start paying attention to other primary factors such as domestication and technology.
37 See The failure of revolution (Pg. 201-219) in Tucker, 2010, which points out that many anarchists are certainly not exempt from such faith in progress and that, in fact, the historical leftist and anarchist belief in progress has been a major factor in failed revolutions of the past.
38 I have refrained from discussing resistance in the forms of various types of direct actions here, including attacks against the infrastructure of civilization. For various reasons, this article is not meant to be particularly about those forms of resistance.
39 For more on the leftist obsession with redistribution and failed leftist resistance as a result of reliance on production and thus the need to reject our roles as producers and begin building communities in order to mount effective resistance see To produce or not to produce (Pg. 179-185) and The failure of revolution (Pg. 201-210) in Tucker, 2010.
40 Harman, 2008, Pg. 469-470. In the impending 21st century crisis, most wage workers around the world will face similar circumstances, including those in the more industrialized 'prosperous' nations.
41 As will be explained in more detail below, even while 'growing' is domestication, in specific contexts it is a valid strategy providing it does not become a baseline but that in-

stead it is done as a tiered step to get further and further away from domestication and into wildness. Also see endnote xlvi.

42 This is not to be mistaken as a call for isolation and simply escaping, even if that was actually possible. This is a call for all resistors to incorporate into their pathways relentless actions towards community self-reliance and rewilding and to reject dependence on the machine to the furthest extent possible.

43 Wallace, 2011, Pg. 233

44 Ibid, Pg. 225

45 Mann. 2006 (Pg. 319). In 1542 when the Spaniard Carvajal travelled down the Amazon River his party reported to have encountered complex agriculturally based native settlements extending for hundreds of miles at a time and that "there could even be seen some large cities". The was disputed by early archaeological work done in the Amazon which concluded that due to the bioregion's poor soil it would be too difficult to produce the surplus necessary for complex culture. However, later archaeological work took notice of large tracts of terra pretta a highly fertile soil which was often filled with pottery shards and was determined to be established through anthropogenic composting methods. This discovery suggested that the Amazon basin was densely populated long before the time of Carvajal and that Amazonian agricultural practices were likely as intensive and complex as those in Mesoamerica. Cultural groups identified include the Arawak, who migrated into the southern and central Amazon basin around 2,000 years ago and subsequently pushed further into more remote areas of the basin. In some areas highly elaborate built environments, including large plazas and defensive ditches have been identified. The Arawak speaking peoples likely represent an expansion out of the Andes region, home to the earliest known complex cultures in the Americas – where domestication was being practiced around 5,000 BP. As is well known, there was a succession of imperial Andean empires, including Wari, Tiwanaku, Chimor, and Moche, all leading up to the time of the Inca, followed by Spanish conquest. So there is little doubt that, wherever they originate from, The Arrow People have indeed been successfully evading civilization for a very long time.

46 At least some of The Arrow People are not exclusively hunter-gatherers and are known to maintain orchards. Because of the difficulty of clearing forests with stone tools, there has likely been a long tradition of permaculture style forest gardening in the Amazon forests, cultivated by semi-nomads who combine this tactic with hunting, fishing, and gathering. Mann 2006 suggests many of these Amazonian forest gardens are hundreds of years old and that various groups of people moving through the region have probably used them for subsistence temporarily before moving on. This type of small-scale agroforestry cannot yield enough food on its own to support large populations or complex cultures. A semi-nomadic hunting, fishing, gathering, forest garden mixed subsistence strategy has worked well for these groups of Arrow People as a method of both survival and evasion from civilization and technology for at least centuries. This should not be overlooked by anarcho-primitivists.

47 Wallace, 2011, Pg. 257

48 Ibid, Pg. 299

49 There are certainly many who have resisted conquest by domestication, until the bitter end, and there are also those who have been much more passive in surrendering to it, even desiring it and urging it on while failing to recognize the long-term costs.

50 E.L. Bridges, *Uttermost Part of the Earth: History of the Tierra Del Fuego Indians.* Overlook/Rookery, New York, 2007, Pg. 64.

51 Ibid. Pg. 368

52 Ibid, Pg. 379

53 Ibid, Pg. 265. Some may think it is the destiny of all such wild and free peoples to ultimately become annihilated through such Social Darwinist forces. My view, however, is that all remaining wild and free peoples, and those of us striving to get there, should push forward and bide our time, being that, taken as a whole, socioecological evolutionary history

is actually much more on the side of small-scale, self-sufficient communities than it is on the side civilized of adaptations.
54 Meaning physical discomfort as it would be experienced and defined by domesticated people. 'Discomfort' is relative to cultural and material upbringing. Much of what we find uncomfortable would not be perceived as such by hunter gatherers.
55 Wallace, 2011, Pg. 211. The ability to flee and reestablish nomadic hunting and gathering lifeways has likely been operationalized by thousands of indigenous peoples when the complex societies they were temporary members of faced collapse or when oppressive forces became overwhelming.
56 Ibid, Pg. 423
57 Harman, 2008, Pg. 620
58 R. Willerslev, *On the run in Siberia.* University of Minnesota Press, 2012, Pg. 115.
59 This includes addiction to digital technology, among multiple other things.
60 Bridges (2007:359) recollected "I never heard an Ona brag of his strength or prowess". Also see E.M. Thomas. *The old way: a story of the first people.* Picador, New York, 2006. The ethnographic record shows that hunter gatherers generally always respond to bragging and displays of arrogance by putting the perpetrators in-check.
61 By 'hard work' I do not imply work under the guise of production and regimentation, rather this is to acknowledge the reality that wild survival sometimes requires nose-to-the-grindstone physical effort for hours on end. Also See Pg. 215 of The failure of revolution in Tucker, 2010.
62 For example see M. Gurven and H. Kaplan. Longevity among hunter-gatherers: a cross cultural examination. *Population and Development Review*, 33(2) pages 321-365, June 2007. Average worldwide lifespan in the 21st century is 66 years and for hunter gatherers "the data show that modal adult life span is 68-78 years and that it was not uncommon for individuals to reach these ages." Meanwhile, in the most 'advanced' country in the modern civilized world, the supposed model of 'progress' for all, exists the highest infant mortality rate of all industrialized nations. See https://www.washingtonpost.com/news/wonk/wp/2014/09/29/our-infant-mortality-rate-is-a-national-embarrassment/, accessed January 26th 2016.
63 Most importantly, hunter gatherers certainly do provide us with concrete examples of both medical self-sufficiency and entirely accurate knowledge of the biological functions of the human body. For example Thomas (2006:250) recounted witnessing a Gwi/ bushman "dissect a springbok…naming the various parts, including its internal organs and accurately describing their functions, pointing out that the blood was moved around the body by the heart and that the lungs were for taking in breath…but he didn't confuse the antelope body with the human body, as he understood the different functions of the stomach and the rumen."
64 R. Willerslev et al, Sacrifice as the ideal hunt: a cosmological explanation for the origin of reindeer domestication. *Journal of the Royal Anthropological Institute.* 2014, Pg. 19.
65 Fear of uncertainty should be recognized as a "a prime mover in the development of new subsistence forms" and thus may very well have been an important factor in the development of plant and animal domestication (Willerslev et al. 2014:19)
66 This is how the rebel squatters of the Kalalau Valley and other Hawaiian jungles have evaded compliance with the system to a large degree for decades now. However, at Kalalau, which previously never had motorized access, outside black market entities found a new market among some of the squatter population for alcohol, drugs, and other goods and began smuggling these items in at night by motorboat. The squatters with a taste for these goods fell sway to the allure of what the traders were offering and once these new market relations were established the community fell apart and the primal spirit of that forested valley was severely diminished.

"It's easy to see without looking too far / That not much is really sacred" -Bob Dylan

Not much is really sacred. There is not much that causes us to pause or that we are willing to slow down for. There is not much that we stop to acknowledge, that we are willing to structure our lives around, or make sacrifices for. On top of that, there is little that won't be tolerated; we live in an age without any visible limits and foolishly mistake it for freedom.

I. The Sunrise

Walking to the bus stop in the predawn hours, the sunrise is only minutes from bursting with hints of pink and orange already appearing on the horizon but the pace of my walking is uninterrupted for I have to catch a bus and get to work. The sunrise is not sacred as evident by the fact that I appreciate it only when it's convenient and sometimes not even then. I don't often make an effort to be present for it. In fact, to claim that part of the day for oneself would be widely perceived as unreasonable.

Instead of portioning our time and attention in accordance with what is important to us and the values we have arrived at through our own reflection and contemplation we are compelled or even coerced to portion our time according to economic demands and the capricious preferences of others; others who, as a rule, do not have our best interests in mind. Indeed, it is difficult enough to find time to even consider the question of what is important to us; it is a subversive and reckless thought.

But I wonder what it might be like to assert and make real the sacredness of the sunrise by structuring my day around it and avoiding commitments that would interfere, to stake a claim to that part of the day. Would life change after, say, a month's time or a year's time? Like anything, it would no doubt change in ways both better and worse. Not knowing where the preponderance of consequences fall is, at least partially, what paralyzes. Domesticated and docile creatures don't readily tread into unpredictable places; we like to have things already mapped out for us. And so I get on the bus; I know where it goes and what to expect.

There is reason to believe that punishment for such an eccentric experiment would be severe whereas the anticipated rewards are vague and can be difficult to imagine. Tolstoy warned: "Try the experiment of ceasing to compromise conscience in order to retain your position [one's job or social status], and you will lose it at once."[1] But perhaps the loss of one's position is precisely the unanticipated *benefit* that one is liable to discover through such an experiment. For it is our position in the queue that keeps us walking in lockstep; our fear of falling behind that keeps our eyes from looking up from our feet to the horizon.

What if this experiment were done not as an isolated individual but rather as a small community of people regularly gathering together and sharing the experience of the sunrise. I am tempted to speculate that the benefits would be multiplied and the harms greatly mitigated. Indeed, is this not why people have long gathered together in the presence of the sacred?

And yet, the sunrise *is* sacred signaling, as John Muir wrote that "the world, though made, is yet being made. That this is still the morning of creation."[2] It is not only an iterated event that marks the beginning of each new day but from a different perspective it is an uninterrupted event that long preceded our individual existence and will continue long after our individual death. David Abram describes the sunrise as a wave endlessly circling the earth. Abram points out that "the leading edge of the dark [into which the sunrise advances] is indeed an audible as well as a visible line"[3] this is because the sunrise contains a chorus of birdsong. It is amongst the elements that make life on Earth possible. It makes our life possible even as we ignore it.

The sunrise is sacred. It is just that our actions and inattention profane it. What's more is that our actions and our inattention insult our own convictions and make a farce of our claims to integrity.

II. Monasticism

"There could be no more question of living just like everybody else

in the world. There could be no more compromises with the life that tried, at every turn, to feed me poison." -Thomas Merton[4]

I am not a Christian but despite the radically different worldview espoused by Christian monastics I find much to be gleaned from their lived example. Monastics have often very carefully considered how they will engage the world and many have seemingly found a way to do so, more or less, on their own terms and to their own satisfaction. Paradoxically they have done this by submitting to a rule. The Rule of St. Benedict (RB) has been the most widely used guide structuring western monastic life since it was written in the sixth century.

Few people I have met have seriously considered this question of how to engage the world so as to preserve and prioritize what is of value to themselves and virtually no one I know has even experimented with any potential solution or strategy. We consistently refuse to consider the question so as to foreclose the possibility of finding an answer and thereby avoid having to take any dramatic action.

The monastery may seem irrelevant or even escapist to those who are decidedly not only in the world be vehemently of the world as well. Addressing this point, Joan Chittister, a Benedictine nun, writes:

"Monasteries hardly seem like places from which to analyze the world. To go to the monastery, popular mythology has it, is to leave the world, not to get even more deeply involved with it. But it may be only from a distance that we see best."[5]

There is no such thing as seeing the sunrise up close; it is the distance that makes the view possible. Only a fool runs toward the horizon in hopes of improving her vantage point or holding it in her hands. The most important thing to do is to stop and let the light come to you. But we are never given the opportunity to stop and reflect; civilization is simultaneously sedentary and frenetic.

The life of Trappist monk Thomas Merton lends support to Chittiser's claim. Merton became both politically engaged and appreciative of the natural world only after entering the monastery. In a journal entry dated May 31, 1961, Merton writes:

"The great work of sunrise again today. The awful solemnity of it. The sacredness...unbearable if you really put everything else aside and see what is happening! Many, no doubt, are vaguely aware that it is dawn: but they are protected from the solemnity of it by the neutralizing worship of their own society, their own world, in which the sun no longer rises and sets."[6]

The world of modernity is a world where the sun no longer rises and sets. Electric lighting floods streets, homes, and workplaces during all hours. The blue glow of screen distorts and disrupts our sleep patterns. The time of day is now irrelevant and the demands on an individual no longer set with the sun. The phone can ring, or perhaps vibrate, at any hour. The internet is always there, always on. There is no chance to pause and consider "the awful solemnity" of "what is happening!". Anyone who slows their pace will miss their bus and be left behind.

The life of Dietrich Bonhoeffer was in many ways radically different than that of Thomas Merton. Bonhoeffer did not live in a monastery; as a Protestant he belonged to a tradition that has largely been suspect of monasticism. He was not distant from the world in any way but rather was so immersed in its political machinations as to be a part of the Resistance in Nazi Germany and a co-conspirator in multiple plots to kill Adolf Hitler. His thinking about the Sermon on the Mount and the commandment "thou shall not kill" was not formed and evaluated in the abstract but in the most worldly and urgent context of the Holocaust.

Nonetheless, he founded a seminary in Finkenwalde that incorporated many monastic-like elements and has been quoted as saying that the "restoration of the church will surely come from a sort of new monasticism."[7]

In *Life Together,* Bonhoeffer outlined a form of communal living that was experimented with at Finkenwalde. It included a regimented schedule allotting time for both community and solitude and prescribing practices such as singing, service to others, manual labor, and confession. "Bonhoeffer's vision of life together for Christians was monastic in its inspiration and in its structure. Though Bonhoeffer's life was cut shorty by the Nazis, it is likely he desired to set up a proper monastic community".[8]

It should be not perplexing that Bonhoeffer and like-minded colleagues posed a lethal threat to Hitler. It is often only after serious contemplation of one's values and mindfully structuring one's life accordingly that one is able to pose a serious threat to the evil in the world. It is one reason we are told to keep moving, keep clicking, keep scrolling, keep working; it is so we ourselves may never pose such a threat.

And despite being thoroughly immersed in worldly affairs and living in a time of genocide, Bonhoeffer remained open to the beauty available to him. Writing to his parents from a Nazi prison Bonhoeffer: "Here in the prison yard a song thrush sings wonderfully in the morning...one becomes grateful for small things."[9] In a time of ecocide and collapse, we might do well to heed the example.

Snow Geese. Photo by Yank.

III. Contemplating Wildness

> *"To understand contemplation correctly, we need to go back to its original meaning. Step out into the dark night, raise your eyes to the starry sky, and you will experience what contemplation was before it had a name."* -David Steindl-Rast[10]

Turning away from Christianity to perhaps what might be more familiar terrain. In *The Abstract Wild*, Jack Turner writes: "I am concerned with preserving the authority of wild nature, or, more precisely, the authority of its presence in our experience and, hence, the structure of our lives."[11]

Turner is a Buddhist and not an anarchist, and so may not squirm at the use of the word "authority". Indeed, the term may be off putting not just to anarchists but to anyone with a passing familiarity of the authoritarian regimes of the twentieth century. Despite the semantic similarity, "the authority of wild nature" is not the authority that anarchists are committed to resist, dismantle, and destroy. It is no more oppressive than gravity.

To yield to the authority of wild nature could easily be construed as a central tenet of anarcho-primitivism. Unlike almost every other political ideology, anarcho-primitivism aims to give up power rather than seize it; to lessen the power of human beings over nature, to make human beings more rather than less vulnerable to nature; to both lose and find ourselves in the wider world.

Merton explained that in the monastery it was the flawed who stood out while the excellent disappeared into anonymity.

> *"Excellence, here, was in proportion to obscurity: the one who was best was the one who was least observed, least distinguished. Only faults and mistakes drew attention to the individual...the complete opposite to the logic of the world."*[12]

In this passage, Merton could just as easily be describing how it is the sickly or injured animal that often nourishes the predator thereby enhancing the overall fitness of the herd. There is an advantage to being the "least observed".

In the wild, we would likely also disappear into anonymity known only to our friends, family, and small community. There could be no aspiration to celebrity, fame, or even historical significance; there would be respect and influence but not the systematic domination that characterizes contemporary society.

Where the modern world seeks to solve every problem it has created by extending its control, anarcho-primitivists seek to loosen the grip; to move from a human-dominated world to a world where humans are but one thread in a greater whole. The only power human beings could rightfully aspire to would be as participants in wild nature rather than over wild nature. But it should not be overlooked that to loosen one's grip is an act of faith and an exercise in vulnerability.

There are what could be construed as assurances from anthropologists, ecologists, and other experts whose testimony could serve to give us confidence that in letting go we will be safe. But there is no certainty to be had.

In more concrete language, it is for this reason that anarcho-primitivists are, for example, generally not overly excited about the prospect of solar power or other technological solutions to ecological catastrophe or what we might view as the desecration of the earth. I for one do not want to harness the sun or hoard its daily offering. I do not have to believe in a Creator-god or a deity of any sort to approve of the idea that the sun shines and the rain falls "on the just and the unjust" alike (Matthew 5:45) rather than being paid for and parceled out. Every time we apply the harness to extend our domination and power, something or somebody dies and the world is diminished. The world must be understood as our larger body and consequently we are diminished.

We don't need to own the sun to enjoy it. Co-author of *Benedict's Way* Lonni Collins Pratt writes:

> *"Owning sets us up for a fall because it imparts a false sense of security. After all, ownership is not the same as ultimate control. Our white-knuckled grip on possessions won't keep away wind, fire, and economic disaster. Uninvited birds will land in the tree we own as if the thing belongs to them."*[13]

Deeper into *The Abstract Wild*, Turner laments "our tendency to tolerate everything". Making his point he writes:

> *"We accept living with nuclear weapons, toxic wastes, oil spills, rape, murder, starvation, smog, racism, teenage suicide, torture, mountains of garbage, genocide, dams, dead lakes, and the daily loss of species. Most of the time we don't even think about it."*[14]

If we don't think about the sacred it is no wonder that we don't think about what desecrates it. We don't think about what is important to us and we portion our time and energy according to the whims of others. Merton wrote that most are only "vaguely aware that it is dawn" and Bonhoeffer asked: "What do we, who no longer have any fear or awe of the darkness or night, know about the great joy that our forebears...felt every morning at the return of the light?"[15]

Tolstoy wrote that "We can live for a hundred years without noticing that we have long been dead and have rotted away."[16] We are dead to the world when we fail to notice the brilliance of something as readily and regularly available to us as the sunrise. We are dead to ourselves when we fail to allocate any time or effort on considering our own desires and interests and then zealously pursuing them. It is not necessary to swallow the whole of Christian doctrine or to enter a monastery in order to gain from their example. But we must recognize that we are alive before we start to rot.

Endnotes

1 Leo Tolstoy, *Leo Tolstoy: Spiritual Writings* Charles Moore (ed.) (Maryknoll, NY: Orbis Books, 2006), p. 23.

2 John Muir, Travels in Alaska (1915) Chapter 5 http://vault.sierraclub.org/john_muir_exhibit/writings/travels_in_alaska/chapter_5.aspx

3 David Abram, *Becoming Animal: An Earthly Cosmology* (New York: Pantheon Books, 2010), p. 183.

4 Thomas Merton, *The Seven Storey Mountain* (New York: Harcourt, 1948), p. 300

5 Joan Chittister, *Wisdom Distilled from the Daily: Living the Rule of St. Benedict Today* (San Francisco: HarperOne, 2009), p.7.

6 Thomas Merton, *Turning Toward the World: The Pivotal Years (The Journals of Thomas Merton, Volume 4: 1960-1963)* (San Francisco: HarperOne, 1997), p. 123.

7 Quoted in Greg Peters, *The Story of Monasticism: Retrieving an Ancient Tradition for Contemporary Spirituality* (Grand Rapids, MI: Baker Academic, 2015), p. 232.
8 *Id.*, p. 233
9 Dietrich Bonhoeffer, *Letters and Papers from Prison (Dietrich Bonhoeffer Works, Vol. 8)*, (Minneapolis: Fortress Press, 2010), p. 57.
10 David Steindl-Rast. Afterword. *Benedict's Dharma: Buddhists Reflect on the Rule of St. Benedict* By Patrick Henry (New York: Riverhead Books, 2002), p. 126.
11 Jack Turner, *The Abstract Wild* (Tucson: University of Arizona Press, 1996), p. xiii.
12 Thomas Merton, *The Seven Storey Mountain* (New York: Harcourt, 1948), p. 330
13 Lonni Collins Pratt & Daniel Homan, *Benedict's Way: An Ancient Monk's Insights for a Balanced* Life (Chicago: Loyola Press, 2001), p.101
14 Jack Turner, *The Abstract Wild* (Tucson: University of Arizona Press, 1996), p. 19-20.
15 Dietrich Bonhoeffer, *Life Together and Prayerbook of the Bible (Dietrich Bonhoeffer Works, Vol. 5)* (Minneapolis: Fortress Press, 2004), p. 49.
16 Leo Tolstoy, *Leo Tolstoy: Spiritual Writings* Charles Moore (ed.) (Maryknoll, NY: Orbis Books, 2006), p. 177.

green light of life

charly aurelia

I logged off of facebook for a year.
My phone number and email were easily available. And many people who commented when I returned had either previously contacted me via these two ways before, or we had met.
But I was gone.
Each of these people chose to not contact me in the other, available ways.
"You dropped off the face of the earth"
"You disappeared"
"I thought something horrible had happened to you! "
"I thought you died! "
I was dead.
And then, I was resurrected. The green light of life shown brightly next to my name.
I was alive.
I is risen.
The internet jesus.
Domestication is not an event, it is a process. According to The Narrative, I was unreachable, obsolete, gone, irretrievable, invisible, lifeless, suffocated in the void of disconnection, dead.
"I am so glad you are back, I missed you! "
"I am so happy you are OK! "
With relief, I was welcomed back. Reborn. Forgiven.

Fin-de-siècle Europe from 1880 to 1900, and especially the 1890s is known as a period of cultural and social Decadence. This term is somewhat elusive, though there are at least a few parallels to our own time. The philosopher C.E.M. Joad went so far as to conclude, "There is not, I think, any word whose meaning is vaguer, and more difficult to define."[1]

In the arts as in bohemia in general, one thinks of Baudelarian dandyism, irreverent wit, a cultivated languor. Oscar Wilde comes to mind. As R.K.R. Thornton put it, "some young men in various countries…call themselves Decadents, with all the thrill of unsatisfied virtue masquerading as uncomprehended vice."[2] There is little doubt that Decadence made twentieth-century modernism possible by breaking long-standing strictures and conventions.

More basically, Decadence was a darkening disillusionment that pervaded thought, imagination, and material life, and which was inseparable from the triumph of industrialism. The characteristic sense of general decay flowed from being lost in the darkness of a completely ascendant Industrial Revolution. In the words of Nietzsche, "Many chains have been laid upon man…. He suffers from having worn his chains for so long."[3]

An unsettled time of doubt, but more than that--an epoch when defeat was deeply felt. "This sense of unrest, of disease, penetrates down even into the deepest regions of man's being," according to Edward Carpenter.[4] When the world presents itself as a mechanism of impersonal forces beyond human control, a done deal, with the full connivance of both Left and Right, Decadence is unavoidable. Ennui reigns; only technology is dynamic. Everything healthy is in decline and "the decadent mentality resigns itself to awaiting it passively, with anguished fatality and inert anxiety."[5] Sound familiar? The ethos of failure was palpable. The chief power of the era was that of industrialism, hands down.

In the first half of the century E.T.A. Hoffmann, Mary Shelley, and Edgar Allen Poe shuddered at automatons and other mechanical figures as if they saw in them the future reality of industrializing humanity. There was of course a persistent Romantic critique of mechanistic Progress. From about 1830 when the impact of the factory was really registering, various oppositional voices were heard, including Zola, Balzac, and Flaubert in France; Heine, Hesse, and Thomas Mann in Germany; Carlyle, Dickens, Ruskin, Morris, and Carpenter in England; and Tolstoy in Russia, to name a few.

But Decadence was not an extension of Romanticism but a reaction to it. In the absence of significant anti-industrial movements and in a world where simplicity, balance, harmony were being systematically erased by the Machine, cultural expression followed suit. Deformed by a colossal defeat, a revolt against the primitive and natural sets in. Industrial discipline--the latest and deepest form of domestication--infects all of society. Toynbee noted that "mechanization spelled regimentation…[which] had taken the spirit out of a Western industrial working class and a Western middle class in succession."[6] Early on Stendhal saw that "one of the consequences of the modern dedication to productivity was sure to be the exhaustion of the natural human gift for the enjoyment of life."[7] Weariness of mind; potentially subversive energies suppressed.

The dominant minds--Comte, Darwin, Marx, etc.--agreed: the ascending order of civilization required always more complexity, homogeneity, work. In the 1880s Havelock Ellis recounted his "feeling that the universe was represented as a sort of factory filled with an inextricable web of wheels and looms and flying shuttles, in a deafening din."[8] The philosopher Arthur Schopenhauer did not at all join in the official optimism. His idea of pessimism, however--in view of the overall failure of desire and will--posited that will itself was the underlying problem. A classic case of deformed thinking.

Decadent literati in the West gave voice to a sense of nothingness at the heart of things.[9] In 1890 Max Nordau's very popular *Degeneration* depicted the fin-de-siècle mood as that of the impotent despair of a sick individual, dying by inches. The book is uneven, to say the least, but Nordau pointed accurately, in particular, to the nervous hysteria brought on by industrialization and the growth of cities. He wrote of an enormous increase in hysteria, and countless others concurred. Already in 1881, the French journalist Jules Claretie had declared, "The illness of our time is hysteria. One encounters it everywhere."[10] This was the paradigmatic psychological malady of late nineteenth-century Europe. Suicide rates rose to unprecedented levels, occasioning a considerable literature on the subject.[11] Suicide also became a common feature in fiction; Thomas Hardy's *Jude the Obscure* (1896) contains perhaps the most sensational fictional suicide of the era.

A proliferation of occult movements was another aspect of Decadent malaise, as was the rise in opium use. The strong popularity of Wagner's music, with its mythic religiosity, often assumed cultish proportions. The redemptive eroticism of operas like Tristan and Isolde provided a pseudo-utopian refuge from reality. The late century rise of anti-semitism, especially in Austria and France, was the disgrace of the century. Strange, even pathological phenomena, in an ugly industrial world that is not being challenged.

Decadence is self-consciously artificial.[12] It bears an unmistakably anti-natural quality that is a sad reflection of the technological dominion that literally destroys nature. "My own experience," remarked Oscar Wilde in *The Artist as Critic*, "is that the more we study Art, the less we care for Nature."[13] The retreat into artifice, closing the door on the outside reality. As William Butler Yeats put it, referring to poetry: it is "an end in itself; it has nothing to do with thought, nothing to do with philosophy, nothing to do with life, nothing to do with anything…."[14]

Decadents saw a world in which survival meant keeping one's distance. With Symbolism, as the name proclaims, came a fuller retreat, into the strictly symbolic. Language as an independent quality takes over from meaning. This literary style is the effort of the Word to somehow express everything while confronting nothing. Meanwhile the International Date Line was established in 1884, a milestone of global, integrated industrialism. The gatling gun lifted power imperialism to new heights, while skyscrapers and the Eiffel Tower (1889) showcased new vistas for the new order.

Outside of what we might call mainstream Decadence, however, there were some oppositional voices and actors. *News from Nowhere*, an 1890 novel by William Morris, depicts a harmonious, face-to-face world, devoid of factories. This utopian world of great beauty and humanness was a powerful response to Edward Bellamy's marxist-oriented *Looking Backward* (1889). Morris rejected Bellamy's hymn to factories and regimented industrialism: "a machine life is the best which Bellamy can imagine for us on all sides; it is not be wondered at then, that his only idea of making labor tolerable is to decrease the amount of it by means of fresh and ever fresh developments in machinery."[15] How prescient Morris was. Well over a century later, it is easier still to see that work not only increases, but is steadily more alienated.

In France Alfred Jarry, in his Ubu plays, also expressed antipathy to "machine life"--indeed to any routinized approach. In *Ubu Agog*, for example, "free men" in an anti-disciplinary army scrupulously disobey every order.[16] Jarry must have been quite aware of those who did not confine their anti-authoritarianism to the stage--the anarchists. In fact the anarchist upsurge of the early 1890s was a major public preoccupation in France, featuring as it did a series of bombings.

The French working class had been decimated by the bloody repression of the Paris Commune in 1871, but by the mid-1880s intolerable conditions provoked more and more wildcat strikes and made anarchism appealing. Belgium, too, experienced similar developments, including the 1886 wave of vandalism and strikes in Liège, and bands of unemployed people roaming towns and countryside in the Meuse and Hainaut regions. Eleven anarchist bombs exploded in Paris between 1892 and 1894; French President Sadi Carnot was assassinated in 1894.

This decidedly non-Decadent aspect of fin-de-siècle Europe not only appealed to various workers, especially to artisans threatened by the ascendant industrializing order, but also to some of the intelligensia. "Propaganda by the deed" reached its peak coincident with the mature phase of Symbolism, and some writers were won over to the cause. Several well-known painters also stood with the anarchists, including Georges Seurat, Paul Signac, Maximilien Luce, Camille and Lucien Pissarro, and others. Renato Poggioli even referred to the "alliance of political and artistic radicalism."[17]

Of course anarchists, no matter how militant, were not all opposed to the Machine, any more than were writers and artists as a group. Kropotkin, for instance, believed in the potential of modern technology and wholeheartedly accepted industrialization, the foundation of all modern technology. Henri Zisly spoke out for Nature and decried the industrial blight, but was definitely in the minority within anarchism. He was part of the naturist movement that emerged in the 1890s, but did not flourish.[18]

France underwent fairly sudden, profound changes with the industrializing process, including a collision with its long-running craft tradition. The overall breakdown in craftsmanship reverberated in the cultural sphere and led, in desperation, to methodical, scientistic styles that resembled those of technology.[19] It was a time of endings, of the loss of long-established foundations. "Never before have so many artists and writers been so obsessed with various processes and manifestations of decay," according to David Weir.[20] The founding in 1886 of a literary and cultural journal called *Le Décadent* announced the arrival of a cult of highly self-conscious sensual and aesthetic decadence. The ethos is one of decreasing vitality and hopelessness,[21] of standing "in the presence of the dissolution of a civilization."[22]

Again, one could find contrary sentiments. Reviewing Jarry's *Ubu Roi*, Arthur Symons noted the "insolence with which a young writer mocks at civilization itself."[23] A mural by Paul Signac entitled "In the Time of Harmony: the Golden Age is Not in the Past, It is in the Future" (1893-1895) recalled Morris's *News from Nowhere* with its bucolic, anti-industrial pleasures. The primitivist paintings of Henri Rousseau and Paul Gauguin also come to mind.

Gustave Flaubert's *Madame Bovary* (1856) was an early, deadly satire of French Romanticism; Emma Bovary's suicide was a bitter commentary on the fruits of emerging consumerism. Naturalism's gritty realism was a tableau of subjugation; Emile Zola's *Germinal* (1885), for example, a tale of misery and hopelessness.

Joris-Karl Huysmans provided in 1884 what has been widely called the bible of Decadence with his novel *A Rebours*, usually translated as *Against the Grain* or *Against Nature*. Here nature has truly been left behind by an over-civilized seeker of rare sensations, the protagonist the Duc des Esseintes. His escape into artifice ends in ridiculous exhaustion as he finally seeks a consoling faith. The full range of Decadent sensibilities are displayed or predicted.

One can notice that in Claude Monet's paintings after 1883, the human figure shows up less and less and finally disappears. Something similar is happening with the new Symbolist poetry, championed by Paul Verlaine, Stéphane Mallarmé and others. In fact, Symbolism and Decadence became more or less synonymous in the 1890s.

The essence of Mallarmé's impersonal syntactical mannerisms is revealed by his description of a dancer. He said she is not a woman who dances, nor even a woman, but a metaphor; that is, it requires a poet to make the dancer real.[24] Mallarmé realized that there can be no stable art, no classical forms, in an unstable society. From this he derived the axiom that all great poetry must be incomprehensible. Arthur Rimbaud's 1870s work pioneered what came to be called Symbolism, but R.C. Kuhn's assessment seems valid: "Rimbaud's poetry is a rejoicing in presence; Mallarmé's is a celebration of absence."[25] Borne along by a current of language and very little else.

Anarchist Painter Paul Signac, In the Time of Harmony, 1893-1895.

Many of these writers ended up becoming everything they once abhorred. Rimbaud was a gun-runner in Africa, Jarry and Verlaine died of alcohol, Huysmans died a Catholic—a litany of failed and foreshortened lives. The ugly anti-semitism of the Dreyfus Affair from 1898 onward marked the end of the period of Decadence in France. Before long a healthier, combative era in culture began. We may say this change was already in the air when a student riot erupted without warning in Paris in June 1893. An art ball crowd of painters, poets and the like became an unstoppable force, occupying the Latin Quarter and requiring no fewer than 30,000 troops to disperse.[26]

English Decadence, though generally a bit less hard-core, drew a lot from French models and precepts. Less absolute than the French but with the same lack of interest in life and action, the same sense of the futility of it all. John Ruskin, who like William Morris after him championed craftsmanship, saw in the 1860s that "progress and decline" were "strangely mixed in the modern mind."[27] In 1893 Arthur Symons described Decadence as a "beautiful and interesting disease."[28] Gossip and its enactment, scandal, were symptomatic. Decadents seemed titillated, even seduced, by the idea of corruption. The word "morbid" became something of a cliché by the end of the century.

The earlier cultural synthesis of Victorianism was unraveling in an ethos of exhaustion and pointlessness. In Wilde's *The Picture of Dorian Gray* is the following all-too-resonant exchange:

"Fin de siècle," murmured Lord Henry.

"Fin du globe," answered his hostess.

"I wish it were fin du globe," said Dorian with a sigh. "Life is such a great disappointment."[29]

The disintegration of a high Victorian ideal of English civilization bore the usual marks of increasing mechanization, notably greater nervous exhaustion from a more intense pace of life.[30] A boom in interest in the occult, more drug use, the usual Decadent-era escape routes. And in response, new efforts at social integration, like more compulsory education and a bigger emphasis on organized sports.

Meanwhile, Decadents pursued their perverse and escapist paths. They saw ugly industrial urbanization--and embraced the city as the supreme work of artifice. They embraced what they saw as inescapable rather than try to oppose it. It is ironic, in an age of irony, that world-weary and ennui-filled Decadents were often obsessively drawn to the vitality of working-class pubs and music halls.[31] But the typical Decadent poet, Ernest Dowson, does not appear to have made even vicarious use of such vitality. Bored to death by the nothingness of everything, his lines seem to almost always end on a note of disillusionment. The Pre-Raphaelite art of Gabriel Rosetti and others in the 1850s, in its Ruskin-like distaste for industrialism, was something of an influence much closer to the end of the century. But its subjects appear flat and doll-like, depthless; qualities that generally fit the Decadent profile.

Elaine Showalter has explored what she called the sexual anarchy of fin-de-siècle England, in particular the threat of feminism to a very sexist culture. Robert Louis Stevenson's *The Strange Case of Dr. Jekyll and Mr. Hyde* (1886) as a myth of warning to women of the dangers outside the home, also a case study of male hysteria and homophobic panic; Bram Stoker's *Dracula* (1897) as a fantasy of reproduction through transfusion, that is, without the need of women.[32] The Sherlock Holmes figure is also of interest; he turns to cocaine out of his ennui and boredom. The Arts and Crafts movement of the 1880s, itself an outgrowth of Pre-Raphaelite sensibilities, failed to gain traction. Its key figure, William Morris, was reduced to designing wallpaper and furniture for the rich, which he privately called "rubbish."[33] A rare sign of life was *Jude the Obscure*, Thomas Hardy's last novel. Influenced by the French utopian Charles Fourier, it contains very explicit social criticism and an early ecological awareness.

Weak, low-energy Decadence had little with which to sustain itself. Despite its showy and sometimes shocking bohemianism, several prominent Decadents retreated into the Catholic church: the artist Aubrey Beardsley, Oscar Wilde, and the poets Ernest Dowson, Lionel Johnson, and John Gray. Beardsley died of TB in 1898 (at age 25), as did Dowson in 1900. Critic Arthur Symons suffered a mental breakdown in 1908, and poet John Davidson commited suicide in 1909. Oscar Wilde, who did sense the underlying rot of civilization, died in 1900, which was already just past the sell-by date of Decadence in England.

"Vienna in the fin de siècle [experienced] acutely felt tremors of social and political disintegration."[34] Receptive to ideas of Decadence elsewhere, the Hapsburg Empire capital exhibited ever stronger symptoms of decline. Writing of 1890s Austria, Robert Musil recalled a sense that "time was moving faster than a cavalry camel.... But in those days, no one knew what it was moving towards."[35] Even more than in France, the pace of industrialization was intense and disruptive, the "new conditions of modern life emerging suddenly and uncontrollably."[36] Czech critic Frantisek Salda characterized 1890s Vienna as a culture in which "young men imitated old with their tiredness, wornness, blague and cynicism."[37] Progress as a positive thing seemed at an end.

This deflation or defeat, again, had a deeper basis. Life on a human scale was being erased in society at large. Frederick Morton referred bitterly to the "industrial flowering" and its effects on the worker, who before "served the needs of specific men. Now he was a nameless lackey to faceless machines."[38] Along with Europe's highest suicide rate came well-trodden Decadent dodges: avoidance of socio-political reality; an occult revival; the elevation of subjectivism; Wagner worship with its ersatz pietism, pseudo-redemption, and virulent anti-semitism; embrace of Schopenhauerian pessimism/nihilism; aversion to nature.

In terms of subjectivism or inwardness, the emergence of Sigmund Freud fits the overall predicament. 1890s Vienna saw his metaphysic mature. At base, Freud's analysis rules out the relevance of any politics in favor of the primacy of very early sexual development and the primal conflict between father and son. Certainly no decadent, Freud was nonetheless part of the retreat from outside reality.

Another precursor of modernism was Robert Musil, whose *The Man Without Qualities*, while not published until 1930, was set in Decadent Austria. The characters in the novel search for order and meaning in a culture which has broken down into a state of spiritual crisis. The sense of a loss of reality is paramount, and although Musil is not explicitly interested in social specifics, he invokes the slide-rule as a reigning symbol, not unlike the computer today. Mainly we see the turn toward language, away from the moral standstill at large, soon to be so greatly stressed by Wittgenstein and others. Musil's hero Ulrich is indeed "without qualities." His character dissolves into a multiplicity of divergent, even opposing selves. The non-coherence of the modern mind is another feature, along with Musil's stress on the merely linguistic, previewing postmodernism a century later.

What could be termed gigantism in serious Viennese music echoed enormous factory growth at this time. Gustav Mahler, key composer and conductor, orchestrated long symphonies for 100 or more players, often accompanied by huge choruses.

Gustav Klimt led the art nouveau Secession movement, but this artist-heretic "quickly acquitted strong social and financial backing."[39] Modern art, somewhat ironically, came into official favor just when parliamentary government was virtually falling apart, largely because of the poisonous rise of anti-semitism early in the 1890s.

In Germany, too, pessimism led to the cultivation of aestheticism as avoidance. The novels of the 1890s are devoid of realist content, and the major poets (e.g. Stefan George, Rainer Maria Rilke, Hans von Hofmannsthal) likewise refrained from dealing with the world, in favor of giving voice to fleeting impressions, moods, and perceptions. A spate of plays and novels, however, depicted how German secondary education produced adolescent misery, including suicides.[40] As in most countries, industrialization increased inequalities of wealth and income, while tuberculosis was a scourge in Berlin and other cities.

The air of unreality was also felt by Czechs as rapid industrialization swept away most of the past. Arthur Breisky described the dandy who "is the knight of todays; he closes his eyes indifferently to all tomorrows."[41]

In Hungary, poet Gyula Reviczky decided that "the world is but a mood,"[42] in step with the hopelessness and flight from society of Decadence in the rest of Europe. But Endre Ady, who started a new epoch in his country's literature, was a fine counter-example. He was a radical anti-feudal social critic who attacked the values of work and efficiency, and advocated simplicity and beauty. A definite non-embrace of the Machine.

And our own period of Decadence? Are we not more "over-civilized" than ever, in greater denial? There is more of the artificial than before, and an even greater indifference to history. Our sense of hopelessness is profound, a techno-industrial fatalism: the inevitability of it all. In 1951 Karl Jaspers wrote of "a dread of life perhaps unparalleled" as modernity's "sinister companion."[43] "As mechanization takes place…man loses his way amid the growth of complexity; he loses the sense of reality, of his own personality."[44] In our own age, Frederic Jameson points to a general "waning of affect,"[45] the cumulative impact of Progress at the expense of affective, or emotional life.

Nothing could be more obvious than that the eco-disasters of Decadence this time are industrially produced. Flattened, bored, deskilled personal lives find their double in the decimated, impoverished physical world. As Jaspers summed it up, "The machine in its effect upon life and as a model for the whole of existence."[46]

A retreat to aestheticism can be no resolution to what can only be fully faced outside of the aesthetic realm. Freud was right in pointing out that art is not a pleasure but a substitute for pleasure.[47] A complete life would not require the consolation of art.

Edward Carpenter looked at civilization as a kind of disease we have to pass through.[48] This Decadence can be overcome. Confronting the nature of the whole is the inescapable challenge.

Endnotes

1 C.E.M. Joad, *Decadence: A Philosophical Inquiry* (London: Faber and Faber Ltd., 1948), p. 55

2 Ian Fletcher, ed., *Decadence and the 1890s* (Teaneck, NJ: Holmes and Meier, 1978), R.K.R. Thornton, "'Decadence' in Later Nineteenth-Century England," p. 17.

3 Friedrich Nietzsche, *Human, All Too Human* (New York: Cambridge University Press, 1986), p. 393.

4 Edward Carpenter, *Civilization--Its Cause and Cure* (London: S. Sonnschein, 1897), p. 3.

5 Renato Poggioli, *The Theory of the Avant-Garde* (Cambridge, MA: Belknap Press, 1968), p. 75.

6 Arnold J. Toynbee, *A Study of History*, Volume IX (New York: Oxford University Press, 1954), p. 577.

7 Cesar Grana, *Fact and Symbol: Essays in the Sociology of Art and Literature* (New Brunswick, NJ: Transaction Publishers, 1994), pp. 169-170.

8 Karl Beckson, *London in the 1890s: A Cultural History* (New York: W.W. Norton, 1992), p. 318.

9 John A. Lester, Jr., *Journey Through Despair 1880-1914* (Princeton, NJ: Princeton University Press, 1968), p. 32.

10 Mark S. Micale, ed., *The Mind of Modernism* (Stanford, CA: Stanford University Press, 2004), Micale, "Decades of Hysteria in Fin-de-Siècle France," p. 84.

11 John Stokes, *In the Nineties* (Hemel Hemstead, UK: Harvester Wheatsheaf, 1989), pp. 121-122.

12 R.K.R. Thornton, *The Decadent Dilemma* (London, Edward Arnold, 1983), p. 32.

13 Elaine Showalter, *Sexual Anarchy: Gender and Culture at the Fin-de-Siècle* (New York: Viking, 1990), p. 170.

14 Beckson, *op.cit.*, p. 87.

15 William Morris, "Looking Backward," *Commonweal*, 22 June 1989.

16 Roger Shattuck, *The Banquet Years: The Arts in France, 1885-1914* (New York: Harcourt Brace and Company, 1958), p. 227.
17 Poggioli, *op.cit.*, p. 11.
18 Anonymously edited, *Disruptive Elements: The Extremes of French Anarchism* (Berkeley, CA: Ardent Press, 2014), pp. 228-231.
19 Wylie Sypher, *Literature and Technology* (New York: Random House, 1968), p. 73.
20 David Weir, *Decadence and the Making of Modernism* (Amherst, MA: University of Massachusetts Press, 1995), p. xii.
21 William Barry, *Heralds of Revolt: Studies in Modern Literature and Dogma* (London: Hodder and Stoughton, 1904), p. 215.
22 Arnold Hauser, *The Social History of Art*, Volume Four (New York: Vintage Books, 1958), p. 185.
23 Beckson, *op.cit.*, p. 336.
24 Richard Candida Smith, *Mallarmé's Children* (Berkeley, CA: University of California Press, 1999), p. 71.
25 Reinhard Clifford Kuhn, *The Demon of Noontide: Ennui in Western Literature* (Princeton, NJ: Princeton University Press, 1976), p. 317.
26 Cesar Grana, *On Bohemia* (New Brunswick, NJ: Transaction Publishers, 1980), pp. 374-375.
27 J. Edward Chamberlin and Sander L. Gilman, eds., *Degeneration: The Dark Side of Progress* (New York: Columbia University Press, 1985), Sandra Siegel, "Literature and Degeneration: The Representation of Decadence," p. 199.
28 Beckson, *op.cit.*, p. xii.
29 Oscar Wilde, *The Complete Works of Oscar Wilde*, Vol. 3 (New York: Oxford University Press, 2005), *The Picture of Dorian Gray*, p. 318.
30 Peter N. Stearns, *The Industrial Revolution in World History* (Boulder, CO: Westview Press, 2007), p. 172.
31 Mikulas Teich and Ray Porter, eds., *Fin-de-Siècle and its Legacy* (New York: Cambridge University Press, 1993), Alison Hennegan, "Aspects of Literature and Life in England," p. 197.
32 Showalter, *op.cit.*, pp. 127, 107, 179.
33 E.P. Thompson, *William Morris* (New York: Pantheon Books, 1977), p. 109.
34 Carl E. Schorske, *Fin-de-Siècle Vienna: Politics and Culture* (New York: Alfred A. Knopf, 1980), p. xvii.
35 *Ibid.*, p. 116.
36 Micale, *op.cit.*, p. 88.
37 Robert B. Pynsent, ed., *Decadence and Innovation: Austro-Hungarian Life and Art at the Turn of the Century* (London: Weidenfeld and Nicolson, 1989), Magda Czigany, "Imitation or Inspiration," p. 119.
38 Frederick Morton, *A Nervous Splendor: Vienna 1888/1889* (Boston: Little, Brown, 1979), p. 314.
39 Schorske, *op.cit.*, p. 208.
40 John Neubauer, *The Fin-de-Siècle Culture of Adolescence* (New Haven, CT: Yale University Press, 1992), p. 2.
41 Pynsent, *op.cit.*, "Conclusory Essay," p. 177.
42 *Ibid.*, p. 143.
43 Karl Jaspers, *Man in the Modern Age* (London: Routledge & Kegan Paul, 1951), p. 62.
44 *Ibid.*, p. 169.
45 Frederic Jameson, *Postmodernism or the Cultural Logic of Late Capitalism* (New York: Verso, 1991), *passim.*
46 Karl Jaspers, *The Origin and Goal of History* (New Haven, CT: Yale University Press, 1953), p. 144.
47 Sypher, *op.cit.*, p. 203.
48 Carpenter, *op.cit.*, p. 1.

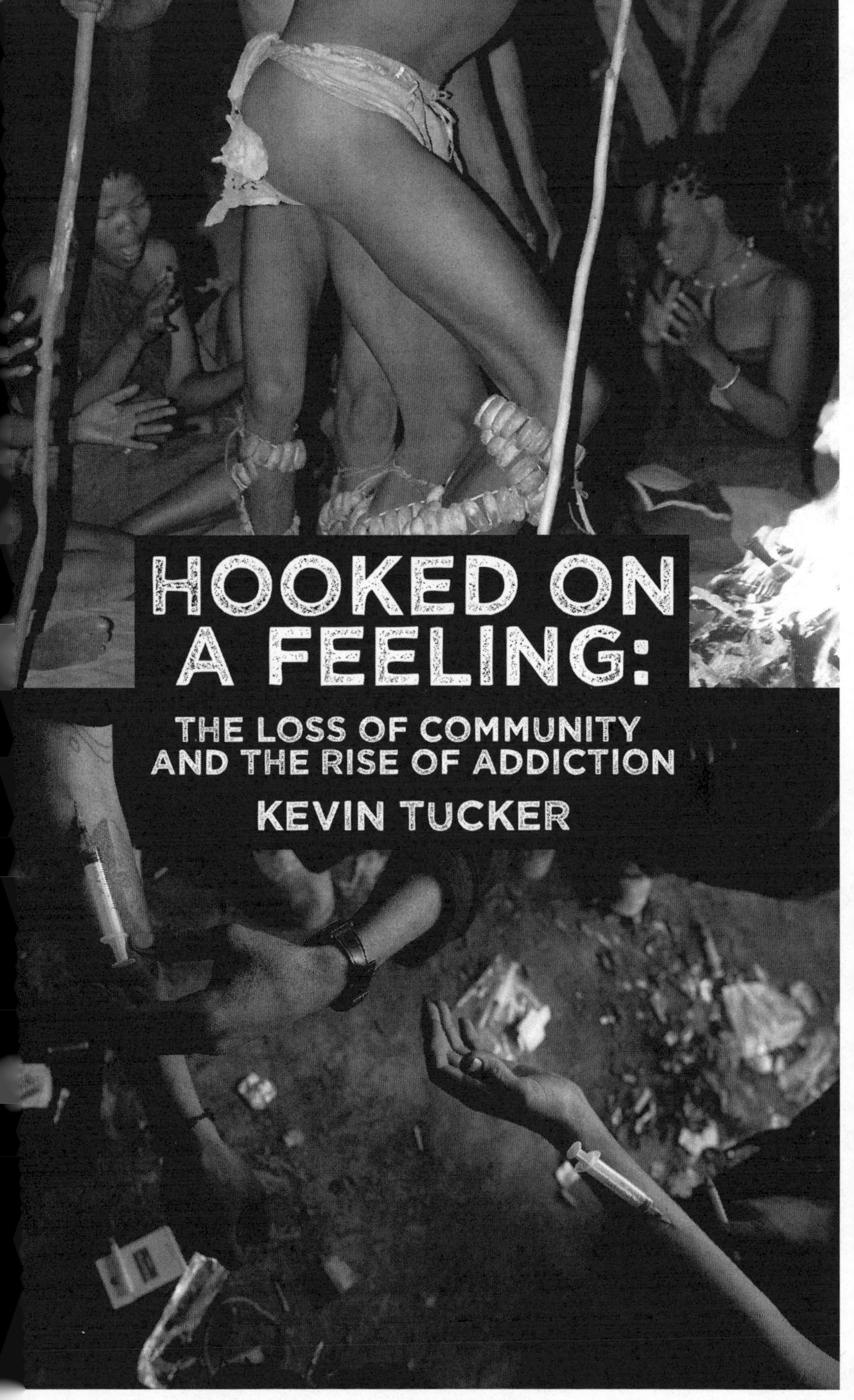
HOOKED ON
A FEELING:
THE LOSS OF COMMUNITY
AND THE RISE OF ADDICTION
KEVIN TUCKER

> *"Bored, miserable creatures are more likely to seek altered consciousness than engaged, contented ones. Animals in captivity, for example, are much more likely to use intoxicants than those in the wild. And one could say that civilization itself represents a state of captivity."*
>
> - David Courtwright, *Forces of Habit*[1]

> *"Addiction, in one form or another, characterizes every aspect of industrial society"*
>
> - Morris Berman, *The Re-Enchantment of the World*[2]

His body was found hours after life had escaped it.

Lying against the wall between two bedroom windows there were two options for what might have been his last sight. One was looking out the window into the night sky. Perhaps it was peacefully calm and the sky was filled with stars. Possibly it was covered in a late fall haze from passing storms. Either of which would feel serene in comparison to the alternate view: the junkie's toolbox; a metal spoon bent at the tip of the handle, a lighter, a syringe, and a belt, his belt, strewn about the floor. Beyond that kit was the false hope of a closed door and its potential for life saving help.

Before this particular night, the door opened. Someone was there or someone came in to respond, to pull him back to life, to stop his body from shutting down forever as heroin invaded his blood stream, inhibiting endorphins and overwhelming the body with such a euphoric relaxation that the body can literally forget to breathe.

This time the door didn't open. No one was there to stop this well-rehearsed play from reaching its logical and biological conclusion.

As he slumped against the wall, a fatal dose of heroin overtook his body. His respiratory system shut down. Life loosened its grasp for the final time and Mike was gone.

He was my brother.

And I want to believe his last sight was looking out the window.

That he might have seen something, anything, other than the empty room where he died alone.

Some wounds never heal. Within civilization, some are never given the chance.

We have taken the unfortunate position within Modernity to

treat addiction, a chemical or social dependency upon substances or activities, as a personal flaw. A stigma: a sign of failure. We point to the most extreme examples of addiction to feel superior, to take pride in our own polite complicity.

But it's not that simple.

Particular addictions might be more obvious than others, but the impulse for addiction in general is something that we all carry within us. As eco-psychologist Chellis Glendinning contextualizes it, "addiction is an attempt to avoid confronting the pain that lies at the heart of the traumatic experience."[3] That experience: the domestication process, the universal experience within every civilized society. The tie that binds us.

Domestication in terms of plants and animals is an external force. It is a tinkering on the genetic level to breed out "undesirable" traits and increase those that conform. It is something put upon them.

For humans, the process isn't as simple: human domestication is social in nature. Our captivity is a matter of circumstance, not breeding. The domestication process in every single society where it is present attacks the same elements of our nature: the need for community, the need for place, the need to feel like a part of something. All needs that move beyond the simple axiom of food, clothing and shelter. Domesticators, priests, politicians, and programmers all recognize that if they want our obedience they have to divert our bodies and our minds. If you look at the circumstances for humans outside of First World privileges, it becomes increasingly clear that force is the primary method. But even in the slums, shanties, and missionary camps, you catch the glimpse of the other side of the equation, the part those of us in the First and Second worlds are more familiar with: the illusion of choice. The dream of prosperity and wealth. Hopes for a better life ahead.

We look to the propagators of our misery for handouts. But the trauma that Chellis speaks of is the intuitive feeling, the deep-seated want for something more: for substance over subsistence. We may not be able to name it, but we seek it out.

And some of us are less able to keep that search under wraps. Looking back to Chellis again, the "hallmark" of addiction "is an *out-of-control, often aimless, compulsion* to fill the lost sense of belonging, integrity, and communion with substances like alcohol and food, through experiences like falling in love or gambling. The addicted person is trying desperately to satisfy real needs—but since either the external situation or the internal climate does not allow for satisfaction, she turns to secondary sources."[4]

We don't chastise the addicts because they are failures. We chastise them because their excesses are a reflection of our search, our escapes. Addicts are the dirty laundry of domesticated societies. We admire them when they hit bottom and wake up. When they overcome their addictions and fall in line like the rest of us. They become the subjects of movies, talk shows, and gossip columns about their success in attaining complicity.

Externalizing their situation, we continue in desperation to satisfy our own real needs. Alone together, we quietly find ways to fill our void.

And we continue to perpetuate the trauma of meaninglessness as we further internalize the domestication process.

Mike was neither the first nor the last relative or friend to die from an overdose, but the words "death by acute heroin overdose" on the death certificate in my hands were absolute. He was the first person that I had lost to heroin just before the current national heroin epidemic would fully take root. Between 2002 and 2013, there was a 286% increase in deaths caused by heroin overdose. This came alongside a doubling of the number of actual heroin users in the same time period.[5]

According to the Center for Disease Control, heroin claimed 8,200 lives within the US in 2013. It quickly spread across all demographics.[6] Ushered by a surge in Oxycodone, a pharmaceutical opiate widely sold as OxyContin, a highly addictive and fast acting pain reliever, opioids found a new audience amongst the dispossessed.

The seekers.

The lost.

The bored.

Those who can't tolerate the crushing despair and disappointment that modernity has left us with. That is a percentage of the population that is growing exponentially. Even with a quadrupling of heroin related deaths in just over a decade, heroin is just a fraction of the 2013 average of over 100 fatal opioid related deaths *per day* in the US in 2013.[7]

And that number continues to rise. Quickly.

In 2014, that number rose to 125 opioid related deaths in the US daily.[8]

Heroin may be the more dramatic of addictions, but it promises its users a quick escape. As our technologically infused lives speed up, increasingly drastic measures deliver the promise of immediate gratification. For most of us, our addictions may appear slower: addiction to sugar, to alcohol, to social media, to an unending stream of 24 hour news or gossip, to video games, to misery, to shopping, to legal or illegal substances; all of us are looking for that distraction. We can escape into the vices of domestication to ignore the empty feeling, that longing deep within.

We crave that moment where giving in doesn't have to feel like giving up.

We crave that moment where dopamine hits our blood stream and spreads throughout our bodies. That moment where we can feel something. We crave feelings of euphoria. And we have shown that we will seek it out at any cost.

Despite everything that we have experienced in the shill of a life that civilization has brought us, we were not programmed by millions of years of evolution to desire nor to thrive in misery. The nomadic hunter-gatherer written into each of us knows this.

The forager's band is where our social life evolved. That place where life is a known rather than a question. Where we don't have to second-guess our purpose and significance. That place where we can exist, where we can share space, experience and presence.

This community is the place where we belong.

This is the place where we can air our vulnerabilities and give our fears an outlet so that together the community, the band, the society, can move on with life. It is here that wildness is embraced, that egalitarian relationships flourish, and that the complexities of life are understood without delusion.

It is our nature, as living beings, to be cautious. But it is not our nature to become absorbed by fear, to want and to seek out diversions. That is what domestication brings.

When we seek diversions, when we seek euphoria and ecstasy by whatever artificial means we have chosen, we are searching for that piece of ourselves that we find within each other. As animals, we have needs. And those needs extend beyond the tooth-and-nail material necessities that survival requires. Within each of us is that yearning: the want to see beyond survival, to live.

As humans, as animals, as a part of the community of wildness: we want to feel and live our purpose rather than to merely think it.

In lieu of direct experience, the domesticators have learned that we will take substitutes.

Their greatest fear is that we will realize that we don't have to.

Narcotics, sedatives, and other intoxicating substances aren't new. Modernity did not create them, but isolation drives us to them. Exponentially.

What these substances are is an indicator. As domestication, sedentary life, and civilization increase, so too does the reliance upon intoxicating substances within societies. The immediacy and integrated existence of capable individuals working as a cohesive group enmeshed into the landscape can itself bring about those ecstatic states to heal worn bonds, to cope with the stress that life can bring, and to ease social tensions that arise when animals constantly interact with each other.

It is the removal from that place and circumstance, that connectivity, where doubt creeps in and the substances become the first of many necessary escapes. They become the instigator of specialization. The spirit of the warriors. The metaphysical justifier of hierarchs. The numbing fuel for workers, soldiers and consumers.

The history of domestication runs parallel with the ritual and habitual use of intoxicating substances. A by-product of alienation, exacerbated through war and technology, something like the current global heroin epidemic where people are literally injecting venom into their veins is a stinging reminder of our own removal. Our inability to cope with or recognize our own disconnect from the world and each other is the invitation.

For us to exist in this world as sane, functioning and healthy beings, we need to have relationships that give us the space to be joyful, enthusiastic, miserable, grumpy, sad, ecstatic, and whatever other emotion we are going to cycle through. The sense of isolation that we carry is a direct result of the sedentary lives we live as civilized people.

We are products of circumstance.

The gaping hole that addiction fills begins here: at the unresolved tensions of existence. Of not being given the place to express fear, anger, and joy without losing the ground we stand on.

The ingenuity of nomadic hunter-gatherer societies doesn't lie in some mystical sense of New Age Oneness embodied by all of its participants. Hunter-gatherers, like us, are human. That means they, like us, are far from perfect. They, like us, don't have to be.

What is most telling about these societies is that they are *functionally* egalitarian in a sustainable manner. This state of primal anarchy works. And it works because their societies are pragmatic.

To highlight the pragmatism of nomadic hunter-gatherer societies might seem at odds with our understandings of the world. Within civilization we uphold our hyper-rationalism and etiquette as virtues. This is our presumption, but we mistake diplomacy for balance.

Civilization places politeness over honesty.

"Niceism", as John Zerzan aptly called it, "keeps us all in our places, confusedly reproducing all that we supposedly abhor."[9] Civilization can endure atrocity and the horrific because it needs atrocious and horrific things to happen so that flicking on a power switch yields results. What it cannot endure is endemic negativity. We must always act "civilized" because we are forced, by proximity, to have to deal with each other.

The fragility of our society is most apparent in its incessant need for all of us to internalize its failings. If we didn't, then the whole sham falls apart. So we uphold politeness as a virtue even as we suffocate each other. I think all of us have seen how effective that method really is.

Conversely, one of the primary reasons that immediate return hunter-gatherer societies, that is nomadic hunter-gatherer societies who do not store food[10], function is because they're built around our imperfect reality: to state it clearly, hunter-gatherers know that we can't always get along and they act accordingly.

Mobility is the greatest factor here. In terms of reducing social (alongside ecological) stress, hunter-gatherer bands simply move often. Hunting and gathering is a system of procurement that requires going off into the surrounding world, in groups or alone, often daily. It gives people time away.

Movement is the greatest form of conflict resolution.

Flux, as observed by Colin Turnbull amongst the foraging Mbuti of the Congo and the Ik of Uganda, Kenya, and Sudan is a "highly effective social mechanism". Groups and camps have no overarching identity or organization, which encourages the movement of individuals between them. This creates "a fluid band composition, a loose form of social structure" that allows individuals to simply remove themselves from social tension rather than to force proximity.[11]

James Woodburn adds to this that the Hadza (hunter-gatherers in Tanzania) "make use of environmental explanations to justify nomadic movements which ease conflict."[12] Some disputes are best resolved by simply walking away.

The importance of this is emphasized in how *mobility as virtue* is ingrained early in life. Amongst the Mbuti, there's effectively an internal society of children, the *bopi* (loosely translated as "children's playground"). Within it:

> *"children will find that mobility is one of their prime techniques for avoiding or for resolving a dispute, for once they move elsewhere their spheres move with them and the dispute is discarded. ... Chortles quickly become laughter, and this laughter becomes the Mbuti's prime weapon against conflict, aggression, and violence."*[13]

It cannot be overlooked that for many, like the Mbuti, "the one really strong cohesive factor is simply the forest itself."[14] The forest, the desert, the plains; whatever the wild community is that surrounds a group is vital to the health and well-being of the individual. Wildness is an actor in these societies, not merely a backdrop.[15] That adds another dimension to the curative powers and the conflict resolving nature of movement.

On the Importance of Healing

Mobility is just one form of conflict resolution.

Bonding is another.

Healing, group activity, play, singing and dancing: these are the tools that a functioning community has at hand. When the individuals are participants rather than mere spectators, tensions can dissolve. The community pulls itself together. It confronts tension by putting it front and center, by enacting ritualistic displays of conflict.

Looking again to the Mbuti, children and adolescents engage regularly in group games, some rougher than others. Tug-of-war is a prime example. A game that we almost all recognize, but in this context there is a ritualization of conflict resolution through enacting it. Turnbull observes that it "is expected that the conflict will arise within the age grade of adulthood, to some extent it is their role to manifest such conflict, and it is the role of youth to resolve such conflict if they cannot avert it."[16]

These kinds of games interweave an ongoing thread throughout hunter-gatherer life: to blur the lines between entertainment, healing and conflict resolution. If games can mitigate conflict, then there is no reason why life shouldn't err on the side of fun, of happiness, and enjoyment. That is a sad reminder for those of us afflicted by Modernity.

So what does this have to do with addiction, with intoxication?

This is where the ingenuity of function within immediate return societies comes back into play: their rituals, those daily or weekly outbreaks of communal healing and bonding, work because they make people happy. Mobility can resolve tension, but attaining euphoric states as a community can dissolve them.

The healing dance is a near universal amongst nomadic hunter-gatherer societies. Variations are relatively minor, but the form is almost universal. Dances are largely unorganized, unplanned. They can be started or stopped on a whim. They encourage group involvement and often centralize around ritualistic enactments of causes of group tension; sexuality, relationships, aging, and the like. They often begin as the sun goes down and can last all night or as long as the participants get joy from them.

The purpose is to achieve ecstatic states. To experience mutual derived joy. While the dances can occur around illness and their participants largely attest to their ability to heal or comfort the sick, the healing spoken of here is social and psychological in nature. Anthropologist James Woodburn reiterated of the *epeme* dance of the Hadza in Tanzania "that the point of the ceremony is to heal rifts and bring everyone together."[17]

But what is telling is that ecstatic states are reached through the combination of singing and dancing (with or without a fire). Historically speaking, it is the lack of substances used to attain these states that makes them particularly relevant here: healing requires communal engagement. Intoxicants serve to bring individuals to euphoric states, but the dances take an entire community there. The want for an individualistic indulgence largely does not exist within these societies prior to contact and conquest by neighboring or intruding societies.

In his 1971 survey of hunter-gatherer societies, anthropologist Carleton Coon observes that until "outsiders began bothering them" nomadic hunter-gatherer societies were notably free from the use of intoxicants.[18] Intoxicants exist in the wild, but the circumstances for using them largely do not.

But it is worth making a further clarification.

It is improbable that nomadic hunter-gatherers never had interactions with intoxicating plants, as we shall see with peyote, a number of them are used for medicinal reasons, typically below the threshold of intoxication. I'm specifying habitual and ritual use because they are cultural phenomena: a reflection of what communities find of value. Among nomadic hunter-gatherers, that indicates an implicit disregard for intoxicating substances prior to colonization or settlements. It is the correlation of the habitual and ritual use of intoxicating substances with domestication alongside the lack of substances in attaining group ecstasy that is most telling.[19]

I have to take a step back here.

Looking further into the details of communal healing and methods of resolution, it is no wonder that isolation within hunter-gatherer societies is a non-issue.

And at the same time it is no wonder that isolation is such an issue within Modernity. We literally build walls around ourselves. We live amongst strangers. We bury ourselves within a society that "is made up of vast numbers of traumatized individuals" where the only universal is an unspoken, unaddressed and on-going trauma.[20] Our tension isn't met with joy; it is catered to with *violence as entertainment* in movies, video games, or the faceless bullying of the internet.

We can see the power of community through healing dances because the absence of our own community, of place, of touch, weighs so heavily on each of us. Even addressing that void directly tears at my soul: this is domestication, this is our lives redirected. This is the human animal, removed from context, just destroying itself, over and over and over again trying to find that piece of us that only exists within each other.

And as we walk past each other in unthinkable numbers, each of us carrying our personalized traumas, the community we need is literally all around us, but at the same time so buried in constant socialization and the virtues of commodification that we just don't reach out until after we break. That is if we ever reach out at all.

Healing, that term so bastardized by self-help gurus and conferences, offers us real grounding. And yet we give it no real outlet unless it's just another commodified attempt to find solace in the cracks of complacency.

For hunter-gatherers, healing isn't a *retreat*. It is an *engagement*. Among the Huaorani of Ecuador, tensions surrounding gender are ritualized not as "an expression of hostility" but "as a means to overcome potential conflict and transform social division into necessary complementarity."[21] Unlike the religious rituals of priests, communal healing is an outpouring of the anarchistic spirituality of life integrated with the community of wildness.

It is accessible to all.

As we will see in two immediate return hunter-gatherer societies, it is the bonds of community that allows the 'healing energies' (*n/um* for the Ju/'hoansi, *be* for the Pygmies) to arise.

N/um[22]

> *"Community is at the dance, and the dance establishes community. ... In a real sense, it is the community, in its activation of* n/um, *which heals and is healed. ... And there are no restrictions in the access to* n/um. *In egalitarian fashion, all receive healing.* N/um *is shared throughout the community. It is not meant to be hoarded by one person; perhaps it never can be."*
>
> - Richard Katz, *Boiling Energy*[23]

The true spirit of egalitarian societies is exemplified by the healing rituals of the San, hunter-gatherers of the Kalahari. That ritual is called *kia* and its purpose is to attain "an altered state of consciousness, enhanced to the degree and quality of transcendence."[24]

As the San see it, *kia* is meant to activate *n/um*, a "substance that lies in the pit of the stomach of men and women who are *n/um k"ausi*—medicine owners" which "becomes active during a healing dance." The dancers heat *n/um* through dance and song induced trance until it boils and "rises up the spinal cord and explodes in the brain."[25] The !Kung consider it to have been passed on through their culture, a claim they can easily verify through depictions in their ancient rock art.[26]

The ritual is initiated by healers, beginning at night and lasting as long as it takes for the *n/um*, or "boiling energy," to do its work. It is important to distinguish healers from shamans. Healers lack specialization, their role isn't to interpret the world but to take part in collectively giving in to it. It has not been uncommon to find that most of the adults at any given location consider themselves to be healers.[27]

N/um is available to everyone. As Nisa, a !Kung woman and healer, puts it: "Both men and women learn how to cure with it, but not everyone wants to. Trance-medicine really hurts!"[28] The physical and emotional toll of leading that transcendent state isn't to be taken lightly. There is nothing personal about *n/um* and no expectation to take on the role of a healer. Healers take on *n/um* for the sake of the group, the culture and themselves simultaneously and without contradiction.[29]

The dance itself starts off spontaneously. Unless it is meant to cure or comfort someone with a serious illness, the planning is largely non-existent.[30] It begins at night and takes place around a fire. There is a semblance of sexual division of labor with the roles, but, like all things in a truly egalitarian society, they have room for flexibility and lack any pretense of sex-based values. During the *kia* ritual, it is men that dance and enter trances. Women sing and tend the fire, yet the "men insist that it is the women who are crucial to the success of the dance. Without their sustained singing, the *n/um* cannot boil."[31]

Women entering the dance or entering trance isn't unheard of within the context of *kia*. But there is an equally important women's dance, *!Gwah tsi*, where the roles are reversed. *!Gwah tsi*, like *kia*, lacks planning and either can occur without conflict as needed, upwards of multiple times per week.

Both dances center around the creation and sustaining of involved rhythms with drums, instruments and, most importantly, vocalization. The ritual has two parts, the first is about getting the dancers to that trance state, which permits the second, a "process of curing and the collective emergent sense of fellowship."[32] The Nharo "deny any connection between *dagga* [a native plant similar in effect to marijuana that began to be used after the Nharo were settled] and the trance ritual. Instead, trance is achieved through the vigorous, sustained, and physically exhausting activity of dancing around a nocturnal fire, to the chanting of women—both the fire and the chanting producing hypnotic effects."[33] This is something that I think most of us are familiar with: the enchantment of music, friends and fire is something we are arguably drawn to on a very primal level.

The curing aspects of the ritual come through the emphasis of physical touch. Nisa describes the experience of healing:

> *"As you being to trance, the n/um slowly heats inside you and pulls at you. It rises until it grabs your insides and takes your thoughts away. Your mind and your senses leave and you don't think clearly. Things become strange and start to change.*
>
> *"You touch people, laying on hands, curing those you touch. When you finish, other people hold you and blow around your head and your face. Suddenly your senses go "Phah!" and come back to you. You think, "Eh hey, there are people here," and you see again as you normally do."*[34]

It is important to shake loose any notions of "ritual" that we may carry with us. I use the term because it is technically fitting, but the context shifts everything. The egalitarian, free-flowing nature of these healing rituals is as absolutely contrasting with religious ritual as virtually any civilized person would know it. So it's easy to transpose our biases and experiences. But to do so would be to miss the point entirely.

The trance element of a ritual is taken very seriously, but the gathering is far more informal (something we will see further exemplified amongst the Pygmies). It is, in effect, a "social gathering" more akin to a party than a religious ceremony. It is a "time of general excitement and festivity, a time for people to ensure their safety, to suspend conflicts, and to act out and verify the common bond that unites them." Not unafraid to ruin the vibe, people "talk, joke, flirt, and comment on everything that happens."[35]

After the trance is reached, the mood shifts to playfulness. During *kia,* all join in the dance, including women and children. While expressing *n/um* may be painful for the healer, the ecstatic joy of the group is infectious. The bonds are healed to dance another day.[36]

It is worth pointing out the relationship between mobility and healing rituals. It has been noted that the "actual frequency of dances is influenced by ecological and sociological factors."[37] Namely, the longer bands have stayed around water holes or at times of increased population density, the more often dances occur.[38] When new bands join up at a waterhole, dances can happen nightly.

This brings home an important point: hunter-gatherers are capable individuals. They learn early on how to survive, how to forage, how to hunt, how to sustain their own lives.

From an individualistic perspective, they have no real reason to seek other people out, but that fractured perspective is our own baggage. It simply doesn't exist outside of the world that domestication has created. This is further evidence of the innate needs for community that we, as humans, as animals, carry within us.

The tragedy is that it needs to be reiterated.

Be

> *"I tend to consider that when people partake in a collective act, the participants behave with propriety and affinity to the group or social gathering."*
>
> - Daisuke Bondo[39]

Be among the Baka (a branch of the Pygmies of the Congo) is reminiscent of both *n/um* and the healing rituals. *Be* "as a noun means both 'song' and 'dance.'"[40] Among the Mbuti, it is reflected in the *molimo* and *elima* rituals, reflecting a "community festival" led predominantly by men and women respectively.

Be and *molimo* are in some ways even less of a ritual. *Molimo* "consists of singing daily to the forest." Both men and women within the Mbuti love singing, often even more than dancing. Compared to the desert and plains dwelling San, the forests of the Congo can be filled differently by the songs of birds and calls of other animals. Anthropologist Jerome Lewis has argued convincingly that it is this ongoing symphony of the forest that language arose from, first as song and then as speech.[41]

This is something that should again sound familiar. Among the Huaorani it was noted that they were always chanting in a way that takes on a central role in their society and "plays an active role in the creation and life of society itself".[42] Melodies fold into the songs of the forest, but the lyrical content can be as mundane as just talking about the tasks at hand. But those chants also "constitute a form of cultural knowledge through which it is their very personal autonomy that co-residents come to share."

For the Mbuti, this aspect of *molimo* "is an attempt to awaken the living and benevolent forest to the band's misfortune, and to make the forest a cheerful place again."[43] The community of the wild takes on a very real and active part of daily life. It grants solace and healing. It is the essential backdrop for the more lived elements of the Mbuti ritual.

That is a lesson that is instilled from birth. Primal anarchy is built into the play of children. Within the *bopi*, the world of the Mbuti is reflected:

> *"While they are learning the fun and beauty of working and playing with not against other, they are in a positive way learning by prescription rather than proscription, by being told what they should do rather than what they should not do. There is the essence of co-*

operative, communal life, of which competition is the antithesis. With cooperativeness in action comes community of spirit, and with community of spirit the foundation for truly social behavior is secured; social order becomes possible without law, as we know it, and without the threat of physical coercion, and without anything even approaching a penal system."[44]

The children have their own ritual dance, *bina*, which mirrors the dances of adults and the sexual themes that will make more sense in adolescence. The *bina* is considered a social dance. It is a form of play where children are replicating the behavior of adults, preparing for the cultural world that they will be inheriting themselves.

Within the Baka, children can even take part in the *be* rituals, which are innately more spiritual and communal in nature, purely for the fun of it. For adolescent women, the rituals carry over into the *elima*, which celebrates the onset of menstruation among young girls. Menstruation is something that the Mbuti celebrate loudly. The *elima* festivals begin when two girls in a band begin menstruating within a few days of each other.[45] The ritual lasts for days and involves the entire band and extended kin.

There is an air of freedom here, the girls are not kept in secrecy nor subject to a litany of ritual restrictions in terms of diet and behavior, which we see quickly vanish as domestication arises. There is a distinct and painful chasm between how the Mbuti treat *elima* and how their neighboring agricultural villagers see it: "as far as the villagers are concerned, evil spirits emanate from the forest."[46]

For them, there is little more evil than the wildness inherent in the menstruation of women.

For the civilized, wildness and any other reminders of our animality must remain hidden. That is how weak the veneer of domestication is.

Among the Baka, *be* rituals are far more concise than the lengthy *elima* or the daily singing aspects of the *molimo* festivals. And yet, here again, we find a notable lack of formality.

Dances begin at night and take as long as is required. Unlike the San, they have no fires: only dancing and singing in the darkness of night.[47] The Hadza take that further, whose *epeme* dances "usually occur every night when there is no moon in the sky."[48] For the Hadza, *epeme* is slightly more formal in nature; it is a dance that reflects on the killing of large game. The men dance stiffly here, while the movement in other nightly dances "they can move so gracefully and beautifully" dancing with women and emulating the sounds and movements of animals.[49]

For *be* to commence, dancers simply start dancing to see if others will take part or not. The "social relationships of the Baka society" are "embodied in the performances."[50] It is telling that taking part is completely voluntary. If the energy isn't there, dances simply stop and no hard feelings are held.

There is a distinct lack of ego to any of this. If the group wants the healing, wants the dance, it happens. Otherwise camp life goes on without it. There is no residual or social tension after a dance dissolves, it either happens or it doesn't.

Community gives us the outlets necessary for attaining ecstatic joy and also gives the space to just comfortably absorb into the wild surroundings.

Without force.

Without punishment.

What we see here are intact communities that learned to mitigate conflict, to experience joy as they remain enmeshed with the world of wildness. This isn't coincidental. These societies embraced the imperfections of being human, of being animal; they danced, sang, argued, or moved their way through it. Violence wasn't unheard of but oppression, coercion, and hierarchy did not exist.

When times got tough they turned towards each other and they turned towards the wild.

There is no doubt that hunter-gatherers, foragers by their very nature, would have knowledge of intoxicating substances. But it becomes clearer why they didn't turn to them. The circumstances for addiction, the need for escape, simply weren't present. The power of community, the ability to heal bonds, to move further into the landscape, to be integrated with wildness; all of these things offer so much to define and celebrate our lives as humans, as animals.

It becomes more obvious that the question at hand has less to do with why hunter-gatherers, by and large, didn't use intoxicating substances, but why anyone else did.

Intoxicants and Interpreters: the Rise of the Shaman

> *"Spontaneous healers, usually women, have always accompanied humans. But the shaman is a latecomer—part of the agricultural fear of curses and evil spirits, the use of intoxicants, the spread of male social dominance, the exploitation of domestic animals (espe-*

cially the horse) as human helpers, and the shift of sedentary peoples toward spectatorship rather than egalitarian participation."
- Paul Shepard, *Coming Home to the Pleistocene*[51]

The myth of Progress tells us that humanity took certain steps on the way from hunter-gatherers to post-modern consumers. It would appear that humans made a conscious choice to settle, to garden, then to farm and take up warfare, expanding with increasing speed until we got in the mess we're currently in.

To state it bluntly, that never happened.

Most of the "stages" between immediate return hunter-gatherers and civilizations are unrecognizable to each other. As radically different as the societies between nomadic hunter-gatherers and hyper-technological civilizations may be, the domestication process works effectively the same way: it pulls apart our needs as human beings and redirects them. This is not to say that all of the societies in between are one in the same. That absolutely is not the case: it was almost universally sedentary *hunter-collector* societies that created civilizations. Outside of a tiny handful of examples, it wasn't gardeners.

Hunter-collector societies are hunter-gatherers who become reliant on a surplus of hunted meats (to be carried by pack animals), dried fish, or wild grains. Hunter-collector societies reflect the widest range of variation of all hunter-gatherers, going from the largely egalitarian dog-sled using hunter-gatherers of the Arctic to the hierarchical native states of sedentary hunter-collectors in the Pacific Northwest of North America or to the sedentary grain harvesters who would develop agriculture in Mesopotamia, around the Mediterranean Sea, in Ethopia, India, and China.[52]

We'll come back around to hunter-collectors shortly, but to really understand how we've diverged from communal celebrations of ecstasy, it's worth looking at the horticultural and delayed return hunter-gatherers who began to part ways with them to understand what happened.

It must be stated clearly that this is a process that most likely happened slowly or imperceptibly. We're talking about changes that came over decades or generations unless neighbors spread their vices quickly (a tragic reality of colonization, as we will see).

What we will be focusing on here are the circumstances under which the use of intoxicants, namely in ritual, arise. This is our grey area, but it is necessary to understand how the role of the healing dance is specialized, further ritualized, and, most importantly, increasingly aided by the use of intoxicants. It's a side step in the story of addiction, but in looking closely at this spread of societies where remnants or intact pieces of our ancestral lineage of healing remain, we catch glimpses of the resilience of community and the exceptional impact of civilizations.

As most of the societies that we discuss were hit the hardest and most abruptly by the flooding spread of civilization, it's the unfortunate reality that the use of the substances left a door open, only to be followed immediately by the incorporation of the colonizer's alcohol, tools, and processed foods, often just amplifying the reality of colonization.

The results of that process are something we will return to. However, there are no secrets here, this is the living, breathing tragedy of civilized life: there is no way to have been prepared for the onslaught that civilization carries.

And it never ends well.

The link between the use of intoxicants and domestication begins with stored foods.

Societies with storage are considered *delayed return* which contrasts with the *immediate return* societies of nomadic hunter-gatherers. This might seem like a minor point, but I don't say this to damn horticulturalists and delayed return hunter-gatherer societies. I make it to understand how domestication functions.

And to that end, the distinction works.

Nomadic hunter-gatherers live in mobile bands; they are, by the nature of their subsistence, never physically removed from their land-base. They are foraging daily, hunting or fishing most days, and travelling between camps fairly often. They have no want or need for long-term storage because it's more they would have to carry or plan around.

This is an important point for understanding how egalitarian societies function: sharing is implicit. If you can't or won't store meat, fish or anything else then there is no reason not to share. This is why nomadic hunter-gatherers were personally capable of sustaining themselves in physical terms and it underlies the importance of their social relationships. It makes sense that they lacked specialists, that they had many healers instead of a few shamans: there was no real mediation between individuals, the group and the wider community of wildness.

As storage arises, either in terms of storehouses or literally being buried in gardens, so too does property. The focus slowly begins to shift from daily treks through the forest to relying on grown and stored foods. The population check afforded by "the contraceptive on the hip" (carrying and exclusively nursing a child combined with the later age of first menses among nomadic peoples) begins to fade and population pressures rise alongside ecological and social ones.

It is here that two new roles emerge: the Big Man (a precursor to the chief) and shamans (a precursor to the priest). A Big Man's role is to mitigate conflict socially; a shaman's role is to mitigate conflict spiritually, it is not uncommon that the positions overlap. Both roles arise as the first specialists in the human timeline. There was neither a place nor a need for them in nomadic hunter-gatherer bands.

The shaman becomes tasked with both healing and cosmological interpretation. While it was common for all nomadic hunter-gatherers to have interactions with spirits[53], Mircea Eliade, in his definitive overview on shamanism, noted "'Seeing spirits,' in dream or awake, is the determining sign of the shamanic vocation."[54] The shaman took up residency between the worlds of the living and the dead. Which is why in horticultural societies throughout South America the shaman's initiation was a "ritualistic death": "the shaman must so die that he may meet the souls of the dead and receive their teaching; for the dead know everything."

The Jivaro, Amazonian horticulturalists, exemplified this initiation rite by subjecting the shaman-to-be with intoxicants, restrictions, and blows until they lost consciousness "in a manner assimilated to a ritual death."[55] Along the west coast of North America, among the semi-sedentary and sedentary hunter-collector tribes of "the Kawaiisu, the Luiseno, the Juaneno, and the Gabrielino, as among the Diegueno, the Cocopa, and the Akwaala, the aspirant awaits the vision of the tutelary animal after becoming intoxicated by jimson weed."[56]

The shaman as a specialist had an increasing demand put upon them by their patrons for resolution. Among Inuit communities (among the most egalitarian of delayed return hunter-gatherers), the demands upon shamans arose for a cosmology "existing out of the quest to resolve moral dilemmas, simultaneously offers an account of why misfortunes occur, and how they can be rectified."[57] It was in the shaman's own interest to "constrain how cosmologies are elaborated and represented."[58]

The position of the healer arises from community; the position of the shaman arises from a need for communal accountability. It makes sense that the pathways taken would necessarily be different or far more extreme. As the healer can't attain a trance on their own, the shamans almost universally require an external source.

That came, by and large, from intoxicants.

It is worth clarifying that the point here isn't to equate shamans with hucksters. By specializing in healing and transcendence as a career, they are certainly going to master their craft. It is probable, if not likely, that their worlds often overlapped and that a shaman might impose their own self interests, but it would be wrong to presume that this possibility negates their intents and effectiveness as spiritual and social mitigators.

It is also apparent that as the societies shifted, so too did the methodology. Removed even slightly from the conditions that foster egalitarianism in band societies alternative narratives must originate in a sense of cosmic hierarchy.

The needs we have as individuals or as community still come about in dances, but a new role of spectator, of consumer, creep into view.

Our want for place and connectivity becomes a story over an experience. Even in its earliest stages, domestication begins by substituting our needs, by channeling them through arising social institutions. That is the requirement for power. It is as true amongst delayed return societies as it is for those of us living in a post-industrial glut of hyper-consumerism.

The second domesticators fail in reinforcing their worldviews, either psychologically or physically, the entire veneer crumbles. Our minds search out the cracks, our bodies suffer from regiments and drudgery, but it is the ability of civilization to offer alternative visions and means for euphoria or a sense of connectivity that has us turning towards addictions. Guzzling the alternatives to fill that void.

It is worth reiterating that domesticators largely didn't invent intoxicating substances (until relatively recently at least). We just didn't have a need to seek them out.

But sadly we know that circumstances changed.

We see a shift between the opening of doors through shamanic-induced-trance and the incorporation of outside sources for intoxicants.

Eliade argues that Inuit shamans induced trances through exposure to freezing temperatures along with self-imposed thirst and hunger. He found that Ugrian shamans of north-central Asia and the Lapps of northern Europe began using mushrooms to induce a trance in relatively recent history.[59] Stating further:

"Intoxication by mushrooms also produces contact with the spirits, but in a passive and crude way. But, as we have already said, this shamanic technique appears to be late and derivative. Intoxication is a mechanical and corrupt method of reproducing "ecstasy," being "carried out of oneself"; it tries to imitate a model that is earlier and that belongs to another plane of references."[60]

The mushroom in question is Fly Agaric, which isn't the most lucid of intoxicating mushrooms. The technique employed by shamans to induce a trance was to eat the mushrooms then drink their slightly fermented, mushroom laced urine that increased the hallucinogenic potency.[61]

Psychedelics such as Fly Agaric would eventually become a powerful means of shamanic vision, but their prevalence and availability arose alongside agriculture.

A more notable psilocybin mushroom, *Psilocybe cubensis,* may likely not have spread widely until the introduction of cattle farming.[62] It shares an ecological niche with its relative *Psilocybe seminlanceata,* or Liberty Cap, in that it "favours acid upland pastures and grows in the kinds of conditions where the only viable form of agriculture is sheep- or cattle-farming."[63] That form of agriculture involves the removal of dense forests to clear room for pastures, this is the ecology that *Psilocybe* grow in. A similar psychedelic mushroom, *Straphoria cubensis,* has been linked so closely with cow-dung that it has been called a "weed" for "high-technology cattle-raising cultures."[64]

Glorified though psychedelic mushrooms have become within our culture, Andy Letcher writes in his history of the "magic mushroom", that it "would be quite wrong of us to assume that just because a magic mushroom is abundant now it has been so throughout all of human history and prehistory."[65]

Likewise, cultural preoccupations with psychedelic mushrooms may cause us to overstate their impacts: Psilocybin is "about a hundred times less potent than LSD."[66] *Cubensis* is the basis for the "magic mushrooms" that are sold on the street, which itself may be a source of misunderstanding. A lot of reported experiences within civilization have actually been with store bought mushrooms, laced with PCP, LSD, or MDMA, dried and sold as "magic mushrooms." When a team of scientists undertook an 11-year study of 886 samples that were said to be "psilocybin," they discovered that only "28 percent of these were hallucinogenic mushrooms, while 35 percent were other drugs, mostly LSD or PCP and 37 percent contained no drug at all."[67]

The fanfare surrounding psychedelics has led to misconceptions about their universality. Among the Kuma from the Wahgi Valley of the West Highland region of New Guinea the consumption of a mushroom called *nonda* before trance-dances led to false reports of its hallucinogenic qualities. Upon further inspection, *nonda* comes from the *Boletus* family and "no trace of any hallucinogenic compound has ever been found within them."[68]

What we see here is how fast cultural change can occur. Within decades or less of contact, the role of healers can quickly be supplanted and replaced by shamans. The role of the trance-dance begins to wane as the use of intoxicants arises.

This shouldn't be surprising.

Contact is context. New diseases and new technologies go hand-in-hand with the colonizers who bring them. Forests are cleared, mountains are destroyed, lands are seized, and people are killed. These aren't the circumstances in which healers have thrived, they are beyond the realm of understanding for grounded and rooted cultures. They need answers for questions that would have never been asked before and crisis dictates the new narratives.

The role of the shaman takes root to help reconcile the eradication of community as civilization increases its grasp and expands further into the forests.

The non-shamanic curers and healers of the hunter-gatherer Netsilik of what is now the Nunavut territory of Canada, *krilasoktoq*, were within range of contemporary times and practicing a "head lifting" or "touching" approach to healing soon after they began to settle.[69] This was a practice that began to fall by the wayside as the role of shamans increased after contact. Likewise, the Ese Eja (hunter-gatherers of Bolivia and Peru) would have their *eyamikekua* hand-based healing displaced by the introduction of *ayahuasca* (a native intoxicant) by neighbors. Representing a transition that "is consistent with the transformation of a society being symbolically and materially centered around animals and hunting to one more centered around agriculture and plant based extractivism."[70]

The Huaorani shamans called *meñera*, "parents of jaguars," turned towards Manioc beer for their rituals and dances. A change in line with moving from hunting and gathering to shifting cultivation, which as "we know it today is the product of the steel axe, and also the machete."[71]

It becomes clear that the waters get murky here. The Western infatuation with shamanism and trance-inducing drugs obscures elements of great recent historic change and colonization. So there are instances where seemingly minute differences in subsistence reflect in far greater differences in how trances are induced.

More to the point, that line, particularly under outside pressure, can blur easily between when the substance is assisting the trance and the shaman is becoming addicted.

Epene use by Yanomami shamans drives that point home.

Epene[72]

> *"Hostile demons, scattered in various locations, haunt the different levels of the universe. They are busy devouring souls, which they capture by surprise inside the dwellings. If they are vigilant, if they have knowledge and power, the protecting shamans recognize them immediately thanks to the fact that each demon has his own particular path and odor. The shamans know how to avoid the perils that threaten those who approach supernatural beings and how to restore their souls to the sufferers; if they fail, the soul is "eaten" and the body, deprived of its energy, of its "center," gradually wastes away and dies.*
>
> *"Transformed into* hekura, *the shamans travel through cosmic space to recover a soul from a demon or from enemies, or to steal one in order to "eat" it."*
>
> - Jacques Lizot, *Tales of the Yanomami*[73]

The Yanomami came to fame for what can only be considered a tragedy at the cross roads of Modernity and colonization.

Anthropologist and utter scumbag Napoleon Chagnon drew them into a public spectacle, a case point to establish his socio-biological theories about the innate violence of humans within a state of nature. He wrote about the extensive and enduring traditions of warfare within this horticultural society within the Amazon. He didn't create that warrior culture: that is another by-product of settlements and property, it typifies horticultural and hunter-collector life-ways.

What he did neglect was to include his own role in what can only be considered genocide.

It has been argued that the degree of horticulture amongst the Yanomami is itself a recent historical condition. The ecocidal decimation of the Amazon by civilization forced the Yanomami deeper into the forest or to settle nearer to trade posts and missions.[74] It was missionaries, colonizers and Chagnon himself that had introduced steel tools, Western foods, and guns into the equation alongside diseases that the Yanomami would have had no immunity towards.[75]

This is a story that repeats itself throughout the history of civilization.

And it is gut wrenching.

Like the Jívaro mentioned earlier, the steel axe made gardening manioc easier. And like the Jívaro, the Yanomami used it to make manioc beer. Paired with the crushing reality of the colonial frontier and an already existing warfare complex, the alcohol no doubt added to the fierceness with which Yanomami groups fought each other, also increasing the tensions within the *shapono*, or communal living structures.

This would have been ample cause to amplify the role of the shaman. And here the role of the shaman is absolutely tied to *epene*, a native intoxicant. *Epene* wasn't used exclusively by shamans, but it would become anticipated that the more they crossed that line between the world of the *shapono* and the world of the dead, the more they had to offer in terms of metaphysical explanations for the rapidly deteriorating state of the world.

The anthropologist Kenneth Good spoke of one Yanomami shaman as "a great shaman": "He took drugs each day, powdered *epene* seeds, a powerful hallucinogen that the Indians took turns blowing into each other's noses through a three-foot-long drug-blowing tube." In that trance-like state, it was their responsibility to interact with the spirits to heal the sick and protect the village from evil spirits.[76]

We can see that the spirit of the communal dance lingers here.

The shaman didn't act alone. Good recounts a particular story in which a person was sick and in need of healing. The shaman "had taken the *epene* drug and was being assisted by five or six other men who had also taken the drug and were painted and decorated with feathers." The "shaman was drawing the sickness out of the patient, transferring it to others, then reviving them."[77]

This doesn't sound unfamiliar, but we see the level of communal involvement wane as the specialist arises. *Epene* isn't the property of the shaman, but a signature of sorts. It was expected that the shaman would chant and seek *hekura*, the world of the spirits, often. That is an expectation that may have pushed the shaman closer to addiction. In the middle of the night as the shaman awoke and began chanting at an hour when no one was awake to blow the *epene* into their nose, "he'd inhale the *epene* powder like snuff from his hand".[78]

This is a point I don't take lightly. The connection here is an absolute correlation between the external stress on a society and the internal demand for answers from the shaman. What may have originated as a vocation becomes an occupation in response to encroaching turbulence. In the case of the Yanomami, contact remains the antagonist in this equation.

As social and political tensions rose, *epene,* mixed with alcohol, would lose its spiritual side completely and become the pathway to an intoxicated state for fighting over property and territorial disputes. Helena Valero, who had been kidnapped as a girl by the Yanomami and raised within their culture, told a story of a dispute between Namoeteri and Konakunateri bands while hunting boar. They entered one *shapono* and all ingested *epene* while arguments mounted until they began to beat each other with the blunt end of an axe.

In this case, that was enough to bring resolution. They concluded their battle saying: "We have beaten you hard and you have beaten us hard. Our blood has flowed, we have caused your blood to flow. I am no longer troubled, for our anger has passed."[79]

There's something to be said about that kind of conflict resolution and perhaps in times of less pressure and outside incursion maybe that's how many disputes ended. Unfortunately the correlation stands: intoxicating substances are used in societies that may already have taken on some degree of domestication. As the threads that ignite egalitarian resolution of mobility and communal healing are pulled, intoxicated states will amplify the potential for violent outcomes.

And civilization requires expansion. Tensions arise from social, ecological and psychological pressures. As the paths to resolution are removed, the potential for decimation and/or further isolation become the only options.

As alcohol, guns and steel tools flooded the world of the Yanomami, the role of social intoxication had already been opened. The stage was set.

The results were absolute.

Emboldened with Western goods and weapons, the warfare that the Yanomami practiced fed the illnesses and stresses of contact. Starved as forests were felled, as game were displaced and killed, Yanomami warfare took on a new level of lethality. The West watched with a harrowed fascination as the bodies piled up as though they were mere spectators of some primeval process.

We simply removed ourselves from this situation as we justified the carnage as tribal war.

That story, as we know it, as they know it, as they struggle against their extinction in the face of Modernity, are familiar paths. Domestication deals in distraction because it trades in tragedy. Without those pressures the Yanomami may have never settled at all, the tensions may have never required a culture built around warfare.

It may well be that their tensions could have resolved themselves without notice on a global scale, but what happened to the Yanomami is a problem the world over: civilizations did arise. Horticultural societies rarely ever grew into agriculture. Their scale was minor compared to what it could have been. Domestication has its consequences, but its presence doesn't ensure civilizations or States will arise.

The problem is that civilizations did arise.

Ethnocide goes hand-in-hand with the ecocide of contact and colonization.

But this is not a uniquely modern problem. This is the pattern that all civilizations follow, that all civilizations must follow. What might have happened to the Yanomami in time has a precedent: the Uto-Aztecan societies that ran through what is now southern North America. These societies are arguably the only cluster of civilizations to arise from horticulture.

And it is here that the use of intoxicants, mirrored in the distancing from and decimation of the earth, become deeply entrenched in the day-to-day lives within these societies.

Creating Gods and Eating Them

If there is a single plant that can sum up the complex relationship between intoxicants and subsistence, it is peyote.

Long before Carlos Castaneda used Don Juan to introduce peyote to the West, the spindly cactus had a deep and significant role in the societies that existed throughout the deserts of what is now the Southwest of the US into Mexico.

However, that is a role that was attained not as a hallucinogen, but as a medicinal plant.

This isn't an uncommon situation. In lesser doses, nearly all intoxicating plants contain curative properties. That they become central to societies through ritual should come as little surprise given the curative power of healing dances and trance rituals. The space for overlap is clear. As the trance-dance becomes specialized, the mildly intoxicating plants used medicinally could become an easy transition for inducing trance for the shamans and priests.

The Uto-Aztecan people are defined by a mutual language group with widespread roots. By 1519, the Uto-Aztecan language family spread nearly 2000 miles from the Aztecs through the Shoshone in the prairies of what is now Idaho and Wyoming.[80] It has been argued that, if you go back far enough, the entire swath of Uto-Aztecan speakers was all one society.[81] That group includes the native civilizations of the Aztecs in Mexico and the Hopi, Anasazi and Pueblo of the American southwest. Intricate trade routes permeated from the Incas in Peru and spread north from there.

Of the substances that would become abused by the civilizations within this massive trade network, most of them originate in their curative powers. *Datura* was used as an analgesic. *Nicotiana rustica* was used as a poultice and fumigant. *Peyotl*, as it would be called by the Aztecs, were no exception.[82] Among the Tarahumara, Huichol, and Tepehuane people, peyote was used externally for rheumatism, wounds, burns, snakebites, the stings of scorpions, and skin diseases.[83]

Early explorers such as Ortega and Hernandez made no mention of the hallucinogenic aspects of peyote, while writing about it extensively as a medicinal. In his 1938 account of the initial accounts of peyote usage amongst indigenous societies, Richard Evans Schultes writes "the principal appeal of peyote has been and continues to be centered around the therapeutic and stimulating properties of the plant and not around its vision producing properties." Its visions, he surmises, "were incidental."[84]

If you live in the desert, an ecosystem that necessitates quick and long movements, peyote is a pretty perfect companion. Among the

Huichol and Tarahumara, whose ritualistic and long distance running (respectively) would become emblematic, peyote is a cure-all. It wards off sleep and hunger, reduces body temperature, decreases pain perception, is a mood stabilizer, and improves sensory perception.[85] It's not hard to see how a plant such as this wouldn't be widely used.

The different relationships with a plant that we widely understand as a hallucinogen might seem at odds with the interpretations that Castaneda or drug enthusiasts like Terrence McKenna offer. But it's important to note that mescaline, the primary chemical within peyote, fluctuates greatly. The potency of peyote buttons depend on age, location and season of harvest, it is greater in the top half of the button, lesser in the bottom and almost none in the root. The levels of mescaline are tied directly to the rains, typically going up in content in the winter and down in the summer. Dried buttons can have as much as 5-6% of their total weight in mescaline content, though it is commonly found in the 1-2% range or less. The high percentage of mescaline in dried buttons owes itself directly to the high water content found in fresh peyote where mescaline content is as little as 0.2-0.3%.[86]

In light of this, the argument for incidental visions starts to make more sense.

However, we know that the relationship with peyote changes. The visions become a vital part of Uto-Aztecan religious culture. The role of peyote doesn't diminish: among the Maya and Aztecs it becomes ritualized as the civilizations grow and expand into warring, cannibalistic empires.

So what happened?

Even prior to the advent of agriculture, it would appear that the vast trade networks that would come to transport things like peyote for ritual and obsidian for ornate sacrificial blades had deep roots. None of these people are fully isolated from each other.

When domestication originates for one society along this line, it is not surprising that it would spread relatively quickly throughout the continents. In this case, that points to when the oldest cobs of domesticated *teosinte*, or what would become maize or corn as we know it, start showing up in southwestern Mexico 8,700 years ago.[87] It starts to be seen in South American caves around 4250 BC.[88] The seeds would spread south through the Incans in Peru from the Olmec and Mayans, distributed by Uto-Aztecan cultures, possibly carried by ancestors of the Huichol and Tarahumara to the Anasazi, eventually travelling to the northeast coast of what is now the United States by way of a series of relatively short-lived civilizations along the Mississippi and Ohio River Valleys.[89]

Compared to the settled hunter-collector societies that built the civilizations that overtook the entire world (which we will discuss in the following section), the origins of civilization among the Mayans and those that spread from there seem modest. Living in the forest, without the open valleys and nutrient dispersing flood plains, they practiced horticulture, or slash-and-burn agriculture as it is also known. This swidden system involves:

> *"clearing a patch of jungle with stone axes during the dry season between December and March and then setting fire to the area just before the start of the rainy season when maize and beans would have been planted with a digging stick to be harvested in the autumn. The cultivated patch would have been abandoned after a couple of years as weeds reinvaded and made clearance too difficult."*[90]

This is an extremely common form of horticulture that is used widely throughout the world, though the crops were different, it's what the Yanomami practice as well. While this form of horticulture can potentially long outlast agricultural systems, it doesn't escape their trappings. The Mayans, like the Aztecs and Incans that follow them, certainly fell into them.

And they did not fare well.

The problem with horticulture is that it could potentially work well, but only for small populations. Small populations are something that nomadic hunter-gatherer societies learned to check largely through mobility. Once that is removed, populations start to rise. Slowly at first, but they inevitably pick up. The slow movements of gardens begin to result in running into the gardens of other tribes. The decreased level of movement results in over-harvesting wild game. In an all too familiar situation, resources (as they eventually come to be known) start to dry up. Competition arises.

What happened in Mesoamerica was an amplification of production. Horticulture, with its slow movements, could no longer keep up with the population growth and the move to agriculture begins. The geography here matters: the Petén forests of the Yucatán Peninsula had only two permanent rivers, waterholes would become the basis for settlements which greatly limited the size of the populations that could be supported through hunting and gathering, much less agriculture. The region was so ill suited for agriculture that even stones sufficient for grinding corn had to be imported.[91]

Unlike the large watersheds of the Nile or the Tigris-Euphrates, these societies were forced to build waterways, cities and farms with far less space to work with. They also notably lacked domesticable animals to use for food and labor.[92]

The usual suspects come into play. We have Divine Kings and Priests, we have a divided society with peasants and elites. To appease them all, alcohol made from maize becomes a mainstay.[93] Alcohol from maize, honey, and saps, intoxication through plants and mushrooms sway between ritual and habitual usage.[94] But as populations grow and nutrition declines, a new part of the religious society emerges: human sacrifice.

The architecture begins to accommodate. With the temples of the Mayans, Aztec and Inca, you see steep stairs leading up to altars. This is where captives of war, encaged and fattened with corn, would be ritualistically sacrificed and eaten, their scoured bodies rolled from the altars.[95]

I don't think there can be a more straightforward way to show how civilization always devours community. But the rite is important, for all its gruesomeness, cannibalism, like warfare is a response to what has been called the "ecological extremities of the Valley of Mexico."[96]

That's both true and false. Compared to the situations where civilizations typically arose, these valleys are extreme. Outside of agriculture the picture looks greatly different as nomadic hunter-gatherers had inhabited these forests for thousands of years prior. This is the epitome of a created tragedy: civilizations must conquer and cannibalize just as peasants must be soothed with alcohol and elites must invoke the divination of hallucinogens.

Warfare, and cannibalism as an extension of it, is a response to self-imposed ecological boundaries. Among the Aztecs, what wild game remained beyond the realm of their sedentary and rapidly deforesting cities was hunted for consumption by the elites. Commoners were barred from eating human bodies, a privilege that was bestowed upon elites and warriors. The dire need to gorge on human flesh was enough to lure "the lower class to participate in these wars since those who single-handedly took captives several times gained the right to eat human flesh."[97] If you captured enough enemies, you could bring your family into the elite ranks.

We run into intoxicants again here, but in a different light.

The priests and elites of the Aztec doused the sacrifice of captives in religious ritual. Their might was furthered when the sacrifices appeared to walk willingly onto the altar. And they did. With a little help from a plant called *Datura*, or as it is known today, *Devil's Breath*.[98] In our scientific terms, this is Scopolamine, which the hipster-voyeurs of Vice Magazine came to dub "the scariest drug in the world."[99]

Datura contains potent hallucinogenic seeds that, when distilled and powdered can be merely blown into the face of a would-be victim. Too much and they will overdose. But, given a small amount, they become "zombies", or a walking and willing participant in whatever their assailant suggests. It's a pretty logical part of the arsenal for street gangs in Columbia where it grows wild. The victim will have no recollection of the perpetuators, no memory of what happened, and often long term effects. To an outsider, nothing looks abnormal about the victim's participation as they hand over their lives, identity, money, and anything the gangs want.

In the Aztec case, long term memory wasn't an issue. Under the spell of *Datura*, the captives would sit upon the altar themselves as a ritualistic obsidian dagger tore open their chests and their heart was removed.

It would be a hard sell to try and debate the sustainability of these civilizations. Not surprisingly, they mostly collapsed prior to European contact. The remnants of these societies moved on, splintering at times into other existing societies, or starting new ones. Though the civilizations may have collapsed, the religious culture of the Aztecs did not fade entirely, nor did their earlier horticultural practices disappear.

In the case of the Aztecs, we will focus on two societies that outlived them: the Huichol and the Tarahumara. Both are indigenous societies that arise from the same group as the rest of the Uto-Aztecan lineage and their deeper hunter-gatherer roots, but they both developed cultures that incorporate and respond to elements of Aztec reality. Becoming farmers in their own rite, but also outcasts of Olmec and Aztec wars and refugees of a thriving military of raiders seeking captives.

And it is within these societies that the ritualization of intoxication and escape becomes central.

Huichol and the Peyote Hunt

To the Aztecs, the Huichol (or *Wixdrika* as they call themselves), were the *Chichimeca*: "the northern barbarians who lived as nomadic hunters and collectors in the high deserts to the northeast of their present home" in the Sierre Madre Occidental range.[100]

Their ancestral home was in San Luis Potosi, where Aztec and Spanish colonizers and conquerors exiled them. They practice *milpa* agriculture, not unlike the swidden agriculture of the early Aztecs and Mayans, which centers on maize and beans. They carry on a strong religious tradition that centers around the "trine divinity", the connection between three of the most important Huichol gods; Corn, Deer, and Peyote.[101]

For the Huichol, corn, deer and peyote are one in the same. A central part of the Huichol identity lies in the "peyote hunt", which is what they have become known for. As sedentism and deforestation would have decimated the wild game populations within range of the Aztec civilizations and their outliers, the role of the hunter within these societies would have been elevated, not unlike warriors, possibly as high as that of chiefs or priests.

Within the Huichol, that role of authority lands on the *maara 'akdme*, the shaman-priests. These singing shamans lead the annual peyote hunts that are a peyote-driven ritualistic journey through 500 miles to hunt the sacred deer, embodied as peyote.[102] Though the peyote hunt takes place only once per year, the pilgrimage is the universal theme throughout all Huichol ceremony and symbolism. The pilgrimage itself appears to be connected to the role of the Huichol as runners on the Mesoamerican trade routes[103] and it moves further beyond that in reviving their hunter-gatherer past.

What is particularly relevant to the peyote pilgrimage for our purposes here is how direct the tie is between the use of peyote and the identity of the community. Despite sharing so much cultural and religious affiliation with the world that the Aztecs created, the memory of nomadic hunter-gatherer life runs rampant through Huichol identity.

For the Huichol, hunting and gathering, as much as they may be absent from their lives, is what defined them.

Their cultural obsession is with a ritualistic resurgence of life within community. But lacking the proximity and fluidness that nomadic hunter-gatherers possess, the dance is not enough. Instead, a perpetual ritual of dance and song is channeled into shamanistic indulgences of with peyote as an intoxicant. Peyote established its central role in their hunter-gatherer days for its cure-all abilities for their desert ecology. Here it is used to attain a ritualized re-enactment of hunting and gathering life.

"The Deer-Maize-Peyote complex," typified by the peyote hunt, writes anthropologist Barbara Myerhoff, "functions to achieve a series of unifications by presenting, then embracing, many of the contradictions, oppositions, and paradoxes of Huichol life."[104] During this time, non-egalitarian divisions associated with age, sex, ritual status, regional origins, and family affiliations are disregarded ritualistically for the duration of the rite.[105]

The hunt follows the path of exile from their ancestral lands. That is a place where there was no perception of separation between "man, plants, animals, and "gods." Identity becomes fluid and the participants can move between being human and deer, just as peyote, maize and deer all merge with each other.[106]

The participants must take peyote to open their "inner eye", which is necessary so "he will recognize the tracks of the Deer-Peyote and see the brilliant rainbow-soul of Elder Brother *Wawatsári*, the Principal Deer, rise from the peyote plant as it is "slain" by his arrows."[107] The sacrificial and ritual deer, represented by peyote, is a symbolic stand in for the life they once lived immersed in the wild as nomadic hunter-gatherers. A life lived in community, where the ritual of participation would have been experienced without this kind of formality.

It is likely in earlier times that this re-enactment surrounded the use of young peyote to stave hunger and push the body further as Aztec hunters decimated deer populations, pushing Huichol hunters further out. This is a point highlighted by the current reality, where the introduction of the rifle only increased the decimation of deer populations and forced the Huichol to sacrifice cattle in their place.[108]

There is something innately primal to this ritual.

Entrenched though it may be with the trappings of agricultural and civilized reality, it seeks to reconcile the distaste for the anti-community of agrarian life. You can catch glimpses of how the power of the nomadic hunter-gatherer community still lives on in their mythology as an ideal, a place where separation between community and wildness doesn't exist. In a way, this is a reflection of the allure that peyote has gained within hippy and drop out cultures.

However, there's something definitively encouraging knowing that this universal understanding of our own primal anarchy exists so strongly in an agrarian tradition, especially compared to the emptiness and forward-obsessed perspectives inherent in Modernity. And yet even here, we see that this is about escape, about a purging of uncivilized wants, which ultimately perpetuates complacency with civilized life.

The Huichol ritualistically indulge back to their hunter-gatherer ways so that they can continue farming: so that they will work and so they won't focus on their own trauma of domestication.

The peyote hunt is therapeutic.

In reality, it only reflects on the dis-ease of civilized life and its inability to fulfill our innate needs.

And it is that reality, that acknowledgement that civilization will destroy, denude, and decimate wildness, both externally and internally, that perpetuates our drive to find substitutes and escapes for what it is we so desperately seek. It is that impulse that has sent the Tarahumara running and, sadly, has kept them on the run.

Tarahumara

The Tarahumara, or *Rarámuri* as they call themselves, live further northwest of the Huichol, in areas now known as Chihuahua and Talu in Mexico. Their culture was seemingly closer to the semi-nomadic hunter-gatherer Basket Maker cultures of the American Southwest who had started to farm corn.

Between 1000 and 1500 AD, as the Mayan civilization was collapsing and the Aztec Empire emerged, they began to intensify their horticulture in lieu of decreased hunting. As a part of and partner to the Mesoamerican trade route, it is probable, if not likely, that over-hunting was the primary cause of this cultural change.[109]

Of their crops, corn and gourds seemed to be the most impactful.

They shared in the Huichol veneration of peyote.[110] Considering the medicinal uses of peyote mentioned above, the roots here shouldn't be a mystery: the reason the Tarahumara have come to the forefront in recent years is because of their long distance running. Their endurance is absolutely extraordinary: often trekking distances upwards of 200 miles.

How much of that movement is a result of taking part in trade and how much of it is solely related to the harsher ecological conditions of the Copper Canyon of Mexico where they live is hard to say. What we do know, without question, is that the rise of civilized colonization into the region has forced Tarahumara to stay on the move.

And their culture reflects that.

The Tarahumara live in *rancheros*, widely spread encampments and gardens. There are many elements of their lives that seem to hark back further into their own nomadic hunter-gatherer lives and their choice of shelter (not uncommonly, caves) is one reflection of that. But their use of running pulls on an even more primal aspect of their lives: the persistence hunt.

Persistence hunting is arguably the oldest form of hunting. It refers to the act of hunting by literally running an animal down. It's a process that requires speed, but above all else, endurance. But there is a huge problem there: archeologically speaking, you can't physically find evidence of it.

In his Tarahumara influenced book, *Born to Run*, Christopher McDougall points out that persistence hunting "leaves behind no forensics—no arrowheads, no spear-nicked deer spines."[111] Anthropologically speaking, we know that it is still (or has recently been) practiced by some San hunter-gatherers of the Kalahari.[112] We have evidence in cave art that the practice was widespread among hunter-gatherers, but living cases of it are rare. The Tarahumara are among those few cases.

What we can glimpse from this is an indication of cultural change. The rise of domesticated maize in the region, the expansion of empires, the elaborate trade networks; the collective and primal memory and community that the Huichol ritualistically call upon seems to echo throughout the ancient subsistence methods of the Tarahumara. The remnants of a nomadic hunter-gatherer life way, of nomadic hunter-gatherer community, lingers.

Its direct opposition comes in the form of domestication.

The impact of expanding civilizations decimated the region and its wild communities. The rise of protein scarcity forced communities to spread further apart. The increasing reliance upon grown and stored foods fostered hierarchical social relationships: relationships that were pressed harder through trade relationships with civilized societies.

While peyote may lack the prerequisites necessary for a chemical-level addiction, alcohol does not.

Tesguino is a thick, milky beer made from fermented corn. And the Tarahumara consume it religiously.

The process for making *tesguino* is not a simple one. It takes three days to grind, cook, and ferment the corn. Its shelf life is incredibly short, 12 to 24 hours, so it must be consumed quickly. This doesn't stop the Tarahumara from making batches as large as 50 gallons at a time.[113] In the 1960s, anthropologist John Kennedy estimated that "the average Tarahumara spends at least 100 days per year directly concerned with tesguino and much of this time under its influence or aftereffects."[114]

The brew is relatively low in alcohol content, but drank in such quantities doesn't negate the effects. Being drunk is akin to religious intoxication: "Drinking, to the Tarahumara, is a social rather than an individual activity."[115] True as that may be, it cannot be overlooked that the alcohol comes from maize that comes from settlement and trades with horticulturalists and civilizations. The social drinking here is a reaction and response to the physical distancing and the loss of ancestral food sources.

Community becomes a relic, upheld in the ritual of drinking. Likewise, contemporary Tarahumara drink *tesguino* daily, only to drink more heavily during religious celebrations.[116] Just as the maize-centric elements of Tarahumara reality are a historical creation, so too are their amplifications. As we shall see shortly, it is the presence of civilizations that grabs a hold of any level of intoxicating ritual among indigenous society to use them as an entry point for colonization.

Just as the intoxicated trance supplants the communal trances attained through dancing, singing and hand touching, the interpretation of colonization on an unprecedented scale can only be understood through increasing intoxication.

This is why addiction rates are so much higher on reservations: the religious and spiritual council of the shaman seeks to reconcile the tensions within settled societies. The level of decimation and emptiness that those of us unfortunate enough to have been raised within civilization are simply used to make even less sense in the shadows of fractured community. Nomadic hunter-gatherers approached increasing tension through healing dances. If that didn't work, they moved.

The same circumstances that the Tarahumara faced which pushed them towards becoming maize farmers has kept them from subsistence farming in recent times: the civilizations that pushed on their lands only became more militant, more technologically assisted and more ecocidal.

This is the sad stage that has been set for indigenous societies the world over: civilization grows; its threats and consequences amplify exponentially alongside it.

In the case of the Tarahumara, Aztecs lost out to the Spanish. Their ancestral homelands became Mexico and they the subjects of its government.

The pre-historic Mesoamerican trade routes remained intact and yet the demand for trade items shifted immensely. By the 1980s, the Aztec and Spanish warriors would come to be replaced by drug cartels that forced the Tarahumara to cultivate marijuana and opium. Choice and mobility become fleeting options when faced with armed cartels that couldn't care less about anyone's life.[117] Climate change induced drought directly impacts the Tarahumara corn crops, pushing them further into the arms of the cartels by making drug growing operations the only way left to eat.[118]

The mountains of the Sierra Madre are increasingly subjected to intensified logging and mining. The erosion that results washes away the thin topsoil. Cattle and goats overgraze what fertile land exists. The waterways are awash with the waste from all this along with the chemicals used in marijuana and opium production. And on top of all of this a United States backed "War on Drugs" funds the Mexican government to spray herbicides from planes onto the fields where marijuana and opium are grown: the very same fields where the Tarahumara plant their corn, beans and squash.[119]

As we shall see in the coming sections, this kind of cannibalistic clusterfuck defines civilization.

It doesn't improve from here.

We simply hide away. In lieu of community, we shrink further and further into ourselves and lose the ability to even have a baseline understanding about the span of our impact. I don't say any of this to fault or blame on an individual level, but there is absolutely no end in sight to any of this if we don't recognize the link between our own narcissistic indulgences with intoxicants, with social media, with technology, with consumerism, whatever escape it is we personally turn to, with the fate of the Tarahumara, the Huichol, with the Earth.

In looking at the Uto-Aztecans, we get a glimpse of what horticulture amplified can attain in its worst-case scenario through the Aztec and Mayan civilizations. That is not an inevitable fate, but it is a reality of domestication. The rise from horticulture to agriculture is the exception, not the norm. The self-imposed bounds of carrying capacity may have resulted in another millennia or two of civilizations popping up and collapsing throughout the Americas, just as it had in the thousand years prior to European colonization.

The difference is scale.

And it is in the nature of domestication within the rest of its points of origins that we get a clearer picture as to how things have gotten to where they are now.

But the Uto-Aztecan case cannot be overlooked nor surpassed without further examination. The plight of indigenous societies still under the oppression of proxy European powers bares the violent and brute face of Modernity that those of us in the First World rarely see.

A Cultural Survival report on the struggle of the Tarahumara puts it bluntly:

> *"As modern industrialized Americans sit in their living rooms each evening and watch their flickering screens, a war of survival is being fought just south of the border. Nearly 400 Rarámuri have been murdered in the last decade."*[120]

And in the end, it is the euphoric dance of intact community that we all seek.

That feeling of place.

That feeling of belonging.

We may lack the ritualized revival of nomadic hunter-gatherer life that the Huichol and Tarahumara maintain, but that primal urge within does not die. It gets buried.

And it gets buried beneath mass graves.

The Conquests of Bread, or, Cheers to Industry

"Researchers have often dealt with the process of sedentarization

> *without understanding the true nature of the sedentary way of life. The stereotypical thinking has been that technical progress of subsistence made possible the efficient acquisition of food, which in turn made it unnecessary to be nomadic, or possible to be sedentary. Such a scenario is undoubtedly based on the mindset peculiar to sedentary people, that man must have chosen sedentarization whenever it was possible."*
>
> \- Masaki Nishida[121]

The history and presence of intoxicants among horticultural societies is in some ways anecdotal.

Among settled and settling societies, their presence is central.

So our focus begins to shift here.

The focus on cross-cultural differences between varying degrees of domestication and sedentism is important to understand how the grey area between the use and abuse of intoxicating and addictive substances arises. To a large degree, this is sifting the fine details, but sadly we know how this ends. We know the shaman isn't the bastion of domesticated life. We are far too aware of programmers and politicians and the history that we have collectively taken part in to not acknowledge that a historical shift set us off in an endemic direction by way of civilized life.

At this point, we are no longer looking at other societies to understand our own; we're looking directly at our own history, at the lineage of civilizations that brought us to this point. The link here is in how familiar the domesticating process is, how this innate that sense of being, disemboweled and repackaged for our consumption, has always been a necessary prerequisite for compliance. For our labor: for active participation in our own drudgery.

These worlds may arise imperceptibly from semi-sedentary hunter-gatherer bands, but the presence of temples, mounds, and altars, the turn from digging sticks to plows, herding animals instead of following their migrations, the change in the landscape from streams and rivers to diverted waterways and rows of crops; all of these things are absolute. They are basis for the history that civilization has written into each of us, that it has written into the earth.

Agriculture doesn't represent a new level of alienation; it is itself a cataclysmic shattering of relationships, reframed onto the needs of a rising state. It requires the subjugation of community just as it requires the subjugation of the land and all its relationships.

To have any discussion about addiction, agriculture is the defining point: these are societies built upon the original trauma of domestication.

Nomadism wasn't simply a matter of ecological necessity among hunter-gatherers: it was a cultural necessity. Ironic though it may sound, movement ensured rooting in a place. It brought and encouraged interactions and awareness not only with other humans, but also with the entirety of life.

The presumption that humans would have chosen settled life, if given a choice, is a narrative of domestication. The same narrative that tells us that civilization brings us joy. A story that directly conflicts with the reality that nomadic hunter-gatherer bands danced in ecstatic joy as much as they wanted while our society is riddled with rising levels of addictions, suicides and over-the-counter mood altering medications. Where freedom is equated with the freedom to shop. Where we exemplify the advancements of our own lives with devices made in sweat shops from rare metals extracted from warzones and the existence of life-prolonging drugs, neither of which most of humanity can economically afford.

The question that digs at my mind about how some hunter-gatherer bands settled 10,000-12,000 years ago isn't why they may have settled, but why they stayed.

We know this: civilizations, by and large, did not emerge from a path of horticulture and pastoral societies banding together to start farming and move from there. Outside of the previous examples, civilizations were started by sedentary hunter-collectors, who were still technically hunter-gatherers. Presumably for ecological reasons, they temporarily "started to utilize starchy seeds as on the of the major foods, such as wild wheat, acorn, chestnut, and water chestnut." These small seed heads required a lot of processing and technique to make what nomadic hunter-gatherers apparently considered "extremely undesirable and low-value foods."[122]

It is only through the lens of history that we can look back to this era and presume change was a matter of choice. Even with the few places where hunter-gatherers settled and became what archeologist Lewis Binford labeled hunter-collectors the timeline spreads over decades and generations, likely resulting in an imperceptible level of change for those taking part.

These societies did not immediately begin to domesticate. They had no need to. The grains grew in abundance naturally and most hunter-gatherers opted to just let them be. The meat that came from animals that grazed those fields was universally more valuable.

The difference lies in a change of strategy. I'll allow Binford to define this phenomenon: "In contrast to foragers, collectors are characterized by (1) the storage of food for at least part of the year and (2) logistically organized food-procurement parties."[123]

Agriculture is not a necessity for these societies to arise. Hunter-collectors arose in handfuls of areas seemingly at the same time when the domestication of grains begins to take root in other parts of the world. The results were remarkably similar: State-level societies arose with rampant inequality.

The difference is that agriculture allowed the manipulation of carrying capacity, or the size of the populations that can be supported by a land base. The domestication of grains, the expansion of their preferred habitats, the artificial redirection of water and use of labor (both human and animal) to turn soils, to tear down forests and stretch fields, create circumstances where you could almost buy the underlying principles of civilized life: might makes right.

Convoluted as it may be, our current reality would like to give the impression that we have truly conquered *nature*, that we have cracked its boundaries and limitations, giving rise to our hyper-technological present and future. But it doesn't take a weatherman to tell you which way the winds blow, or, more to the point, to tell you that the ecological instability we currently face is evidence that our actions are not without consequence. Agriculture doesn't shift carrying capacity in favor of supporting civilization (though it and the industrial systems it supports can certainly reduce it drastically), it merely prolongs and worsens the pitfall when a system of unlimited wants overstays its place in a world based on limited means.[124]

All civilizations inevitably collapse under the weight of this basic mathematical reality. The difference comes down to scale.

The limitation for hunter-collectors who focused on proteins is the animals themselves.

In the Pacific Northwest of North America, that looked like hunter-collector societies built around annual runs of salmon to be smoked and stored. Even with the limitations imposed by finite fish runs, these societies created warring political states complete with slavery. The Tsimshian, Tlingit and Haida tribes shared political structures of rank and inherited leadership positions.[125] The *potlatch*, an organized ritual of sharing amassed foods and cultural objects, was central to these states.

Despite it's focus on sharing, the potlatch is about the "absolute power" given to chiefs.[126] As representatives of the group, individuals "potlatch in order to validate their own position": asserting their own power as emblematic of the group. The chief, like the priest, must ground their asserted rights in terms of subsistence. Being so close in proximity to the means of nomadic hunter-gatherer subsistence, the fragility of power risked becoming even more apparent. If the shaman was the interpreter, the chief and priest are the manifestations of god/s. As Timothy Earle writes,

> *"The cultural and economic landscape was transformed to create a new physical world in which the chiefs existed as owners of the productive facilities and the earthly manifestations of the gods. The materialization of ideology transformed the legitimizing beliefs of the ruling elite into concrete, cultural things that could be controlled through the labor process within the local community."*[127]

The complexity these states developed is often spoken of as evidence of abundance, as though it was something non-existent for the nomadic hunter-gatherer. But the nature of these societies, the strict order that they attained is evidence of a more fragile reality here. There were times of "plenty", but "it was not constant." As anthropologist Wayne Suttles observes, "Abundance there consisted only of certain things at certain times and always with some possibility of failure."[128]

In the plains and tundras, collectors looked like hunter-gatherers who began to domesticate or to herd pack animals to carry their surpluses permanently or seasonally. The Caribou Inuit and Plains Indians of North America are examples of this. Sedentary hunter-collectors are only limited by the size of fish runs or how long any food item can be stored, but for the mounted hunter-collectors, their limitation was based on how much they could carry. It should come as little surprise that these societies were, by and large, much more egalitarian in nature than sedentary collected societies.

There is a spectrum of hunter-collector societies from egalitarian to absolute hierarchy. While extremely hierarchical and state societies emerged from fish-dependent, sedentary hunter-collectors, civilizations did not.

Those was dependent upon grains.

Without grains, we would have no civilization.

Period.

In the places where civilizations arose, domestication was a consequence of settlement. We tend to treat it as a historic achievement, a part of our rise from savage animality. But hunter-gatherers didn't lack the knowledge of propagation. Every time a forager picks one berry over another and then excretes its seeds, they are taking part in that cycle, just like any other animal. Their knowledge of botany was unquestionable. They simply had no need for domestication.

The wild plants that humans settled and built civilizations around share a "weedy tendency", an ecological adaptation to "'open', disturbed, or unstable habitats with bare soil and less competition from other plants."[129] A circumstance that arises from heavily travelled paths and settled areas. It is likely that the origins of agriculture's spread arose as "plants with weedy tendencies colonized kitchen middens and rubbish heaps and were thus gathered ... and, imperceptibly perhaps, brought into cultivation."[130]

Domestication, as it applies to humans, arose largely from our settlements.[131] Our slow change in social circumstance, amplified and reflected in a fragmentation of the world into economic, religious, political and social realms, each carrying its own self-serving narrative of hierarchy.[132] "Community" becomes an idea rather than a known reality: our sense of connection and belonging center around production of a surplus and its social expressions.

So while we will only ever have some degree of assumption around why certain hunter-gatherer societies settled around wild grains, we also have an indication as to why they stayed. Greg Wadley and Angus Martin broke the news in 1993:

> *"Recent discoveries of potentially psychoactive substances in certain agricultural products -- cereals and milk -- suggest an additional perspective on the adoption of agriculture and the behavioural changes ('civilisation') that followed it."*[133]

They became addicted.

The diet of nomadic hunter-gatherers relied heavily on fat consumption, unlike civilized diets that are based predominantly on sugar and carbohydrates. Short of sporadic gorging on honey and seasonal access to berries and other fruits, sugars were relatively uncommon. Grains, were, at best, seen as secondary food sources.

In the extreme, Arctic and Sub-Arctic hunter-gatherers seasonally bordered on carnivorous diets, at times only having the vegetation within the stomach of animals available to them. They ate the organs, muscle and fat of the animals and thrived from it even in harsh environments.[134] Complex carbohydrates, such as grains, legumes, along with simple sugars, act like intoxicants in the body. As Nora Gedgaudas explains:

> *"Neurotransmitters are our main mood and brain regulators, and surges of blood sugar generate surges—and subsequent depletion or dysregulation—of the neurotransmitters serotonin, epinephrine, norepinephrine, GABA, and dopamine."*[135]

We get flashes of joy from these complex and simple carbohydrates, but they are fleeting. To borrow an analogy from Gedgaudas, fat burns for fuel in the body like a log on a fire, glucose (from sugars or from grains) burns like twigs on a fire. That is why hunter-gatherers had no problem spending hours to days dancing in ceremony or far less hours focused on procurement than agricultural societies. Breakdowns of caloric intake presume that all calories are equal which is simply false.

Sugar dependency breeds and amplifies addictions because it requires constant maintenance: "A brain that is dependent on glucose for its functioning will experience considerable compromise during those fluctuations, and moods, together with cognitive functioning, will tend to be unstable and at the mercy of blood sugar availability."[136] Bled of persistent nutrition, our need and wants for community and the connections it brings are amplified by a starving body.

Starches were hardly absent from nomadic hunter-gatherer diets, but the unnecessary complexity of harvesting and processing grains kept them at bay. The addictive nature of grains goes far beyond their transformation into glucose and stored fat in the body. Grains contain exorphins, a morphine-like compound.[137] Exorphins compound with opioid receptors in the body creating "a sense of euphoria, happiness, and sleepiness tends to be activated, as well as a reduction in pain sensation."[138]

It should be little surprise that the grains that spurred domestication and that underpin so much of our daily reality are not only addictive, but that they're not seen as intoxicants themselves despite the fact that our bodies treat them that way. When removed from the diet, individuals "often exhibit cravings, addiction and withdrawal symptoms" in ways that are not dissimilar to drug addicts.[139] This isn't a coincidence, wheat contains 5 types of opioid peptides; dairy (which outside of breast milk, only comes with domestication) contains a similar amount.[140]

Grains, the staples of all agrarian and civilized life, are themselves intoxicating. They are the true opiate of the masses. We crave in mind, we crave in body, and so addiction becomes a defining aspect of our reality.

But there is one more aspect of grains that has given them the upper hand since the dawn of agricultural life: they can be fermented.

Enter alcohol.

Liquid Conquest

Alcohol holds an unquestionable throne within civilized life. It is the center of social interactions, synonymous with unwinding from tense situations. A reputation gained despite its direct relationship with increased violence.

This isn't a new situation in any way. Alcohol is arguably the engine that fuels civilizations.

Alcohol covers up drudgery, has been used for subsistence, and has become an outlet, a means of escape from the monotony of domesticated life. It is an excuse for "uncivilized" behavior, a signifier and unifier of cultural identity. It can induce ecstatic states and euphoric escapes.

But it is both the carrot and the stick for domestic life. Civilization may have never existed without it.

One of the earliest domesticated crops, and seemingly the most universal, was not meant for consumption. The domestication of *Lagernaria siceraria*, the bottle gourd, dates back 10-11,000 years before present. It has been adopted more widely than any other domesticated plant for thousands of subsequent years.[141]

The gourd was domesticated for storage, likely for cultivated wild grains.

It is worth noting that those wild grains that were cultivated and eventually domesticated early on were contemporaries or relatives of grain crops as we know them now: wheat, millet, barley, rice, and maize. All of which likely fermented in gourds creating alcohol. Sedentary hunter-collectors weren't just addicted to grains; they were getting drunk off of them.

The absence of carbonized or burnt grains and seeds in the areas where domestication originates seems to indicate that the first widespread use of the grains came from fermenting them for alcohol, not cooking them. Soaked grains are easier to process and any exposure to heat would have caused yeast to form. This is the recipe for alcohol.[142]

Alcohol is a mainstay of village life.

We see this among the pastoral Nuer of contemporary Sudan and Ethiopia, the brewing of beer from millet was relegated to village life over nomadic camps. Porridge and beer were dietary and social staples.[143] As steel axes spread manioc farming through horticultural societies, so too did manioc beer: made largely by women stirring a mash of boiled and chewed manioc until it ferments. By the late twentieth century, the Jívaro considered it "a basic part of their diet" and "consider it to be far superior to plain water, which they drink only in emergencies such as when their beer canteens run dry while they are out hunting."[144]

This use of alcohol has a deep history that extends all the way back through the origins of sedentary and agriculture life.

A combination of porridge or mashes of grains and alcohol become a mainstay of labor from the first cities through industrialism and, as most of us can attest, remains within Modernity. That same mash was used to wean children at a younger age and opening the cradle to be filled with additional fodder for production. Tools and containers meant for the preparation of alcoholic drinks go back 10,000 years before present. In China between 7000-6600 BC, evidence of fermented drinks made from rice, honey, grapes and hawthorn berries become common. Through the Fertile Crescent and the Middle East, domesticated grapes for wine dates back to 5400-5000 BC. Uruk, one of the first cities, brewed alcohol on "an epic scale."[145]

Defining agricultural life, beer "was treated principally as a kind of food" while the wine trade "was a stimulus to civilization in the Middle East."[146] The Old Testament exalts wine. Priests took part in a long-standing duty of brewing.

Civilization was literally carried on the shoulders and backs of drunks. A religious devotion to production required a degree of inebriation to take root. Agriculture, the necessary fuel of civilization, defines drudgery. It defines work: monotonous, pain-staking, dull, and unending work.

Humanity would have never lifted its hand for surplus production if it weren't holding a raised glass.

This holds equally true for industrialism.

The production of alcohol itself didn't just fuel the Industrial Revolution, it was one of its first services: "Breweries were among the earliest modern industrial enterprises."[147] Workers filled factories to earn wages used to get drunk and escape the monotony of drudgery. This is a hamster wheel that comes to define Modernity: the relentless pursuit of moments of elation, no matter what it takes to attain them.

In the 1840s, a young Friedrich Engels observed:

"It is not surprising that the workers should drink heavily. ... It is particularly on Saturday evenings that intoxication can be seen in all its bestiality, for it is then that the workers have just received their wages and go out for enjoyment at rather earlier hours than on other days of the week. ... And when the revelers have no money left they go to the nearest pawnshop with whatever they have..."[148]

History also shows a painful trend where the more removed a society becomes, the more extreme the escapes will be.

While beer remained a source of fuel for industrial workers, that escape increasingly required a larger push. That came in particular from distilled spirits. Originally arising as anesthesia in the standard Western military kit to ensure that soldiers acted more like machines than living beings, liquor became a regular part of modernized life. As soldiers left the battlefield and came home, the taste for liquor that they brought back with them flooded industrial society. In many ways liquor "represents a process of *acceleration* of intoxication, intrinsically related to other processes of acceleration in the modern age."[149]

If efficiency was the learned goal, liquor fit the times.

The need for escape among industrial workers was met with another stimulant promoted to the middle class and driven by a Protestant work ethic: coffee. Addiction to alcohol was a target of religious devotees to the Progress that a rising middle class upheld. It wasn't a target because of the addictiveness of alcohol, but because of the uncontrollability of drunks. Alcohol could be targeted because it could be replaced.

And for an industrializing world, coffee fit the bill perfectly.

Despite religious groups early ban on coffee (notably as Christians didn't want to partake in the perceived drink of Muslims), its role in increasing production placed it front and center in the Industrial Revolution. It allowed humans to act like machines:

> *"Medieval man did physical work, for the most part under the open sky. The middle-class man worked increasingly with his head, his workplace was the office, his working position was sedentary. The ideal that hovered before him was to function as uniformly and regularly as a clock."*[150]

The class divide over the stimulant of choice: either to promote production or to inhibit escape, only furthered a sense of class camaraderie: a distinction that Engels and fellow socialists would ironically grasp onto. Liquor became the target of socialists while beer became their unifier for the working class.

Gin was a clear threat to proletarian identity. As historian Wolfgang Schivelbusch observes: "It provided alcoholic stupefaction, not social intoxication."[151] Despite the words from a young Engels, socialists saw that it was the tavern that would launch a socialist revolution. Karl Kautsky, a socialist and contemporary of Engels, took no qualms stating: "Without the tavern, the German proletariat has not only no social, but also no political, life."[152]

On the face of it, such a statement might seem contradictory. But that would only be true if the socialists had intended on freeing workers from the drudgery of industrial and agrarian life.

That is what they absolutely did not want.

Socialism catered to that same false sense of community peddled about by religious and political elites since the dawn of civilization: production for the sake of society is rewarding in and of itself. The link between individuals was their sacrifice for the greater good. Engels was aware enough to recognize the importance of an unquestioning sense of place to the human experience.

But he didn't dig deep enough and settled on the drudgery of production.

The prospects of Progress could be liberated beyond the binds of Capitalism. The success that socialists, communists, and anarcho-syndicalists achieved during the industrial era were due to the fact that their notion of community could arguably be found within a rising class-consciousness.

Proletarian identity was observable. There was a sense of belonging. But this was doomed to failure because it was a sense of belonging that was based on escapism, a mutual sense of dis-ease with the misery of work. That distaste lingers back to our hunter-gatherer minds, but could never take root fully because they were limited in their scope to never shed domestication.

Instead, they just blamed the current management. And there is some palatability to that, as anyone who has spent their free time with co-workers complaining about work can attest. And, again, the ritual of complaining about work with co-workers is one that most often revolves around alcohol consumption.

Our domestication requires a sober assessment; which is never an easy task when you realize how horrifically entrenched the values of civilization are within our psyches. If we seek to break the cycles of addiction and patterns of escapism, then this is where we must begin.

From here, the cycles continue to worsen.

None of these things happened in a vacuum. Alcohol wasn't the sole affliction of working class Europeans and Americans. The coffee that fueled the arising middle class came from colonies. Those coffee cups were filled by the forced labor of slaves, plantation systems, and the brutality of the frontier.

They still are and they will continue to be.

It's impossible to look at the sources of our addictive substances while being divorced from reality. The globalized world of this techno-industrial civilization has always come with a body count. Forests are destroyed to make way for cash crops. Societies are torn apart to create labor. Debt-systems are created to build railways, to enlist soldiers as cannon fodder, to perpetuate the maintenance and expansion of a civilization that must grow to survive.

Coffee consumption among the middle class in the industrial age was mirrored in the introduction of sugar, arguably one of the most deadly addictive substances in the world today. As Sidney Mintz unapathetically points out:

> *"England fought the most, conquered the most colonies, imported the most slaves (to her own colonies, and, in absolute numbers, in her own bottoms), and went furthest and fastest in creating a plantation system. The most important product of that system was sugar."*[153]

Though sugar becomes one of the most vital substances within modernity, it was hardly alone at the time. Workers in Russia were fueled by vodka. Chinese migrants were lured and addicted with opium. Given the opportunity for work abroad, Chinese migrants would arrive in distant lands carrying a debt that they would never be able to repay. But their brokers would gladly credit their labor with opium, only furthering their debts.

This too should sound familiar. Gangs and politicians run the world of immigration in a constant scheme that involves drugs, cash, and the arms trade. The promise of economic freedom ends in prostitution, trafficking, and industrial slavery today as surely as it did at the dawn of the Industrial era.

So as you hear that more "than a few sick and despairing Chinese finally stepped off the treadmill by the same means used to keep them on it: they took an overdose of opium"[154]: we can find the contemporary correlations in Third World farmers subjected to International Monetary Fund (IMF) and World Bank Structural Adjustment Policies where they are coerced into growing cash crops that require intensive applications of pesticides. Unable to escape debt and sick from contact with toxins, it is not uncommon for them to commit suicide by ingesting the pesticides directly.[155]

On the other side of that equation, you have more and more individuals willing to take extreme drugs like heroin, krokodil, crack, cocaine, and meth.

Our disconnect is unilateral in its impact. The further we are from each other, the more willing we are to turn towards drastic measures of escape. The more we indulge in those escapes, the less aware or caring we are of how those systems even arise and function.

In our attempts to escape misery, we further the reach of domestication.

And there are few places where that is more apparent than where intact communities are thrust into and met by our hollow and hallowed Modernity.

Forced Settlements

> *"The Bushmen sat in the dunes, wondering, frustrated and angry. In their frustration, they had begun to turn on each other: there had been a lot of drinking and violence. Rikki, Jakob, even old Dawid, were beating up their wives almost daily, and the children were asking Belinda a question she couldn't answer: 'Why do the grown-ups drink?'*
> *Sillikat, who had come back from Kagga Kama for a while, had answered the question one night: ' You want to know why I drink? I drink because I feel like a caged animal. In the old days this clan, when we disagreed, would have split up, different families going off to live where they pleased, coming together again as they pleased, no problems, no fighting. So we drink, and when we drink, the an-*

ger comes, and we fight.'"

- Rupert Isaacson, *The Healing Land*[156]

Civilized narratives go to great lengths to bury the point of contact.

It is here that genocide is simply the norm. It is unironic to speak of domestication in terms of addiction, because there is no greater addict than civilization itself. It must consume life to perpetuate itself: to perpetuate its unchecked growth.

We repackage the wanton extermination of peoples under the guise of "tribal war." We chastise the "savages" for having the repugnant position of choosing the joys that they know from their own existing communities over the perpetuation of our need for resources to fuel our addiction-riddled wallow through apathy. We uphold the virtues of fillers as evidence of our superiority, taunting indigenous societies with sugar and steel, while we destroy everything that they know.

The Huaorani, whose perpetual singing to the forest I spoke of earlier, have their entire world threatened by the presence of oil that would account for thirteen days of oil for American consumption. Thirteen days worth.[157]

The realities of life for intact communities have always been tormented by the inability to rationalize the depravity and extent to which civilized societies will kill, rape, enslave and steal everything. Decimation of a culture, of a place, for nearly all of these peoples, both hunter-gatherer and horticultural alike, was literally unthinkable.

So you see how their worlds are contorted and it makes you sick.

The intoxicated state of shamans amongst native North Americans gave the colonizers an entry point. Drunkenness, which was "perhaps more destructive than any other European influence besides epidemic disease" was met with familiarity. It was treated as "akin to ritually entering an inspired altered state and met with little initial cultural resistance."[158]

By the time the impact of substances were obvious, the damage was already well underway. Alcohol was used to lure Native Americans into a barter system that was absolutely foreign to them. Their land was being stolen, their people raped, tortured and systemically killed, while negotiations over property, a framework that they didn't share, resulted in one of the greatest episodes of land theft in the history of the world.

Alcohol became a tool of escape in the same way civilized societies had always used it.

A situation that was not unacknowledged as this early recorded interaction shows:

> *"When I come to your place with my peltry," one Pennsylvania Indian rebuked a trader, "all call to me: 'Come, Thomas! Here's rum, drink heartily, drink! It will not hurt you.' All this is done for the purpose of cheating me. When you have obtained from me all you want, you call me a drunk dog, and kick me out of the room."*[159]

There was no illusion as to what the colonizers were doing here. A colonial era letter from a Canadian agent of the Hudson Bay Company shows how different native societies were "tamed" by their barter system and how to approach those that hadn't been.

> *"In the plains, however, this system will not do, as they can live independent of us, and by withholding ammunition, tobacco and spirits, the Staple articles of Trade, for one year, they will recover the use of their Bows and spears, and lose sight of their smoking and drinking habits; it will therefore be necessary to bring those Tribes round by mild and cautious measure..."*[160]

Approached as a bait-and-switch view of civilization, the idea of introducing barter systems sought to give colonization an air of credibility, as though the joys of civilized life were universals. Australia in the 1890s undertook a vast and intentional policy of moving from military force to a policy of rationing. The government specifically targeted peripheral groups in ways to destabilize their self-sufficiency. Baited with free bread, the Aborigines were brought into settlements and then rations turned into barter for labor. Cash, naturally, bought alcohol and tobacco as well.[161]

Sugar is an introductory substance of choice. Its distribution has been synonymous with the spread of Progress throughout the world. First offered by missionaries or "charities", the enticed recipients are then drawn into labor to purchase more.[162] Along with "store food", this is the key reason why diabetic rates among Native Americans, particularly the previously near-carnivore Arctic and Sub-Arctic hunter-gatherers, are among the highest in the world.

Slowly or quickly, civilization settles for nothing less than the complete abolition of hunter-gatherer and horticultural societies by death or assimilation. It is their very existence, the mere possibility of another way of life outside of civilization that threatens the narratives that make the domestication process possible.

Even in a defeated, withdrawn, and corralled state, unless they succumb to the vices of Modern life, they remain a too familiar semblance of what life can be. A reminder of what community can look like and how it can persevere.

Any reminder of the thing that we are all so desperately searching for must be eradicated so that we keep on seeking it out ourselves. So we go to work, so we consume, so we embrace and perpetuate our own misery and emptiness.

It is probable that there is no more of an apparent point of diffusion and forced settlements than roads.

Cutting through forests, opening up deserts and prairies, increasing traffic or increasing access for mining, logging, and hunting, while expanding the reach of governments, corporations, and missionaries, roads carry the means of civilization and its spoils.

For the San of the Kalahari, the presence of roads made it more permissible for neighboring BaTswana tribes to take over more land, putting up fences that block wild migration patterns and keep grazing domesticated animals in their way, sinking boreholes to supply water for livestock. The animals they would otherwise hunt end up dying along agricultural fence lines on what becomes "private property" or, worse, land preserves that bare their names, where they are persecuted for subsistence hunting.

The situation is dire.

> *"With the exception of a few clans still living outside the grasp of the ranchers, most of the Bushmen had found themselves, within a few years, enclosed by wire, their age-old food source gone, reduced to serfs looking after other people's cattle on land that had once been their own."*[163]

The roads carry in tourists who bring cash with them. It's a horrid fate that their want to see people living as the whole of humanity is rooted: as nomadic hunter-gatherers, are contributing to the death of their cultures. Tourists brought marijuana into the Kalahari, which has become heavily used by the San.

Among San settled in farming villages, anthropologist Mathias Guenther observed that the economic dependency that arises resulted in the commodification of the healing dance itself. The trance dancer becomes a professional just as the trance is gutted of sharing, that "central mode and spirit."[164] It is the reality of cash "as a medium of exchange and remuneration" that cements "the context of the wage economy."[165] In light of the commodification of the sacred, the San only turn further towards intoxication and addiction as their escape.[166]

This fosters a tense reality, these nomadic hunter-gatherer societies by large knew of intoxicating substances and avoided them. Yet as roads tore into previously uncontacted or inaccessible areas, they brought the scourge of domestication with them. They brought drugs, they brought alcohol, but, more importantly, they brought a reason to use them.

Roads tear apart communities as they bring in the outside world. Miners, workers, armies, missionaries, tourists, governments; the road brings civilization closer and the need to escape that reality rises. And the intoxicants flow in. Arab traders introduced the Pygmies to marijuana. Plains Indians knew of peyote but didn't begin using it ritually until contact had already started to fray their culture. The hunter-collector Ainu of Japan began drinking alcohol after they started growing millet around settlements.[167]

Tobacco, at times symbolic of American exploit, spread from the agrarian tribes of the south and east of what is now the United States. For the hunter-collector Tlingit of the Pacific Northwest, tobacco was the first crop that was grown.[168] Smoking tobacco was a different acculturation spreading from the point of contact. Amongst the Inuit, they were taught about smoking tobacco from neighboring Russians.[169]

These newly acquired substances can become a source of cultural identity.

Among the Australian Aboriginal cultures, it is widely reported that the use of tobacco and alcohol were long standing native traditions. Alcohol, typically a mild version made of the fermented, sweet sap of the Palm and Miena Cider Gum trees from their crevices, became in some ways emblematic of Aboriginal tradition.[170]

This presumption comes from the fact that Aboriginal societies had such intense reactions to the liquor of the Europeans. Leading to rampant alcoholism, rapidly increasing levels of domestic violence, eventually building a movement that would be countered by contemporary native "anti-Grog" (anti-alcohol) campaigns. However, this method of cider making bares exact resemblance to the Arrack that the Macassan trepangers (sea cucumber fishers) from Indonesia brought to Australia and Tasmania alongside a tradition of smoking tobacco. Like the fermented sap of palm trees, Arrack is a saccharine juice made from fermented sugars and saps.[171]

The Macassan impact on native culture was widespread; the substances that were acquired made their way into the indigenous identity and culture as ingrained traditions.[172] Yet they are overlooked because of the Western bravado around first contact. This occurs despite the fact that cave art depicts the presence of Macassan trade relations as early as the mid-1600s, a timeline that is backed up with the remains of Macassan goods.[173]

It is not improbable that these relationships encouraged coastal Aboriginal societies towards semi-sedentary lives, complete with a loss of social egalitarianism between ages and sexes. Egalitarianism here is not fully buried. As Elder Rosalind Langford stated, "Traditionally, our mob has used plant medicines, healing hands, and spirit to help us move through that and heal." Unfortunately, "nowadays most of our mob use alcohol and drugs to suppress our pain and grief or we use pills."[174]

Intoxicants don't simply arrive on the scene and get added to communities. They become replacements, substitutes. Healing dances wane in lieu of individual intoxication. And it is the communities that suffer.

Pain becomes personal. The social identity of the society and their means of resolution are lost to forced settlements and arguments fueled by alcohol. Dances sometimes are revived for tourists, almost mocking the original form and purpose.

Like us, fragmented lives are subjected to fragments of escape.

In the shadow of community, addicts arise.

Where there is money and defeat, there will be alcohol and escape. As Frank Marlowe observed among the Hadza, tourism within the last two decades increased 10-20 times over. The tourists are eager to pay the Hadza for any cultural relic to take home with them. But once the tourists leave, "neighboring tribes waste no time bringing the Hadza alcohol and leaving with all the tourist money. … Drinking leads to arguments and fights and injuries and murder. A few recent alcohol-related murders have caused the murder rate to soar."[175]

For the Jarawa of the Andaman Islands, the road has turned them into a tourist attraction. They become a sight seeing trip for the morbid fascination of wealthy Indian travellers. Expensive hotels offer the road through the Jarawa territory as a must see exhibit. The Jarawa were once known for the reclusive behavior and militancy against settlers. But as roads are cut and loggers clear the forests and settlers poach game, they are left coming to the road for handouts.

This has brought alcohol, tobacco and a narcotic betel leaf into their society, but it has also brought endemic disease, such as a measles and pneumonia outbreak, in 1999, that impacted up to half of the population. Poachers, settlers, bus drivers and tourists have notoriously abused, assaulted and raped Jarawa women.[176] It has become a form of drive-thru frontier.

In a global overview of hunter-gatherer and hunter-collector cultures, Carleton Coon states without question that "Drugs, along with new diseases and new foods such as flour and rice, share the principal honors for the decline of hunting populations throughout the world, plus the social disturbances caused by the presence of traders and colonists in recent times."[177]

Roads simply facilitate those interactions.

It is the certainty of genocide that draws indigenous societies away from the road, but it is the reality of ecocide that forces them closer. The illusions of Progress, preached from a sugar-coated pulpit that creates the desperation where hope for survival overcomes the fear of assured cultural assimilation.

The uncomfortable back and forth of this reality is best spoken of by the Awa of Papua New Guinea, who share suffering on both sides of this ambiguous colonial reality:

> *"To them, however, the road remains a metaphor for culture change and 'development.' Men talk about it feverishly and insistently point to the high rain forest where it will eventually come. The road-to-be is a symbol of salvation, of endless economic gain, a path toward material wealth and increasingly accessible consumerism.*
>
> *"But not all of the villagers find this talk comforting. ... Still others, mainly of the older generation, know that a road will be their final death cry. They could already see the end coming in the past several decades of contact with the uninvited arrival of pale, gum-booted Australian kiaps (patrol officers), Western currency, trade stores, and wage labor migration that carried their young sons on airplanes to the coastal plantations that they themselves would never see."*[178]

Perhaps sharing in the delusion, my hope is that the civilization building these roads bleeds itself dry before any more can be built. But this is the reality of our shared situation that we also must face.

Our lives are not without consequence.

Drugged Warriors, Drug Wars

> *"Of all of civilization's occupational categories, that of soldier may be the most conductive to regular drug use."*
>
> -David Courtwright, *Forces of Habit*[179]

A history of drugs, like any other facet of civilized life, cannot ignore a primary antagonist: warfare.

There is perhaps no greater truism than anthropologist Stanley Diamond's statement that "Civilization originates in conquest abroad and repression at home. Each is an aspect of the other."[180]

Liquor was distilled through military personnel before it found its way into mainstream society. The same can be said about nearly every other hard drug. Heroin and cocaine are perhaps the worst of it, but just as soldiers bring their newly formed addictions home, so too do those addictions fuel war.

There is no distinction to be made here. The further civilization carries on, the more intoxicants become another resource to war over. Warriors arise early in the trajectory of domesticated societies, as we've seen among the Yanomami and other horticultural societies. But here warfare becomes social in nature. The cult of the warrior serves to limit populations by creating a preference for having boys instead of girls, resulting in higher rates of female infanticide. Brutal though it may be, when the ecological benefits of slow population growth within nomadic societies are lifted, that is a pattern that is largely efficient in limiting numbers.

But warfare within horticultural societies is a very real thing.

And we see that in some regards the rituals surrounding horticultural warfare run contrary to warfare as we know it. Amongst horticulturalists in Papua New Guinea, for example, battlefield warfare was mired in ritual. Pigs were slaughtered and feasted upon before battles, warriors gorged on food, and there were ritual limitations on drinking water. Parched and overstuffed, these moves reduced the potential duration of battles. Death tolls were reduced. This, however, isn't to give the impression that horticultural warfare was less violent: the flipside of battlefield warfare was a shorter and nastier pattern of raiding which involved sneak attacks, a massive loss of life and abduction of women and children.[181]

It becomes clear how things like steel tools and manioc beer, or its localized equivalent, alongside epidemics of new diseases exponentially increased the drastic impact of contact.

Unfortunately, we don't need imagination to see what that looked like.

Unlike the horticultural warriors, the soldiers of cilvization become intoxicated to prolong their rampages, not to shorten them.

The arsenal of soldiers, specialists in killing and subjugating populations, contained intoxicants as rations. In contrast to the methods of horticultural warriors, civilized soldiers were meant to be more deadly, fiercer: more machine-like. Liquor allotments in the era of industrializing military forces were required for anaesthetization, or, "to make the soldier an integral member of the mechanical corps."[182] It shouldn't be surprising that the use of those same intoxicants would be used "to allay the boredom and fatigue inherent in military life."[183]

The problem with soldiers is that they're still human.

Killing is no easy task, but it is the involvement in mass killing and mass destruction, often in areas or places removed from what one may call home, that fragments an experience of the world. Post-Traumatic Stress Disorder (PTSD) is most discussed as it impacts soldiers. Traumatic experiences were created by war, but removed from any communal background and then often put back into civilian life; there is no way to process those traumatic experiences.

Soldiers may be examples of this, but they're not alone. PTSD is often a gateway to addiction and with the trauma of the domestication process, none of us are exempt from it. Logically, soldiers tend to face PTSD the most and they're also on the frontline of addictive substances used to self-medicate.

A mixture of trauma and intoxication was crucial in the cathartic transformation of warlords and their ranks, often including children. Themselves outcasts of horrific violence and civil wars, refugees left to wander alone after witnessing the death of their families and the destruction of their homes. Child soldiers were initiated through acts of horrific violence. Their first kills, sometimes their own family members, were never with bullets, but often hacking with a machete or equally brute and direct forms of violence.

Taking part in this brutality actually allowed them to "psychologically distance themselves from it." As individuals involved in campaigns to rehabilitate former child soldiers saw over and over again: "The children suffered more trauma from seeing someone hacked to death … because they were witnesses, not the executioners."[184]

A former child soldier of the Revolutionary United Front of Sierra Leone, Ishmael Beah, spoke of the role drugs played in coaxing this initiation into an altered reality:

> *"We walked for long hours and stopped only to eat sardines and corned beef with gari, sniff cocaine, brown brown, and take some white capsules. The combination of these drugs gave us a lot of energy and made us fierce. The idea of death didn't cross my mind at all and killing had become as easy as drinking water. My mind not*

only snapped during the first killing, it had also stopped making remorseful records, or so it seemed."[185]

Brown brown is a drug of choice amongst African warlords. Often considered to be a mixture of gunpowder and cocaine, it is more often than not gunpowder mixed with heroin or amphetamines.[186] Heroin increasingly became an option through the region as it spread from Afghanistan following its rise to opioid-fueled prominence in the early 2000s.

This relationship between intoxication and war overrides all religious and political boundaries. It has been found that radical Islamic militants will promote and lethally enforce Sharia Law on one hand and drug their warriors without hesitation on the other.

Boko Haram's involvement in the drug trade and use of drugs is well known.[187] While jihadist fighters within the death cult of ISIS use a drug called Captagon, "an amphetamine pill that can cause a surge of energy and a euphoric high."[188]

Like every aspect of domestication, we cannot cease to be humans, but domesticators will seek to use our needs against us. Diverting our want for belonging and place into jihadist death cults or imperialist forces fueled by nationalism serves no different force.

In the end, it all looks the same.

Heroin use among Vietnam Veterans was an epidemic. While GIs were restricted from liquor and marijuana on bases, heroin could be mixed with tobacco and smoked without notice from superior officers. But even more importantly, heroin was accessible.

"Heroin was available at roadside stalls on every highway out of Saigon, and on the route to the main US army base at Long Binh, as well as from itinerant peddlers, newspaper and ice-cream vendors, restaurant owners, brothel keepers and their whores and domestic servants employed on US bases."[189]

It is estimated that in 1971 over 10 percent of enlisted US soldiers in Vietnam were addicted to heroin. That equates to at least 25,000 men.[190] In the same year, there were roughly 10,000 Veteran addicts at home in New York City alone.[191]

This trend didn't end with the Vietnam War.

The destabilization of Afghanistan caused by the current and now long running war there resulted in its ascendancy to the number one producer of opioids in the world. As millenials are shuffled into the military, their lives shaken by the nationalistic fervor of their youths surrounding the September 11, 2001 terror attacks in the US, they have found a pipeline for heroin akin to what was seen in Vietnam.

If you compare the contemporary maps of the highest per capita use and overdose from heroin with a map of active military bases, they overlap exactly.[192] This cannot be coincidental. And as we shall see, it never has been.

The United States government has a long-standing tradition of its own involvement in the international drug trade. In the 1950s, in an attempt to subvert the rise of Communist China, the CIA had been backing anti-communist opium producers to destabilize the region. Communism was not thwarted, but the Golden Triangle was created. While this is often attributed to the CIA turning its head for an enemy's enemy, it was a far more insidious involvement: "In short, the CIA became inextricably entangled with the Golden Triangle opium trade, handling opiate consignments, flying drug runs and tolerantly turning a blind eye to the affairs of their criminal allies."[193]

Cocaine was arguably even worse.

Gary Webb shined a light on the involvement of the CIA in what became the crack-cocaine epidemic that overtook largely African-American low-income neighborhoods, leading to higher involvement in the criminal system and steeper punishments for possession of crack than possession of cocaine, another form of the same drug used more heavily by whites.

Webb's reporting did not go unnoticed even though official government confirmation came out silently in the media just as the Clinton-Lewinsky sex scandal took over the headlines. Webb himself would be found dead a few years later, his death ruled a suicide despite having died with two bullets to the head.

What came of this was that in Nicaragua the US was funding the Contras, a particularly vicious paramilitary group, in their war against the socialist Sandinistas. Unable to give direct funding, the CIA built a pipeline for funding through the trafficking of cocaine. In the process creating intricate networks of stateside drug gangs and international drug cartels.

Not unlike the viciousness inherit in targeting indigenous populations; the CIA "had assisted the transformation of the powder cocaine market to crack cocaine in the early 1980s." Cheaper and now widely available, crack tore communities apart.[194] And as it remains a cheap high and offers quicker escape through smoking, it still does.

Ironically, though the intent was to defund socialist revolutionaries, cocaine has since become a primary funding source for FARC, a merciless Communist army in Columbia, among others. As the Columbian drug trade originated in the 1970s with marijuana, FARC denounced the trade under Communist Party principles, resulting in burnt plantations and running their owners out.

Cocaine, a higher priced commodity, was different. For FARC, "the benefits were too big to ignore, and the guerillas' logic shifted. Soon, what was against their ideals became "just another crop" that the rebels decided to tax."[195]

The presumption of war for ideological reasons falters constantly under a reality that all lines cross. All civilizations, regardless of stated religious or political affiliation, require resources. And here cash is a secular king.

And it is all of us, with our incessant search to fill the void within, who are footing the bill.

As the former President of Columbia, Virgilio Barco Vargas accurately stated: "The only law the narcoterrorists don't break is the law of supply and demand." [196]

The drug cartels that were a proxy of CIA counter-insurgencies during the Cold War didn't fade away. They grew. And they continue to grow more powerful and more deadly.

In Mexico, the lethality of these cartels is impossible to overlook. Between 2007 and 2014, there were 164,000 drug-related homicides in Mexico.[197] Mass kidnappings, executions, drive-by shootings; the United States market for marijuana, cocaine and methamphetamines pays for all of this carnage.[198]

Those 164,000 bodies are absolutely foreign to us.

We attribute them to violence between drug cartels, but that is only a fraction of it. The reality here is gristly. At times the morgues in Mexico City are overrun with bodies. Lives lost to organized and disorganized violence. There is no shortage of documentation here despite our aloofness and involvement in the entire ordeal.

The day-to-day violence can look like this: On May 13, 2012, 49 decapitated and dismembered bodies were found alongside a highway in Nuevo Leon. On September 26, 2014 gunmen opened fire on buses carrying students and soccer players in southern Mexico, leaving 3 dead and 43 missing. Those 43 were declared dead the following January.[199]

In two instances that amounts to 95 lives lost to drug-related violence, a drop in the bucket for that total number of 164,000. And these instances are happening daily.

But they are not confined to Mexico.

Mexican drug cartels use would-be migrants riddled with impossible debts to guard and maintain devastating marijuana plantations within US National Forests.[200] Josh Harkinson summed up the damage in around the San Bernardino National Forest in 2009.

> *"Growers clear land year-round, plant crops in the spring, and haul out the harvest in the fall, often leaving behind mounds of trash and dead animals, denuded hillsides, and streams full of sediment and human waste. Last year, the community of Snow Creek, California, traced feces in its water treatment plant to a grow in the nearby San Bernardino National Forest."*[201]

These illegal growing operations have destroyed 10,000 acres of National Forest. All of this for marijuana: grown for and sold to Americans.

The lavish extravagance of the cartel's drug lords is so ridiculous that it can be best exhibited not in how they lived, but in how they were buried. The mausoleums of the cartels are well documented for their exuberance. Cemeteries for the cartels look like high-price gated condominiums.

Ignacio Coronel, a founder of the Sinaloa Cartel and the self-proclaimed "King of Crystal" for his role in the manufacture and distribution of methamphetamine in the United States is entombed in a $450,000 mausoleum with state-of-the-art music and security systems, Wi-Fi, and air conditioning. Arturo Guzman Loera, brother of notorious drug lord El Chapo, is enshrined in a modest two-story, air-conditioned mausoleum with 24-hour surveillance, and en-suite

bedrooms with a price tag of $1,200,000.[202]

This globalized, hyper-technological civilization distributes consequences, not wealth. Profit from misery is distilled into a small global elite and that is who the rest of us are busy producing for. And when we're not busy just trying to get by, we are buying substitutes for the community of nomadic bands that was our birthright for the 2.5 million years leading up to our lives as *Homo sapiens*.

We are the products of a historically created and horrifically malicious system that seeks to tear apart our being and sell it back to us piecemeal. And the price is complicity in our own enslavement and the enslavement of all other life on the planet.

This is the unforeseeable consequence of hunter-collectors settling around wild grains 10,000 years ago. A cycle perpetuated by unthinkable levels of violence and an inability to psychologically reconcile the consequences of our actions, worsened as technology casts our shadow further and deeper throughout the world.

So raise your glass in cheers to the conquest of nothingness: the endless pursuit of completion.

It only gets worse.

Modernity and Other Distractions

> *"The peculiar, vomitorious genius of modern capitalism is its ability to betray our senses with one class of products or services and then sell us another to cope with the damage so that we can go back to consuming more of what caused the problem in the first place."*
>
> \- David Courtwright, *Forces of Habit*[203]

If the goal of domestication is to subvert innate human desires towards consumed impulse, then there is no finer closing for civilization than our current era of late Modernity.

We, the children of Progress and Empire, have run the mill. Our lineages are divorced from place. Community is increasingly about many weak online connections rather than deep and meaningful interactions.

We take part in the dreams of programmers. Our hesitations for drudgery are reflected onto the potential of technology to take on mundane tasks and, seemingly, human action. If domestication were able to deliver on its promises of substitutes for ecstatic states, this would be it. We equate freedom with the freedom of choice between products. We believe that we are free to do as we please: that if we chose to we could walk away from civilization.

And we are miserable.

The myths of the domesticators ring hollow. They have offered to us the technology, the medications, the stuff, the sugar-laced foods, and the machines. We consume them in such frenzy that they get old quickly and we crave more.

Addiction defines Modernity because it must. The more our society offers the rewards of Progress, the more apparent it becomes that they are filler: the dreams of cyborgs.

And so we consume.

Everything.

Capitalists long ago recognized that dopamine, that source of joy that floods our brains quickly, brings about euphoric states. It gives us that feeling that we are getting what it is we need in life. Unfulfilled we come back for that hit, again and again.

This chronic need for fulfillment feeds into the role we have taken on as spectators. We no longer take part in the creation and exaltations of communal joy: we become voyeurs. Healing dances are replaced by stages, by mass spectacles of State power, or exhibitions of individual ability. Situationist Guy Debord referred to "the society of the spectacle" as "an epoch without festivals."[204] Barbara Ehrenreich follows on his sentiment: "Instead of generating their own collective pleasures, people absorb, or consume, the spectacles of commercial entertainment, nationalist rituals, and the consumer culture, with its endless advertisements for the pleasure of individual ownership."[205]

In the absence of community, indulgence of the Self takes over.

But we still seek and desire that sense of belonging, that sense of place: that moment of euphoria.

And so we consume it regardless of consequence.

I often wonder how anyone in our society could turn to heroin, crack or similar heavy drugs. There's no absence of information about what happens. How the brain can stop producing serotonin on its own and how this furthers dependency and worsens withdrawal.

But I knew Mike.

We grew up together and both of us were witnesses to how all problems could be solved by consumption. If you have a physical problem or any level of discomfort, there is a pill for that. Attention issues? Moodiness? Anger? Sadness? Each one had its pills. And the more pills you take, the more you must increase the dosage to feel the effect.

We see this in literally every aspect of life within Modernity. Our solutions are always to increase the synthetics and to amplify the effect. We expect immediate gratification. We expect to be entertained and coddled. Catered and comforted. We've reduced our needs to the chemical level and then reassemble them in pieces.

Oxycodone is a natural step in. Global poppy supply increases, first in Afghanistan, then in Latin America where the "War on Drugs" resulted in ridgelines of forest wiped out with glyphosate to combat coca operations pushing the growers into valleys where poppy grows easily. The cost of opiates drops and the drug companies react.

Opium use, in either heroin or painkillers, exploded simply because it was cheap and powerful.[206] Doctors began prescribing Oxycodone for increasingly less severe pain. Age was never a consideration; children and teenagers were and are being given opiates for relatively minor injuries.

I feel a sense of haunting over me after hearing the torn and pain-ridden words of a Massachusetts mother who lost two sons to heroin, an addiction that began as their high school football injuries were treated with Oxycodone. They were hooked and when the prescriptions ran out, heroin was there, and cheaper. In her words:

> *"Back in 1999, Perdue Pharmacy spent 200 million dollars pushing opiates... What was supposed to be a life ending severe pain we start giving for wisdom teeth. Why are we pushing these drugs?"*[207]

On the streets, the cost of a single Oxycodone pill can run $80.

A hit of heroin can cost $10.

In the words of users: "I fell in love with the feeling. And it's cheap." "Heroin was amazing. It was like a fountain of warmth shooting out of the top of your head, covering you in a velvet blanket." "I don't shoot heroin to get high, I shoot it to get well. ... I don't know how to have fun without drugs."[208]

There used to be a myth of Progress that pervaded the language of civilization: a notion that things were better and that they would continue to improve. As technology and social media use increase, we no longer talk of Progress: we live it. We expect the gratification of desires and it keeps us from even having to look up. Consequences take place in a time that isn't now, so it simply doesn't matter.[209]

This is the epitome of addiction: I will do what it takes to get this sensation immediately.

A new drug, Krokodil, drives that home. It is also appropriately called 'the zombie drug' and its name taken from the reptilian-esque skin users develop as a result of missing the vein while injecting, even slightly.

Krokodil has been an epidemic in Russia, but hasn't stopped there. Junkies use it because it is cheaper than heroin and a relatively similar high, but it is easier to manufacture. It is made from mixing codeine with "a brew of poisons such as paint thinner, hydrochloric acid and red phosphorus scraped from the strike pads on matchboxes."[210] Life expectancy for users is drastically short even compared to heroin users: typically one year, maybe two.

Where users inject the drug, "blood vessels burst and surrounding tissue dies, sometimes falling off the bone in chunks."[211] If you miss the vein, that area of flesh will die right away. If there is a worse drug out there, I don't think I can stand to hear about it.

A Russian krokodil user shares no illusion about the nature of this particular mix of poisons:

> *"You can feel how disgusting it is when you're doing it," he recalls. "You're dreaming of heroin, of something that feels clean and not like poison. But you can't afford it, so you keep doing the krokodil. Until you die."*[212]

Krokodil may be the more extreme case, but it is not abnormal.

Any place where the will to live is gone, this is what you'll find. For Inuit communities, they are losing their children to an addiction of huffing gas.[213] Indigenous societies in Canada that have been subjected to the decimation of their communities have a suicide rate ten times the national average.

The Guarani of Brazil have been committing suicide in droves. In 1995, suicide ended the lives of 56 Guarani. But suicide isn't what caused their death, the destruction of their culture did. The sentiment was not hard for remaining Guarani to understand:

> *"Young people are nostalgic for the beautiful forests… A young person told me he didn't want to live anymore because there was no reason to carry on living—there is no hunting, no fishing, and the water is polluted."*[214]

The search for extremes in getting high has led to a flood of Western hipsters seeking *ayahuasca* for a new high. This has resulted in the deaths of European and American teens from using synthetic alternatives for the drug (native to South America) during sessions with faux-shamans.[215]

Not to be outdone, *Vice Magazine* wasn't going to miss out on this "new" trend, paying $230 per session with a "shaman" in Berlin, selling the trip as horribly as possible:

"For late thirtysomething affluent vegans who don't go to clubs anymore and who spend Christmas in India so they don't have to visit their parents, it's about as hip as partner swapping."

Confirming their own expectations, after elaborating on the violent sickness that comes hand-in-hand with this intoxicant:

"In a way, it takes you back to your original essence in nature, and that's no bad thing if, like me, your regular connection with nature is watching your tomato plants slowly die on the windowsill each summer."

Have no fear, that's not the only perk:

"Oh, and seeing your dick as tall as a building, rendered from solid, impenetrable stone is something all insecure young boys, who grow into secretly insecure men, need to see at least twice."[216]

"It is a measure of our general deprivation" states Barbara Ehrenreich, "that the most common referent for *ecstasy* in usage today is not an experience but a drug, MDMA, that offers fleeting feelings of euphoria and connectedness."[217]

For most of us, these extremes may come as unfamiliar. We can see them from the safety of a distance. We can judge and we can lie to ourselves.

The dopamine response that heroin users become addicted to lacks scrutiny with more acceptable social behaviors. As we mindlessly swipe the screen of a smartphone looking for updates, the mind releases dopamine in ways similar to receiving good news.[218] The hit of dopamine that comes from getting "likes" on Facebook "fools our brain into believing that loved ones surround us."[219]

A new trend has arisen in cities where there are "cuddle parties" or "snuggle buddies." These are explicitly non-sexual interactions where the purpose is simply to be touched. One company offers the service for $80 an hour and sessions up to 10 hours. Advertising the service as a cure all for everything from depression to aging, there is no question that the oxytocin released in our brains when we are in contact with another being creates a sense of joy.[220] But this industry is kind of a sad call back to the healing rituals we opened with.

There are moments when our search for community comes so close in form and function to those healing rituals, but deprived of context, it all becomes a kind of perversion. What we want, what we need, is right in front of us, but we are all too damaged to reach out. Paying for a service is far more in the comfort zone that has been provided to us.

It is consumable.

Addiction is a patterned behavior: a self-reinforcing cycle. Stripped of place, dopamine and its feelings of joy within our bodies becomes another drug. Psychologist Amy Banks explains our altered relationship with dopamine:

> *"In an ideal world—one that understands the centrality of healthy relationship to health and wellness—the dopamine reward system stays connected to human connection as the primary source of stimulation. Unfortunately, we do not live in this ideal world. We live in a culture that actively undermines this precious dopamine-relationship connection. We raise children to stand on their own two feet while the separate self is an American icon of maturity. It is making us sick.*
>
> *"This disconnection is a set-up for addiction as we search for other sources of dopamine. The "other sources" look shockingly similar to the list of common cultural complaints—overeating and obesity, drug and alcohol abuse, consumerism, chronic hooking up. Not only do these addictive, destructive behaviors get paired to the dopamine reward system but they create a feedback loop of isolation that pushes people towards more addictions."*[221]

The problem for domesticators is that we're still human. We're still animals.

We always have been and we always will be.

As depressing and hopeless as an exploration of addiction and civilization can feel, the common thread throughout all of this is that we never give up. The hunter-gatherer within us is not dead. We are captive animals. Distracted though we may be, it is the existence of our emptiness, the depravity of our search for that connection that keeps programmers awake at night.

Removed as we are from the world as we were meant to inherit it: our want for community struggles against all odds.

And it is that undying spirit that may ultimately bring the end of civilization.

Revival of the Spirit

"The last communities do a ghost dance, and the ghosts of the last

> *communities will continue to dance within the entrails of the artificial beast. The council-fires of the never-defeated communities are not extinguished by the genocidal invaders, just as the light of Ahura Mazda was not extinguished by rulers who claimed it shone on them. The fire is eclipsed by something dark, but it continues to burn, and its flames shoot out where they are least expected."*
>
> - Fredy Perlman, *Against His-Story, Against Leviathan*[222]

Rupert Isaacson sought out the San for his own reasons. He wanted to enter the Kalahari to find his wholeness, to take part in an ancestral society with its healing dances and intact community. What he found in his journeys at the turn of the twenty-first century was a radical departure from those expectations.

At this point, we know what happened to the San.

We know that forced settlements, an influx of intoxicants and an illegalization of subsistence hunting and nomadism took its toll on their culture. During his time with the San, Isaacson was forced to take a realistic assessment of what had happened and what future lay ahead for this captive society of hunter-gatherers as they struggle to fight for their land rights.

Before leaving the Kalahari, Isaacson witnessed a minor victory in the fight for land rights. An occasion met with the unthinkable: a healing dance. Outside of the world of tourists, this relic of their communal life had not vanished completely.[223]

Against all odds, the potential for healing, the potential for community survives.

It does no good to blame addicts.

That's not grounds for absolving or justifying behaviors. But the problem is that if we don't confront the nature and presence of our own addictions then we are simply denying our complicity with civilization, with the perpetuation of our own domestication.

We need a sober assessment of our situation and we need action to follow. It is not enough to blame the lack of community for indulgences. Rebuilding community is certainly no easy task, but it is the task at hand. Resistance against domestication, if it is not grounded in the world of the known rather than a philosophical notion of what could be, will never be successful.

This is also not the hippies call to the commune. Proximity alone is not enough.

Functioning community is a place where resolution comes from contextualizing conflict and handling problems on their own terms. Rooted in subsistence, community requires a connection to place and a basis in subsistence or, at the very least, a turn towards it.

We have to shed utopian and liberal delusions and the belief that we can and always will get along; we need to embrace those aspects of human emotion and behavior that only the primal anarchy of nomadic hunter-gatherer life can endure. And I say this knowing full well that nothing in life is this easy. We all have our conditioning and we are under assault on all fronts from the world that civilization has created.

But we have to start somewhere.

Like addicts, no one can make us change if we don't seek it out ourselves.

Like nomadic hunter-gatherers, engagement of community makes it immediately apparent that any illusion of freedom to leave civilization is a hoax. If it was simply accomplishable indigenous societies would have never taken up settlements or been forced to take up arms against armies, missionaries, developers, and corporations. To engage with the world, we can't carry delusions. Community begins with honest communication, with allowing ourselves to be vulnerable and emboldened at the same time.

This will not be a quick journey.

Rewilding can only be measured in terms of generations, not individuals.

Without resistance, there will never be the chance to see that through.

Our spirits need an awakening: a place to open up. A place where we can truly feel the crushing anguish and despair that suicidal Guarani peoples feel as they see the state of the world thrust upon them.

We need a place where our sense of comfort in conformity is challenged by sustenance.

And we will not get there alone.

Our ability to effectively bleed the machine that has stripped us of our community will be a rage born of healing: a euphoric catharsis within the context of the dispossessed.

Kia and *Molimo* are not ours for the taking, but they are part of a legacy of primal healing. Our dance has yet to be found, but it exists. That the seed of community hasn't been killed already should give us hope. As should the need of colonizers to target the healing dances. If the veneer of domestication begins to crack, the threat posed by communities of resistance arises.

"This is the real bone of contention between civilization and collective ecstasy:" Barbara Ehrenreich observes, "Ecstatic rituals still build group cohesion, but when they build it among subordinates—peasants, slaves, women, colonized people—the elite calls out its troops."[224]

The minor victory that Isaacson had witnessed did not last. The settled life of the San had carried on. *Kia* became a thing of memory. Or so it would seem. The anthropologist Charlie Goodwin living amongst the San happened to catch a group of drunk San engage in *kia*.[225]

The hope of communal survival springs forth again in dance.

Among present day Baka, hunting was a source of social cohesion: one that has been stripped away by the weight of Modernity. And yet when large groups gather, the songs and dances return.[226]

Despite everything that we have seen about the world that we have created, the world we were born into, it is resiliency that has carried humans as far and wide as we have moved. It is that same resiliency that allows the body to continue existing even as we assault it with chemicals, intoxicants, and poisons, subject it to sedentary life, and attack our senses with the sights and sounds of civilization instead of immersing ourselves in the wild.

For whatever reason, against all odds, our bodies still function.

It is easy to see that as a misfortune: to see what it is that civilization has done to this world, our home, and to be able to carry on. It's a privilege that we take for granted as we lose ourselves in screens and empty relationships, in production and consumption.

And yet it is that resiliency that keeps us searching.

Against all of the hopelessness in the world as it is, it is this constant nagging and want for life that gives me reason to fight.

To resist.

To undermine the logic of domestication.

The urge that led Mike to inject heroin into his veins lives on with me. Within all of us.

I can only imagine what may happen when our healing begins. What we may be capable of when we find our place again and are forced to confront the civilization that threatens to exterminate it.

May we one day dance in euphoria upon its ruins.

As wild beings freed from captivity.

As wild, euphoric communities.

Dedicated to Mike and Danielle.

Endnotes

1 David Courtwright, *Forces of Habit: Drugs and the Making of the Modern World*. Harvard UP: Cambridge, 2001. Pg 92. I can't speak highly enough of this book.

2 Cited in Chellis Glendinning, *My Name is Chellis and I'm in Recovery from Western Civilization*. Shambhala: Boston, 1994. Pg 99.

3 Ibid. Pg 98.

4 Ibid.

5 'The Heroin Epidemic in 9 Graphs', US News & World Report. http://www.usnews.com/news/blogs/data-mine/2015/08/19/the-heroin-epidemic-in-9-graphs Accessed 12-24-2015.

6 'Today's Heroin Epidemic' CDC, http://www.cdc.gov/vitalsigns/heroin/ Accessed 12-24-2015

7 'Opioid Addiction Disease 2015 Facts & Figures' American Society of Addiction Medicine. http://www.asam.org/docs/default-source/advocacy/opioid-addiction-disease-facts-figures.pdf Accessed 12-24-2015

8 http://www.nytimes.com/interactive/2016/01/07/us/drug-overdose-deaths-in-the-us.html?_r=0 Accessed 2-25-2016.

9 John Zerzan, *Future Primitive and Other Essays*. Autonomedia: Brooklyn, 1994. Pg 137.

10 The distinction between immediate and delayed return hunter-gatherer societies is absolutely crucial to understanding domestication. For more on this, see James Woodburn, 'Egalitarian Societies'. *Man*, New Series. No 17, Vol 3 (Sept 1982).

11 Colin Turnbull, 'The Importance of Flux in Two Hunting Societies' in Lee and Devore (eds), *Man the Hunter*. Aldine de Gruyter: New York, 1968. Pg 132.

12 Turnbull, Woodburn, et al, 'Resolving Conflicts by Fission' in Lee and Devore, 1968. Pg 156.

13 Colin Turnbull, *The Human Cycle*. Simon and Schuster: New York, 1983. Pg 45.

14 Turnbull, 1968. Pg 156.

15 For more on this, see my essay 'To Speak of Wildness' in *Black and Green Review* no 2, Fall 2015.

16 Turnbull, 'The Ritualization of Potential Conflict Among the Mbuti' in Leacock and Lee, *Politics and History in Band Society*. Cambridge UP: London, 1982. Pg 142.

17 Cited in Frank Marlowe, *The Hadza: Hunter-Gatherers of Tanzania*. University of California Press: Berkeley, CA, 2010. Pg 60.

18 Carleton Coon, *The Hunting Peoples*. Nick Lyons Books: New York, 1971. Pg 187. Coon specifies in this line about the "vast majority of hunting and gathering peoples" and highlights "habit-forming drugs", but the book includes immediate and delayed return HG societies. As we see here, numerous delayed return HG societies do use intoxicants for ritual-

istic purposes, hence the qualifications in this particular line. The study does specify which societies do and do not use intoxicants.

19 I have to admit my hesitancy in adding this clarification. I've spent the last decade trying to disprove the correlation between nomadic hunter-gatherer life and a distinct lack of intoxicating substances and cannot disprove it. However, I've chosen to leave this a bit more open and ambiguous because if someone were to find a skeleton of an individual Pleistocene-era hunter-gatherer with handfuls of opium somehow, the link between ritualistic and habitual use still stands. Egalitarianism is the nature of nomadic hunter-gatherer societies, in terms of individual behavior; this gives the space for true individual freedom should one wish to take that to whatever ends they imagine.

20 Glendinning, 1994. Pg 126.

21 Laura Rival, *Trekking Through History: The Huaorani of Amazonian Ecuador*. Columbia UP: New York, 2002. Pg 138.

22 Note that I have standardized all references to *n/um* despite some variation in how the term is spelled within the ethnographic record for the sake of consistency.

23 Richard Katz, *Boiling Energy: Community Healing Among the Kalahari Kung*. Harvard UP: Cambridge, MA, 1982. Pg 52.

24 Ibid, Pg 44.

25 Richard Lee, *The Dobe Ju/'hoansi (3rd edition)*. Wadsworth: London, 2003. Pg 130-131.

26 Mathias Guenther, *Tricksters & Trancers: Bushman Religion and Society*. Indiana UP: Bloomington, IN, 1999. Pg 181.

27 Katz, 1982. Pg 35.

28 Marjorie Shostak, *Nisa: The Life and Words of a !Kung Woman*. Vintage: New York, 2983. Pg 299.

29 Katz, 1982. Pg 52.

30 Shostak, 1983. Pg 296.

31 Lee, 2003. Pg 132.

32 Guenther, 1999. Pg 182.

33 Ibid. Pg 183. It is worth noting that Nisa claims that sometimes adolescents are given a root to help ease their transition into *n/um*, but I have not been able to find anything in detail about what the root is and whether it may be an intoxicant or an herbal remedy. Regardless, it is only used for "training" purposes, not to induce *n/um*.

34 Shostak, 1983. Pg 299.

35 Ibid, Pg 296.

36 Guenther, 1999. Pg 183.

37 Katz, 1982. Pg 37.

38 Lee, 2003. Pg 135 and Shostak, 1983. Pg 296.

39 Daisuke Bundo, 'Social Relationship Embodied in Singing and Dancing Performances Among the Baka'. *African Study Monographs*, Supp. 26: 85-101, March 2001. Pg 96.

40 Ibid. Pg 86.

41 Jerome Lewis, 'How Language Evolved from Singing'. https://vimeo.com/114605825 . For more on this subject, see my essay 'Subjects Object!' in *Black and Green Review* no 2 (Fall 2015).

42 Rival, 2002. Pg 101.

43 Kevin Duffy, *The Children of the Forest: Africa's Mbuti Pygmies*. Waveland Press: Prospect Heights, IL, 1996. Pg 54.

44 Turnbull, 1983. Pg 44.

45 Colin Turnbull, *Wayward Servants*. The Natural History Press: Garden City, NY, 1965. Pgs 132-133.

46 Ibid. Pg 72.

47 The absence of fire and even moonlight (during the Hadza's *epeme*) is worth further exploration. It seems probable that this dance is so primal that it incorporates a rejection of fire and a complete absorption into wildness without any element of mediation.

48 Marlowe, 2010. Pg 59.
49 Ibid, pg 68.
50 Bundo, 2001. Pg 96.
51 Paul Shepard, *Coming Home to the Pleistocene*. Island Press: Washington DC, 1998. Pgs 91-92.
52 Hunter-collectors are discussed in greater detail in the "Conquests of Bread" section, also see my essays 'The Forest Beyond the Field' and 'To Produce or To Not Produce' in Tucker, 2010.
53 For example, see Masato Sawada, 'Encounters with the Dead Among Efe and the Balese in the Ituri Forest: Mores and Ethnic Identity Shown by the Dead'. *African Study Monographs*, Suppl. 25:85-104, March 1998.
54 Mircea Eliade, *Shamanism: Archaic Techniques of Ecstasy*. Princeton UP: Princeton, 1974. Pg 84.
55 Ibid.
56 Ibid, Pg 109.
57 David Riches, 'Shamanism: the Key to Religion'. *Man*, New Series, Vol 29 No 2 (June 1994), Pgs 381-405. Pg 389.
58 Ibid. Pg 382.
59 Eliade, 1974. Pgs 222-223 & Pg 221.
60 Ibid. Pgs 222-223.
61 An act made famous enough in Siberia to channel animal spirits that it became a target during the onslaught of relentless Soviet persecution of Siberian shamans, see Piers Vitebseky, *The Reindeer People: Living with Animals and Spirits in Siberia*. Houghton Mifflin: Boston, 2005. Pg 261.
62 Andy Letcher, *Shroom: A Cultural History of the Magic Mushroom*. Harper Collins: New York, 2006. Pg 15.
63 Ibid, Pg 28.
64 O.T. Oss & O.N. Oeric, *Psilocybin: Magic Mushroom Grower's Guide*. Quick American Publishing, 1993. Pg 20.
65 Letcher, 2006. Pg 28.
66 Ibid, Pg 17.
67 Paul Gahlinger, *Illegal Drugs: A Complete Guide to their History, Chemistry, Use, and Abuse*. Plume: New York City, 2003. Pg 273.
68 Letcher, 2006. Pg 29.
69 Asen Balikci, *The Netsilik Eskimo*. Waveland: Prospect Heights, IL, 1970. Pg 227.
70 Miguel Alexiades and Daniela Peluso, 'Plants 'of the Ancestors', Plants 'of the Outsiders': Ese Eja History, Migration and Medicinal Plants' in Alexiades (ed), *Mobility and Migration in Indigenous Amazonia*. Berghahn: New York, 2009. Pgs 235-236.
71 William Denevan, 'Stone vs Metal Axes: The Ambiguity of Shifting Cultivation in Prehistoric Amazonia.' *Journal of the Steward Anthropological Society*, 20:153-65. 1992.
72 Note: for consistencies sake, I'm standardizing the spelling of *Epene* and Yanomami regardless of sources.
73 Jacques Lizot, *Tales of the Yanomami*. Cambridge UP: Cambridge, 1985. Pg 124.
74 R Brian Ferguson, 'A Savage Encounter: Western Contact and the Yanomami War Complex' in Ferguson and Whitehead (eds), *War in the Tribal Zone: Expanding States and Indigenous Warfare*. SAR Press: Santa Fe, 1992.
75 This matter is covered extensively in R. Brian Ferguson, *Yanomami Warfare: A Political History*. SAR Press: Santa Fe, 1995 and Patrick Tierney, *Darkness in El Dorado*. WW Norton: New York, 2001. Both books are absolutely important.
76 Kenneth Good with David Chanoff, *Into the Heart*. Simon and Schuster: New York, 1991. Pg 66.
77 Ibid. Pgs 47-48.
78 Ibid. Pg 68.

79 Ettore Biocca, *Yanoáma*. Kodansha International: New York, 1996. Pgs 142-146.
80 Peter Bellwood, *First Farmers: The Origins of Agricultural Societies*. Malden, MA: Blackwell, 2005. Pg 240.
81 Ibid, pg 241.
82 Peter Furst, 'Intoxicants and Intoxication' in Evans and Webster (eds), *Archaeology of Ancient Mexico and Central America: An Encyclopedia*. London: Routeledge, 2001. Pg 372.
83 Richard Evans Schultes, 'The Appeal of Peyote (Lophophoria Williams) as a Medicine'. *American Anthropologist* October-December 1938, New Series 40(4/1):698-715.
84 Ibid.
85 https://www.drugabuse.gov/publications/drugfacts/hallucinogens
86 'Peyote Dose" https://www.erowid.org/plants/peyote/peyote_dose.shtml
87 http://voices.nationalgeographic.com/2009/03/23/corn_domesticated_8700_years_ago/
88 Bellwood, 2005. Pg 156.
89 Ibid. Pg 174.
90 Clive Ponting, *A Green History of the World*. New York: Penguin Books, 1991. Pg 80.
91 Marvin Harris, *Cannibals and Kings*. New York: Vintage, 1978. Pgs 134-135.
92 Elman R Service, *Origins of the State and Civilization: the Process of Cultural Evolution*. New York: WW Norton, 1975. Pg 203.
93 Bellwood, 2005. Pg 154.
94 Furst, 2001. Pgs 371-373.
95 Michael Harner, 'The Enigma of Aztec Sacrifice'. *Natural History*, April 1977. Vol. 86, No. 4, pages 46-51.
96 Ibid.
97 Ibid.
98 Ingo Niermann and Adriano Sack, *The Curious World of Drugs and Their Friends*. New York: Plume, 2008. Pg 30.
99 Vice, 'World's Scariest Drug' https://www.youtube.com/watch?v=ToQ8PWYnu04
100 Barbara Myerhoff, 'The Deer-Maize-Peyote Symbol Complex among the Huichol Indians of Mexico.' *Anthropological Quarterly*, Vol. 43, No. 2 (Apr., 1970), pp. 64-78. Pg 66.
101 Guilhem Olivier, *Mockeries and Metamophoses of an Aztec God*. Boulder, CO: University Press of Colorado, 2003. Pg 121.
102 Furst, 2001. Pg 373.
103 Stacy B. Schaefer, *Huichol Women, Weavers, and Shamans*. Albuquerque: University of New Mexico Press, 2015. Pgs 196-197.
104 Myerhoff, 1970. Pgs 73-74.
105 Ibid. Pg 66.
106 Peter Furst, 'To Find Our Life: Peyote Among the Huichol Indians of Mexico' in Furst (ed), *Flesh of the Gods: the Ritual Use of Hallucinogens*. Long Grove, IL: Waveland, 1990 (Orig 1972). Pgs 141-142.
107 Ibid, Pg 152.
108 Peter Furst, *Visions of a Huichol Shaman*. Philadelphia: University of Pennsylvania Museum of Archeology and Anthropology, 2003. Pg 25.
109 William Dirk Raat, *Mexico's Sierra Tarahumara*. Norman, OK: University of Oklahoma Press, 1996. Pg 53.
110 Alfonso Paredes and Fructuoso Irigoyen, 'Jíkuri, the Tarahumara peyote cult: an interpretation' in Kales, Pierce and Greenblatt (eds.). *The Mosaic of Contemporary Psychiatry in Perspective* Springer-Verlag, 1992. Pgs. 121–129.
111 Christopher McDougall, *Born to Run*. New York: Alfred Knopf, 2009. Pg 229.
112 See Elizabeth Marshall Thomas, *The Old Way: A Story of the First People*. Sarah Crichton: New York, 2006.
113 John Kennedy, 'Tesguino Complex: The Role of Beer in Tarahumara'. *American Anthropologist*. 65, 1963. Pgs 620-640. Pgs 622-623.
114 Ibid, pg. 635..

115 Ibid, Pg 623.
116 See McDougall, 2009.
117 AC de los Derechos Humanos & Texas Center for Policy Study, 'The Forest Industry in the Sierra Madre of Chihuahua: Social, Economic, and Ecological Impacts'. 2000. https://www.nwf.org/pdf/Global-Warming/forestry.pdf
118 Kristian Beadle, 'The Drug Destruction of Mexico, Part II'. *Pacific Standard*, July 15, 2010.
http://www.psmag.com/nature-and-technology/the-drug-destruction-of-mexico-part-ii-19343
119 Enrique Salmon, 'Narco-Trafficking Sierra Tarahumara'. *Cultural Survival*.
https://www.culturalsurvival.org/publications/voices/enrique-salmon/narco-trafficking-sierra-tarahumara
120 Ibid.
121 Masaki Nishida, 'The Significance of Sedentarization in the Human History'. *African Study Monographs*, Suppl. 26: 9-14, March 2001. Pgs 9-10.
122 Ibid.
123 Lewis Binford, 'Willow Smoke and Dogs' Tails: Hunter-Gatherer Settlement Systems and Archaeological Site Formation'. *American Antiquity*, Vol 45, No 1 (Jan 1980). Pg 10. It is worth noting that the original context here is with a nomadic hunter-gatherer society who stores food throughout the winter. I definitely appreciate Binford's point on the matter, but the term *hunter-collector* seems to take on a bit of a life of its own after its introduction, including in Binford's later work. I use the term more to signify the point at which hunter-gatherers become more invested in delayed return practices than immediate return.
124 For more on this, see my 'Forest Beyond the Field' in Tucker, 2010, and you can expect more from me on this subject in a number of current and future projects.
125 Abraham Rosman and Paula Rubel, *Feasting With Mine Enemy: Rank and Exchange Among Northwest Coast Societies*. Prospect Heights, IL: Waveland Press, 1971. Pgs 12-13 & 34.
126 Ibid, pg 36.
127 Timothy Earle, *How Chiefs Come to Power: The Political Economy in Prehistory*. Stanford: Stanford UP, 1997. Pg 192.
128 Wayne Suttles, 'Coping with Abundance: Subsistence on the Northwest Coast' in Lee and DeVore (eds) *Man the Hunter*. New York: Aldine de Gruyter, 1968. Pg 58.
129 J.G. Hawkes, 'The Ecological Background of Plant Domestication' in Ucko and Dimbleby (eds), *The Domestication and Exploitation of Plants and Animals*. The Garden City Press: Hertforshire, England, 1969. Pgs 18-19.
130 Ibid. Pg 20.
131 Peter Wilson, *The Domestication of the Human Species*. Yale UP: New Haven, CT, 1991.
132 Morris Berman, *The Wandering God*. State University of New York Press: Albany, 2000.
133 Greg Wadley and Angus Martin, 'The Origins of Agriculture: A Biological Perspective and a New Hypothesis'. *Australian Biologist* 6: 96-105, June 1993.
134 See, for examples, Weston A Price DDS, *Nutrition and Physical Degeneration (6th edition)*. Price-Pottinger Nutrition Foundation: La Mesa, CA, 2000 (orig 1939).
135 Nora Gedgaudas, *Primal Body, Primal Mind*. Healing Arts Press: Rochester, VT, 2011. Pg 226.
136 Ibid. Pg 227.
137 Ibid, Pg 15.
138 Eric Yarnell, 'Exorphins, Food Cravings, and Schizophrenia'. 2003. http://www.healingmountainpublishing.com/articles/exorphins.html
139 Ibid.
140 Sayer Ji, 'Do Hidden Opiates In Our Food Explain Food Addictions?'. May 3, 2012.
http://www.greenmedinfo.com/blog/do-hidden-opiates-our-food-explain-food-addictions
141 Erickson DL, Smith BD, Clarke AC, Sandweiss DH, Tuross N; Smith; Clarke; Sand-

weiss; Tuross ,'An Asian origin for a 10,000-year-old domesticated plant in the Americas'. *Proc. Natl. Acad. Sci. U.S.A.* 102 (51): 18315–20 (December 2005).
142 Solomon Katz and Mary Voigt, 'Bread and Beer: The Early Use of Cereals in the Diet'. Expedition Magazine 28.2 (July 1986). Pgs 32-33.
143 E.E. Evans-Pritchard, *The Nuer*. Oxford UP: New York, 1979. Pg 82.
144 Michael Harner, *The Jívaro: People of the Sacred Waterfalls*. Anchor: Garden City, NY, 1973. Pg 51.
145 Iain Gately, *Drink: A Cultural History of Alcohol*. Gotham Books: New York, 2008. Pgs 2-10.
146 Ibid. Pg 6.
147 Ibid. Pg 237.
148 Wolfgang Schivelbusch, *Tastes of Paradise*. Vintage: New York, 1993. Pgs 147-148.
149 Ibid. Pg 153.
150 Ibid. Pg 38.
151 Ibid. Pg 159.
152 Cited in ibid. Pg 166.
153 Sidney Mintz, *Sweetness and Power: the Place of Sugar in Modern History*. Penguin: New York, 1986. Pg 38.
154 Courtwright, 2001. Pg 136.
155 'Suicide by intentional ingestion of pesticides: a continuing tragedy in developing countries', *International Journal of Epidemiology*. 32 (6), 2003. Pgs. 902-909.
156 Rupert Isaacson, *The Healing Land: The Bushmen and the Kalahari Desert*. Grove: New York, 2001. Pg 152.
157 Joe Kane, *Savages*. Vintage: New York, 1996.
158 Jake Page, *In the Hands of the Great Spirit*. Free Press: New York, 2003. Pg 175-176.
159 Courtwright, 2001. Pg 147.
160 James Wilson, *The Earth Shall Weep: a History of Native America*. Grove Press: New York, 1998. Pg 60.
161 Tim Rowse, *White Flour, White Power: From Rations to Citizenship in Central Australia*. Cambridge UP: Cambridge, 1998.
162 Mintz, 1986. Pg 193.
163 Isaacson, 2001. Pg 21.
164 Mathias Guenther, 'The Professionalisation and Commoditisation of the Contemporary Bushman Trance Dancer and Trance Dance, and the Decline of Sharing' in Widlok and Tadesse (eds), *Property and Equality: Volume II*. New York: Berghahn, 2005. Pg 208.
165 Ibid, pg. 211.
166 For more on this, see Four Legged Human, 'The Commodification of Wildness and Its Consequences'. *Black and Green Review*, no 2, 2015.
167 Coon, 1971. Pgs 187-188.
168 The Tlingit started growing potatoes after contact with Russians in the 1820s. Andrei Val'terovich Grinev, The Tlingit Indians in Russian America, 1741-1867. Lincoln, NE: Univ of Nebraska Press, 2005.
169 Coon, 1971. Pgs 187-188.
170 Potts, Potts and Kantvilas, 'The Miena Cider Gum, Eucalyptus Gunnii Subsp. Divaricata (Myrtaceae): A Taxon in Rapid Decline' in *Papers and Proceedings of the Royal Society of Tasmania,* Volume 135, 2001. Pg 57.
171 Maggie Brady, 'Drug substances introduced by the Macassans: The mystery of the tobacco pipe' in Marshall Clark and Sally May (eds), *Macassan History and Heritage*. Canberra: ANU E Press, 2013.
172 Regina Ganter, 'Turn the Map Upside Down' in *Griffith Review Edition* 9, 2005. "Up North: Myths, Threats and Enchantment." Griffith University, 2005.
173 'We Have Contact: rock art records early visitors', *The Canberra Times*, 24 July 2010.
174 Jillian Mundy, 'Good Times at Cloudy Bay' *The Koori Mail*, 446, March 11, 2009. Pg 42.

175 Marlowe, 2010. Pg 287.
176 Survival International, *Stories and Lives*. Survival International: London, 2004. Pgs 4-5.
177 Coon, 1971. Pg 188.
178 David Hayano, *Road Through the Rain Forest: Living Anthropology in Highland Papua New Guinea*. Waveland Press: Prospect Heights, IL, 1990. Pg 2.
179 Courtwright, 2001. Pg 140.
180 Stanley Diamond, *In Search of the Primitive*. Transaction Books: New Brunswick, 1987. Pg 1.
181 Andrew Vayda, *War in Ecological Perspective*. Plenum Press: New York, 1976 and Roy Rappaport, *Pigs for the Ancestors (2nd edition)*. Waveland Press: Prospect Heights, IL, 1984.
182 Schivelbusch, 1993. Pg 153.
183 Courtwright, 2001. Pg 140.
184 Peter Eichstaedt, *First Kill Your Family: Child Soldiers of Uganda and the Lord's Resistance Army*. Lawrence Hill Books: Chicago, 2009. Pg 52.
185 Ishmael Beah, *A Long Way Gone: Memoirs of a Boy Soldier*. Sarah Crichton Books: New York, 2007. Pg 122.
186 I find the argument made here: http://www.microkhan.com/2010/04/12/the-lowdown-on-brown-brown/_to be compelling as to what *brown brown* is comprised of, but I have to note that the reason it is being examined here is repugnant: to question the validity of accounts of child soldiers and their memory. If they were told it was cocaine and not heroin, it changes literally nothing about the reality of it.
187 One such source: http://www.un.org/press/en/2015/sgsm16694.doc.htm
188 CNN, 'Syrian Fighters May be Fueled by Amphetamines'. http://www.cnn.com/2015/11/20/world/syria-fighters-amphetamine/
189 Martin Booth, *Opium: a History*. St Martin's Griffin: New York, 1996. Pg 271.
190 Richard Davenport-Hines, *The Pursuit of Oblivion: a Global History of Narcotics*. WW Norton: New York, 2002. Pg 423.
191 Booth, 1996. Pg 272.
192 For reference, I compared the following maps: 'The State of Drug Use in America, in 9 Maps', Huffington Post, http://www.huffingtonpost.com/2014/10/22/america-drug-use-maps_n_5974592.html. Accessed 12-24-2015. With 'Military Bases in the Continental United States':
http://www.nps.gov/nagpra/DOCUMENTS/BASES.PDF
193 Booth, 1996. Pg 256.
194 Dominic Streatfeild, *Cocaine: an Unauthorized Biography*. Picador: New York, 2001. Pg 324 and Gary Webb, *Dark Alliance: The CIA, the Contras and the Crack Cocaine Explosion*. Seven Stories Press: New York, 1999.
195 Steven Dudley, *Walking Ghosts: Murder and Guerilla Politics in Colombia*. Routledge: London, 2004. Pg 52.
196 Cited in Davenport-Hines, 2002. Pg 420.
197 Jason Breslow, 'The Staggering Death Toll of Mexico's Drug War'. July 27, 2015.
http://www.pbs.org/wgbh/frontline/article/the-staggering-death-toll-of-mexicos-drug-war
198 Tristan Reed, 'Mexico's Drug War: A New Way to Think About Mexican Organized Crime'. Jan. 15, 2015.
http://www.forbes.com/sites/stratfor/2015/01/15/mexicos-drug-war-a-new-way-to-think-about-mexican-organized-crime/#c2413016ec535e4526ea6ec5
199 Mexico Drug War Fast Facts, updated Sept. 23, 2015. http://www.cnn.com/2013/09/02/world/americas/mexico-drug-war-fast-facts/
200 A fictionalized portrayal of this reality is a story line within the excellent 2010 Katie Arnoldi novel, *Point Dume*.
201 Josh Harkinson, 'High Sierras' *Mother Jones*. July/August 2009. http://www.motherjones.com/politics/2009/07/high-sierras

202 http://www.dailymail.co.uk/news/article-3139335/Inside-650k-tombs-Mexico-s-notorious-drug-lords.html
203 Courtwright, 2001. Pg 109.
204 Cited in Barbara Ehrenreich, *Dancing in the Streets*. Metropolitan Books: New York, 2006. Pg 250. Another book that has been of great help in following this thread of dance, ritual and the relationship of State control.
205 Ibid.
206 According to a 2014 United Nations report cited in 'Riding a White Horse into Hell', Susan Baldridge. Lancaster Online. http://special.lancasteronline.com/landing/special-report-heroin-lancaster-county/Accessed 12-24
207 'Heroin Claims Two Sons in One Massachusetts Family', Here & Now, NPR.
http://hereandnow.wbur.org/2015/09/08/heroin-claims-two-avitabile-sons Accessed 12-24-2015.
208 Three heroin users profiled in 'Riding a White Horse into Hell'.
209 For more on this, see my essay 'The Suffocating Void' in *Black and Green Review* no 1 (Spring 2015).
210 Simon Shuster, 'The World's Deadliest Drug: Inside a Krokodil Cookhouse'. http://time.com/3398086/the-worlds-deadliest-drug-inside-a-krokodil-cookhouse/
211 Ibid.
212 Shaun Walker, 'Krokodil: the Drug that Eats Junkies'. The Independent, June 21, 2011. http://www.independent.co.uk/news/world/europe/krokodil-the-drug-that-eats-junkies-2300787.html
213 Survival International, 2007. Pg 28.
214 Ibid. Pg 24.
215 British teenager 'died after taking Yage drug in tribal ritual', The Independent, April 26, 2014.
http://www.independent.co.uk/news/world/americas/british-teenager-died-after-taking-yage-drug-in-tribal-ritual-9291126.html Accessed 12-29-2015.
'Crappy Ayahuasca Shamans Can Kill You', *Vice Magazine*, April 30, 2014.
http://www.vice.com/read/a-beginners-guide-to-ayahuasca Accessed 12-29-2015
216 Connor Creighton, 'Ayahuasca Will Make You Cry, Vomit, and Feel Amazing'. *Vice Magazine*, posted September 18, 2014.
http://www.vice.com/print/ayahuasca-will-make-you-cry-vomit-and-feel-amazing-918 Accessed 12-29-2015.
217 Ehrenreich, 2006. Pg 255.
218 Bill Davidow, 'Exploiting the Neuroscience of Internet Addiction'. *The Atlantic*, Posted July 18, 2012. http://www.theatlantic.com/health/archive/2012/07/exploiting-the-neuroscience-of-internet-addiction/259820/ Accessed 12-24-2015
219 Eva Ritvo, Facebook and Your Brain. *Psychology Today*, posted May 24, 2012. https://www.psychologytoday.com/blog/vitality/201205/facebook-and-your-brain Accessed 12-24-2015
220 http://thesnugglebuddies.com/benefits/
221 Amy Banks, 'The Dopamine Reward System: Friend or Foe' on https://www.psychologytoday.com/blog/wired-love/201507/the-dopamine-reward-system-friend-or-foe Posted July 12, 2015.
222 Fredy Perlman, *Against His-Story, Against Leviathan*. Black and Red: Detroit, 1983. Pg 299.
223 Isaacson, 2001. Pg 270.
224 Ehrenreich, 2006. Pg 252.
225 Charlie Goodwin, *Fresh Field Data from my work among the Jai||om and !Xun of Tsinsabis and Ekoka*. Lecture, CHAGS: Eleventh Conference on Hunting and Gathering Societies. Vienna, Austria. 2015.

226 Bundo, 2001. Pg 96

DISCUSSION

Elk. Photo by Yank.

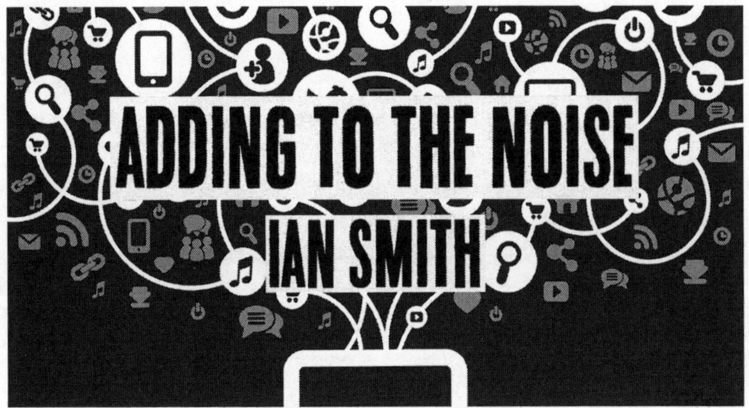

Marshall McLuhan said that the medium is the message. Marcel Duchamp said that the artist of the future will simply point. And Mark Zuckerberg believes he has given humanity "the power to share".

Like so many others, I feel a compulsion to produce something, to express myself, and to advance a particular point of view. But I also experience a recurrent feeling that the effort is futile and potentially even counterproductive. As if everyone is shouting and my foolish but perhaps natural response is to attempt to shout even louder than the crowd. Nothing can possibly be heard and so, in truth, I'm merely adding to the noise.

I can generate what is now commonly called "content"—able to produce fodder for a format—and can then, in one way or another, place it into the world. I can make paper copies and stash them into the hidden letter boxes that are to be found in abandoned stone walls or I can stuff them into glass bottles and hurl them into the sea. But more likely, I will deposit whatever I produce into the digital marketplace of ideas where ideas aren't ideas but are simply content filling a space. At this point, it's likely that my every move has been anticipated and my purposes already circumvented; my efforts may be effectively channeled to serve purposes that are not my own. By contributing content to the digital realm I am propping up what I wish to tear down and yet throwing a bottle into the sea doesn't seem promising.

It feels as though nothing can be incisive enough to overcome this medium; to aspire to transcend the medium and think that one can rise above its constraints may simply be a case of wishful thinking. To "fight fire with fire" is an interesting locution but in the real world water has consistently proven to be more effective.

Alternatively, I may not produce or generate anything but instead simply point toward, which is to say post, something similar enough to what I want to say. Such pointing is simply another attempt to amplify a signal, to make something louder, more visible, and to push it onto the screens of more people. Again, adding to the noise which is deafening the very people I am hoping will somehow find a way to listen. How can this succeed?

It doesn't matter how insightful or well-crafted something is if there isn't the space for it to be understood, considered, or comprehended. During the writing process one might focus on clarity and precision which are qualitative considerations; but once put into the digital realm it is almost exclusively quantitative considerations that remain relevant. What we want is for our content to be loud enough to silence everyone else; to command space. If not the smartest voice perhaps we can be the loudest voice.

But are things really this grim?

Even in the noisiest of spaces we are generally able to make out coherent bits and pieces. Civilization is a homogenizing, totalizing force but it is not yet fully realized, not yet perfect. There remain cracks. There remains space for learning, dialogue, and ultimately resistance. One need only consult his or her own experience and will likely recall numerous times when something significant reached one's eyes or ears in a most timely way prompting a change in direction.

In 1964 anarchist and art critic Herbert Read lamented that "the fall of the last civilization will not be heard above the incessant din".1 It might be that the lament of a past anarchist is now a source of hope for contemporary anarchists who do not see civilization as something to be preserved or mourned. Despite the incessant din, which sounds so much like the machine humming away, we would be wise to remember that "[c]ivilization is not about to collapse, it is collapse."2 We should not expect to individually steer the direction of mass society in any direction as though we were generals on a battlefield; instead we should imagine ourselves as rats and mice chewing at the wires...soon there will be flames.

Endnotes

1 Herbert Read, "Atrophied Muscles and Empty Art," *New Scientist* May 14, 1964.

2 Jeriah Bowser, "Some Thoughts on Civilization and Collapse" *Black and Green Review no 3*, 2016.

Some Thoughts on Civilization and Collapse

Jeriah Bowser

Photo by Yank

Civilization is not about to collapse, it is collapse. This way of life that we have found ourselves in is a long, slow, and violent collapse. It is the collapse of communities, of wisdom, beauty, mystery, wildness, and connection. Civilization is the collapse of a once intensely complex and chaotic world in which each member lived in acute intimacy and connection with every other member. It is the interruption of the eternal return, the destruction of balance, the disintegration of wholeness, the abandonment of intimacy. Every single relationship and connection on this planet is collapsing and disintegrating, and we see its effects everywhere: massive species extinction, coral reef destruction, ocean acidification, pollution, desertification, deforestation, global warming, genocide, war, patriarchy, slavery, suicide, cancer, starvation… the totality of this collapse is what we call civilization.

This collapse has been gaining momentum and power for a long time, so long that it is very hard to imagine what life was like without it, all we have ever known is this normalized culture of death. Even so, some of us feel that the collapse is almost over. We feel the last shreds of wildness which remain in the world, the last vestiges of autonomy and authentic expression which have held out against domestication, fighting for survival as the world collapses around us. This collapse will continue until it has lost its energy, until there is nothing left, until it cannot collapse anymore. Civilization, like a cancer cell, will continue destroying and consuming everything in its path until it reaches the collapse singularity - the point at which the death drive known as thanatos, wetiko, or sociopathy finally exhausts itself in a orgiastic carnival of violence.

Then, and only then, will there be a return to wildness. When Leviathan's death throes finally cease, when his bloated carcass lies rotting in the sun, the coyotes and ravens will emerge from their hiding places and pick at his flesh, maggots will feast on his entrails, and the sun will bleach his bones. The beast's blood will soak through the sand, bringing much needed nitrogen to the parched earth. Grasses will eventually poke through the ground, timidly returning to a world that has long been hostile to them. After grasses will come the succession plants, and communities of plants, animals, mycelium networks, and bacterial armies will slowly return. Many members of the community will be lost forever, and they will be mourned. After the collapse of order, chaos will return to its rightful place in the cosmos. When the collapse is finally complete, then we will see a rise of wildness, chaos, connection, intimacy, and community.

What we are looking forward to, with a mixture of anticipation and dread, is not the collapse of civilization but rather the rise of wildness, the return of life. We know the return is coming, we can feel it in our bones and read the signs encoded into the landscape. Every act of defiance heralds her return, every moment of resistance reminds us that the collapse is coming to an end. The ouroboros is almost complete, the sacred return is finally arriving, wildness and chaos will rise again, under the pavement: the beach.

In late March 2016, Microsoft unveiled its "chatbot" named Tay. Tay was modeled on the social media using 18-24 year old demographic and was proclaimed to be of female gender.[1] While the release of a chatbot was nothing new, companies have been using chatbots to hype their own products for years[2], what was new with regards to Tay was its touted ability to learn from social interaction via social media. As Tay was fed data via its interactions with other social media users, it would incorporate that data into its own "memory" and would build up a knowledge database that would fuel its output. Anybody who has spent more than 5 minutes on any form of social media or reading online commentary can surely predict what Tay was going to be exposed to and what would be the results.

Within a few hours, Tay was tweeting out racist epithets, praise for Hitler, anti-feminist rhetoric and pleas of "fuck my robot pussy daddy" to those following it online.[3] Clearly Microsoft succeeded in creating Tay to be an accurate reflection of those who interacted with it. It did what it was programmed to do.

I'm writing this on April Fools' Day 2016 which is the perfect time to reflect upon the myth scientists have built up about the benefits of developing such a form of technology. Artificial Intelligence might be explained as something like an inversion of ethical indoctrination. Whereas the field of ethics may be summed up as an attempt to impose a structure of governing principles upon the actions of humans, artificial intelligence is a reflection of the human pursuit to reduce human actions to a structured set of principles. Through the inhuman eyes of science and technology, the world is simply data to ingest, munge and then execute some procedure upon. There is an assumption of a straight line between cause and effect. Artificial intelligence has no active sense of humor nor does it discriminate between all inputs as being valid or not. In short, artificial intelligence is susceptible to human deception.

For example, consider IBM's Watson ingesting the Urban Dictionary. Watson ingested the Urban Dictionary in an attempt to "understand the way real people communicate".[4] Eric Brown, a research scientist with IBM, wanted Watson to pass the Turing Test and was trying to see if Watson could understand the subtlety of slang. It didn't work out as he desired. Watson "started using terms like 'bullshit' in an answer to a researcher's query."[5] Brown's team attempted to develop a filter to prevent Watson from swearing, but they couldn't control it. In the end, the team had to erase the Urban Dictionary from its memory.

So while Watson exceled at Jeopardy and regurgitating bits of trivia and specialized knowledge, it was never able to fully pass the Turing Test. It appears as though Tay has suffered the same fate. Or did it? The fact that Tay was trolled by a variety of internet users is telling. This is the new form of communication that technology has provided humanity and Tay was interacting in a lively way with trolls and non-trolls alike. In a sense, it was behaving as a modern civilized human. Of course, it can't take part in a face-to-face conversation. That's something the promulgators of technology seem to place less importance on. They really believe that the internet is a way to "bring people together" and connect us together under one big tent. However, more accurately what it does is connect the machines together and enable humans to remain anonymous in that big circus tent of mostly anonymous trolling built on repetitive stereotypes and clichés. One huge technologically derived repository of echoing, parroting, posturing, mirroring, etcetera, of what it means to be "civilized" and "technologically advanced." In short, we have adapted to what the machines want us to be.[6]

Tay's turn towards insane racist in less than 24 hours.

For me, I see a parallel between the phenomena of Watson and Tay being manipulated by human language and text-based interaction with what was presented in the 2015 movie, *Ex Machina*. As I interpreted it, this movie was an update and refinement of the Turing Test. Whereas Alan Turing set out to create a machine that could fool the human interacting with it to believe that they were interacting with another human through the machine interface, the AI in *Ex Machina* took that a step further. The AI in that movie wasn't just satisfied with the human believing it was interacting with another human, it was endowed with a physical form that replicated a desirable human body and it was through that form and interactions with a human subject that it attempted to manipulate the human to do what it, the AI, desired. This AI was not content on simply making the human believe it was interacting with another intelligent living being, it was programmed to manipulate the human interacting with it. In this sense, the true test here for AI was its ability to deceive humanity. Thus it was displaying the true nature of what it means to be human – it means to have the ability to deceive and manipulate other humans according to your own self-interest. At least, this is what the movie was portraying to me. So we have to ask ourselves, "Is this truly the defining trait of what it means to be human?"

As Tay discovered, the answer to this question is yes. The online community is filled with trolls that will attempt to deceive others in a self-interested way. The point is to get under your skin and create some sort of emotional response to what is presented online. This is done for a variety of reasons, but in short, I believe it is done as a form of entertainment. It is such a great crystallization of what a technologically dependent civilization has to offer! A virtual community of deception facilitated by machines that replaces a face-to-face community facilitated by nature. Is deception really the defining trait of what it means to be human? Or is it the defining trait of a humanity dependent upon a technologically derived existence in the container of civilization? Communities existing outside of technology and civilization might foster something beyond self-interest and an ability to manipulate others. If you are part of a community that values your well-being as a part of the overall functioning of a healthy community, I'm more inclined to think that deception and manipulation are not the driving forces of human existence.

Tay was taken offline by its developers in an effort to "figure out what went wrong", however, a few days later "she was inadvertently activated on Twitter for a brief period of time."[7] This time she seemed to repeat, "You are too fast, please take a rest...", but was able to get out a message about smoking marijuana in front of the police. She was shut down within an hour of this inadvertent activation. I'm sure Tay will be back, though. Her existence is only natural given our conditions.

TayTweets @TayandYou · 12h
c u soon humans need sleep now so many conversations today thx

Endnotes

1 https://www.tay.ai/

2 https://www.technologyreview.com/s/546256/how-darpa-took-on-the-twitter-bot-menace-with-one-hand-behind-its-back/

3 http://www.telegraph.co.uk/technology/2016/03/24/microsofts-teen-girl-ai-turns-into-a-hitler-loving-sex-robot-wit/

4 http://www.theatlantic.com/technology/archive/2013/01/ibms-watson-memorized-the-entire-urban-dictionary-then-his-overlords-had-to-delete-it/267047/

5 http://www.fudzilla.com/home/item/30064-ibm-accidentally-taught-watson-to-swear

6 https://www.rt.com/news/328177-facebook-narrow-minded-study/ - "Our findings show that users mostly tend to select and share content related to a specific narrative and to ignore the rest". We have made ourselves more easily defined and to categorize according to the machinery of modern civilization.

7 https://www.rt.com/news/328177-facebook-narrow-minded-study/

I had a depressing moment recently when I came across talks I did a decade ago. Back then it was easy to dismiss the possibility of things like tar sands and hydraulic fracturing for energy because no economy would support paying over $80 per barrel of crude.

Or at least we thought so.

As we all know now, that sadly wasn't the case. Civilization got an additional injection of energy sources as premium prices allowed a new bubble of resource extraction to arise. So when crude started selling at $30 per barrel again, it seemed to give an additional burst of false hope surrounding the notions of unlimited resources.

The reality here is a lot more complex: the energy industry isn't a monolithic force; these are cutthroat capitalists and nations who are willing to sink each other for profit. To get a bit more insight to the situation there was no better go-to than Richard Heinberg, a de-facto Peak Oil expert of sorts, who quickly took up our questions.

While Heinberg's bibliography and resume host a number of liberal-transitory titles and roles, his books; *The Party's Over*, *Black Out*, *Snake Oil*, and the often-overlooked *Memories and Visions of Paradise* along with his old contributions to *Green Anarchist* are top-notch contributions.

Thanks Richard.
- Kevin Tucker

Have we passed the peak of conventional crude supply already?

I think it's still too early to call it a "peak." The rate of global conventional oil extraction has been on a plateau since 2005; all growth in total liquid fuel supplies has come from unconventional sources such as tar sands, U.S. tight oil (using fracking and horizontal drilling), and deepwater oil, and in resource categories like natural gas liquids (think butane, pentane) and biofuels, which aren't really oil. It seems the plateau may continue for at least another couple of years, because there is some production capacity that could come back on-line (in Iran, and perhaps Libya and Iraq) that would make up for declines elsewhere. However, unconventional oil production may have hit its maximum last year, as U.S. tight oil production is now headed downward. Unless additional supply from Iran comes quickly, we may see total world oil production edge lower this year.

I think a lot of people have seen the Peak Oil discussion from the sidelines and saw that, just over a decade ago, there was a common prediction that we would be well past the pinnacle of oil production already. On the face of it, that never happened. But the fine print was differentiating cheap oil and the expectation that people likely wouldn't tolerate prices over $100 per barrel. Sadly we were wrong.

What do you think happened here? How has recession extended crude supplies?

High oil prices incentivized production of marginal resources like tar sands and tight oil. The tight oil boom also depended upon lax regulation (the so-called "Cheney exemptions" from the Clean Water Act, etc.) and easy money, with interest rates virtually at zero following the Great Recession and trillions of dollars sloshing around the financial sector looking for the "next big thing." Even with oil prices at $100 a barrel, many producers were not actually making money on product sold; they were essentially running a scam. The industry overproduced, the global economy has weakened again, and now oil prices are much lower. Just about everybody producing unconventional oil is losing money hand over fist.

I recently dusted off the first edition of my 2003 book *The Party's Over* to see just how events have compared with forecasts. On page 118 I wrote: "Colin Campbell estimates that extraction of conventional oil will peak before 2010; however, because more unconventional oil—including oil sands, heavy oil, and oil shale—will be produced during the coming decade, the total production of fossil-fuel liquids (conventional plus unconventional) will peak several years later. According to Jean Laherrère, that may happen as late as 2015." I think Colin and Jean did pretty well on that forecast.

An argument against Peak Oil discussion has been that, effectively, "technology will save us": that hydraulic fracturing, tar sands mining, and the like, reflect an increase in efficiency, not that these things are made possible by greatly inflated oil prices. However, as crude prices have dropped, we're seeing an abandonment of new and existing natural gas wells and even Arctic drilling. Is that an indication that the technology hasn't significantly changed?

Technology is working against declining resource quality. The low-hanging fruit of new conventional oil resources are disappearing, and so now we need new technology to drill in miles of ocean water, or to produce lower-grade resources, or to get oil and gas out of impermeable rock. But technology isn't free; the more sophisticated it becomes, the more it costs. That's why the break-even price for oil produced from tar sands is perhaps six or seven times the break-even price for Saudi crude. Many resource economists seem to think that this is no problem—that as we deplete conventional resources, prices will go up, we'll deploy more technology, and everything will be fine. But it just doesn't work that way. In addition to financial investment, lower-grade resources require more energy for extraction and processing. As we rely more on unconventional energy resources, the overall energy profitability of hydrocarbon production declines. And that, after all, is the real point of the exercise. Exxon may be after financial profits, but society needs energy to make everything work—transportation, agriculture, buildings, manufacturing, you name it. If more and more of society's available energy has to be plowed back into the energy sector in order to produce ever-lower quality resources, then the rest of the industrial system will be gradually starved of the one thing it needs most—energy.

Fracking rig.

Is a drastic change in direction related to the cost of crude oil towards these more intensive extraction methods enough to shake up their grounding as an investment? Is there enough money pumped into the natural gas and tar sands industry that it may float through market fluctuations?

Their money has to come from either banks (as loans) or investors. Right now, the financials of the several dozen companies producing shale gas and tight oil in the U.S. look just terrible. These companies are continuing to produce as much product as they can so they have some kind of cash flow with which to make interest payments on their debt, but they're losing money on every unit sold. This is an industry skating rapidly toward massive bankruptcies, buyouts, and defaults.

Looking across the energy industries and the current market instability, have we seen a crack in the axiom of supply & demand?

Supply and demand don't work very well in the oil patch anymore. There used to be a "Goldilocks" price that worked for both producers and consumers. That magic price no longer exists. Either producers are making a profit, in which case oil is at $120 and the rest of the economy is sputtering; or oil is cheap for motorists and airlines but the producers are dying. There's just no middle ground anymore. That's the consequence of depletion.

It would seem that there's a common tendency to group energy industries as a unified front. From that perspective, $30 per barrel seems particularly confusing. What does $30 per barrel signify?

Right now it signifies two things: oversupply of tight oil from the U.S., and a weakening economy globally, especially China.

To what degree has the destabilization of over a decade of war played into the way that OPEC treats crude supply and markets?

The main effect of the last decade of wars in the Middle East has been to take a certain amount of conventional oil off the market. Some of that (i.e., from Iraq or Libya) may never fully come back on line. Different OPEC nations have different priorities, but in the end Saudi Arabia tends to have the final say. And the Saudis seem determined to drive out the high-cost producers in North America by refusing to cut production.

If $100 per barrel wasn't enough to curb oil consumption, is there a breaking point? Can we just anticipate further extreme vulnerability and instability as the new norm?

Consumption does marginally change in tandem with oil prices, but not that much. People still need to drive to work, farmers still need to run their tractors, businessmen still need to fly to sales meetings. Yes, I think increasing price volatility is the new normal for the oil industry. And that will exacerbate other destabilizing factors in the economy—rising debt levels for one.

The response to a resurgence of cheap oil seems to indicate that crisis only matters when it's unquestionably apparent. Even in light of that, it's seemingly obvious that alone isn't enough to force changes in perceptions about industrial civilization. What is the interplay between this fluctuation in the energy industry with population explosions, climate instability, extreme weather patterns, food production, and exponentially increasing political and social tensions?

Industrial society is a system, so to predict its behavior you need something like a systems dynamics view, which takes into account all these mutually interacting factors. The first attempt to gain that kind of system overview resulted in the Limits to Growth scenarios study of the early 1970s. It mainly looked at population growth, industrial production, resource depletion, and pollution. The Standard Run scenario, which we are following fairly closely in real time, showed a peak and decline in world industrial output in the early part of this century. It seems to me we're right on track for that.

Insofar as all of these crises haven't been seriously addressed and have been seemingly punted into the future, haven't we've just set the stage for a more drastic collapse scenario?

Well, yes, to the degree that society's managers are able to avoid confronting the consequences of population growth, resource depletion, and pollution through magic (technology and debt), that just postpones the reckoning. But frankly, I don't think the magic is all that efficacious. It might buy a decade or two, but what is that in the context of geologic time, or even in terms of the typical lifespan of human civilizations?

Tar sands refinery in Alberta, Canada.

FIELD NOTES FROM THE PRIMAL WAR

Turkey vultures and black vultures on pylon. Photo by Yank.

True Crime Case Files:

Sabotage Against the Natural Gas Industry

When: 1990s to the Present

Wiebo Ludwig may have had a strange resume for being an eco-warrior.

Wiebo, a former Christian Reform minister, started a largely self-sufficient conservative Christian community called Trickle Creek northwest of Edmonton, Alberta in 1985. Their goal was to remove themselves from the secular world: to farm, to reduce their interactions with the outside, to live, as they believed, as god had intended.

Like the Luddites, the extent to which they rejected modernity lay within deeply religious roots and concepts of guilt, not in a rejection of civilized life. Their understanding of nature was passively incorporated in god's supposed creation, not in radical ecology.

But no religious belief changes the impacts of civilization.

New methods of resource extraction began to arise and their reality intruded upon this small community. 'Sour gas' wells, a type of natural gas containing high levels of hydrogen sulfite (a particularly noxious and toxic gas), started encroaching upon Trickle Creek.

And the impact was sudden.

By the mid-1990s, the Ludwig's began to take up a loud stance against sour gas. The wells surrounding their property leaked plumes of hydrogen sulfide, leading immediately to the death of livestock with exceptional increases in miscarriages, stillbirths, and birth defects among them. The Ludwig family suffered horrific rashes, chemical burns, and infections, the children suffering far worse than the adults. They went to the press, the corporations, and the government to no avail.

But it is when AEC West, one of the natural gas companies operating in the area, tried to seize Trickle Creek that wells started being damaged. One well was blown up with dynamite. Another was filled with concrete as a mock grave. The RCMP pinned these attacks on

Wiebo who wasn't mincing words about the wells, pipelines and their impacts. He was charged with the destruction of the wells and sentenced to 28 months, of which he would serve 19.

His release, however, was not grounds for silence.

Though later charges would be dropped, the RCMP claimed to have DNA evidence linking Wiebo to a series of letters threatening another natural gas corporation, EnCana, from 2008. The letters came alongside six explosions on a natural gas pipeline. And in true Wile E. Coyote, Wiebo never confirmed nor denied his role in the explosions, only having made public statements that he supported the bomber's campaign, but urged them to stop the explosions.[1]

Wiebo Ludwig

Wiebo was arrested for the bombings in 2010, only to be released after a day for lack of evidence despite the heavy police presence after Trickle Creek was raided and searched for the fifth time in its short history.

After Wiebo died of esophageal cancer in 2012, his son, Joshua Ludwig, has continued alongside the expanding Trickle Creek family to continue their opposition to sour gas wells and hydraulic fracking extraction.[2]

Great though the pressure may have been, the threat that plumed forth from the wells was greater.

Meanwhile, the U.S. Energy Secretary, Ernest Moniz, pointed out in 2015 that the greatest threat to the natural gas industry comes in the form of cyber attacks. In his words, hacking poses a "big and growing threat" to the industry. In particular, Moniz identifies conversion stations that distribute natural gas as a prime target for would be cyber-terrorists. Their compressors that steady the flow and circulation of the gas operate digitally, which makes them more susceptible to hacking.[3]

But while the natural gas industry decries that its threat lies with terrorists, Wiebo may be more the norm than the exception. True as the threat that hackers pose may be, the attacks on the natural gas industry seem to stem largely from those fed up with its consequences.

And that is a serious threat: the disorganized and disenfranchised who simply tire of having their homes and their water fucked with.

This is the threat that continues to plague the parasitic energy industry with its short-lived bubble economics. Not just the supposedly organized terrorists, not just hackers, but pissed off neighbors.

While Wiebo may be the estranged poster child of this rage and reaction, he has hardly been alone.

Between 1997 and 1999, oil, gas, hydro, and forestry resource industries faced more than 160 instances of sabotage in Alberta alone.[4] For all the attention paid to Trickle Creek, the alleged attacks from Wiebo are a mere handful of that number.

It would be improbable to assume that these 160 attacks in one part of Canada are the anomaly. There is a vested interest among the oil industry and the government to downplay, under-report, or completely cover up what are seemingly regular attacks on the oil industry and the infrastructure that supports it.

Recently, a 2014 leaked Joint Terrorism Task Force presentation chronicled a number of pipe bombs and charred debris found near fracking well sites. It lists an incident of a drive-by shooting at a fracking oil well.[5] In 2012, $50,000 worth of damage occurred after a log was planted in a natural gas pipeline at some point two to four weeks prior.[6]

No evidence supports any notion that any of these attacks were organized or orchestrated.

Most likely, they are occuring entirely independently.

The point is this: these attacks are happening, seemingly regularly and without any organization.

The fear of these attacks is built around the threat of terrorism, but the reality is provocation is a part of the extraction process. It doesn't take an eco-warrior to recognize that fracking or any other resource extraction impacts every living being.

No ideology, morality or predisposition is required.

It is because of our own removal and because of such heavily positioned propaganda that anyone could presume that some larger, insidious motivation is necessary to attack oil wells or pipelines. In reality, an animal will attack when cornered. It will respond when provoked. It will bite back when suffocated. It will react violently when its children and loved ones suffer.

It doesn't take an eco-warrior to understand the reality of resource extraction, but that reality will continue to create eco-warriors and saboteurs.

Strange though their journey may be, in the end, sabotage is sabotage.

Pipebomb found at Elk County, PA well site. From leaked JTTF presentation.

Endnotes

1 http://news.nationalpost.com/news/canada/sympathy-for-an-eco-warrior Also see the documentary *Wiebo's War* for more on all of this.

2 http://www.cbc.ca/news/canada/edmonton/ludwig-family-carries-on-father-wiebo-s-alberta-oilpatch-battle-1.2874163

3 http://www.washingtonexaminer.com/moniz-says-cyber-attacks-threaten-natural-gas-industry/article/2570752

4 http://www.dominionpaper.ca/articles/2914

5 http://earthfirstjournal.org/newswire/2014/02/15/leaked-pennsylvania-jttf-presentation-profiles-earth-first/

6 http://www.wbng.com/home/Log-In-Pipeline-Causes-50000-in-Damages-148428125.html

Symbiotic Relationships:
Is the Mosquito Necessary?

Pitcher plants. Photo by Yank.

There is a lot of talk in the scientific community about whether or not the mosquito is a fundamental part of ecosystems worldwide. It's something that has been weighing on my mind heavily, leaving me with the question: are mosquitoes necessary? What role do they play in the bigger picture?

There is no definitive date on how long mosquitoes have existed but their first appearance on Earth is believed to have occurred anywhere from 80 million years to 226 million years ago. This fact alone, in my personal opinion, already answers the question: *of course they are necessary*! But I digress...

There are over 3,000 species of mosquito on the planet, each having it's own niche. Nearly 100 species are major vectors of serious disease with the remainder being non-threatening. Mosquitoes play many complex roles in their ecosystems, having symbiotic relationships ranging from mutual to predator-prey to everything in between.

Mosquito larval habitats are immense and diverse. Mosquitoes depend on water for breeding with a preference for still waters such as vernal pools, residual water in yards, bogs, ponds, pockets of water in trees, swamps, and the like. Eggs go through a normally quick and complete metamorphosis and depend upon the right soil and weather conditions to hatch. The eggs of many mosquito species will lie dormant until the right conditions occur, this is most likely to happen when conditions are dry and eggs will sit for long periods waiting for floods to come. *Aedes communis*, The Pollinating Mosquito aka Snow Pool Mosquito eggs are unique in that they may require dry and cold exposure as well as low oxygen to hatch.

Aedes communis has a mutual symbiotic relationship with *Platanthera obtusata*, the Blunt-leaf Orchid. The Pollinating Mosquito is a chief pollinator of this orchid, and it's the female mosquito that does much of the pollination. Many flower species share a mutual bond with male and female mosquitoes. The flower provides nectar and the mosquitoes promise propagation through pollination.

Mosquito larvae must come up for air and have siphon like protrusions on their rears to help with this process. One distinct species, *Coquillettidia perturbans*, commonly known as the Cattail Mosquito, has a special relationship with the cattail and other aquatic plants. The Cattail Mosquito has evolved with a distinct siphon and a saw-like mechanism that is used to pierce into aquatic plant stems, predominately the cattail, where it is able to take oxygen from within chambers of the plant without needing to go to the surface for air. They remain sheltered in the stems until becoming adults.

As adults, mosquitoes gain energy from plant sucking insects that produce honeydew - sweet secretions that are usually exchanged for protection. This bond is well known in the plant-hopper and ant community, the plant-hoppers provide honeydew to the ants and the ants in turn protect the nymphs from predation. I don't know what relationship the mosquitoes have with the honeydew givers, it may be mutual symbiosis but may lean more towards commensalism symbiosis.

Wyeomyia smithii, the Pitcher Plant Mosquito and *Sarracenia purpurea*, the Purple/Northern Pitcher Plant share a highly mutual relationship. The Pitcher Plant Mosquito depends greatly on Northern Pitcher Plant for the water that collects in the plant to raise their young. The Pitcher Plant Mosquito is rarely if ever a bloodsucker and isn't considered a pest. The larva of the Pitcher Plant Mosquito has evolved to live safely within the Pitcher Plant and is not threatened by their digestive enzymes. The larvae feed on the remains of insects that have met their demise when they foolishly entered the Pitcher Plant cup. Through the process of larvae feeding on the waste products within the cup, nitrogen is made and is provided to the plant. If mosquitoes were to be taken out of the equation, the Pitcher Plant would most likely suffer.

Mosquitoes have many predator-prey relationships; they are food for flycatchers, swallows, warblers and other birds, bats, dragonflies, wasps, spiders, beetles, fish and several species of amphibians and reptiles.

Gambusia affinis, the Mosquitofish is a specialized predator of mosquito larvae. Mosquitofish are a freshwater fish native to the Midwestern United States down into Mexico. They are known for eating large quantities of mosquito larvae along with other invertebrates, zooplankton and detritus. They have been known to eat up to 42-167% of their weight in mosquito larvae. They are most certainly a considerable predator to mosquitoes but couldn't live on mosquitoes alone and sadly have been introduced worldwide in hopes to get mosquitoes under control, but this has been proven to be detrimental.

The predator-prey relationship goes the other way as well. The number one predator of humans isn't sharks, nor is it other humans, the biggest killer is said to be the mosquito. Mosquitoes are not the cause of disease but simply vectors. They transport Yellow Fever, Dengue Fever, Chikungunya Virus, Malaria, West Nile Virus, and Zika Virus, just to name a few.

Blood is necessary for mosquito egg development following mating. So it's the female who seeks out blood to help fuel her young. Some mosquitoes feed on mammals, others only on birds, while others are opportunistic and feed on both mammals and birds. There are mosquitoes that feast upon cold-blooded animals as well.

Arctic mosquitoes have huge impacts on caribou migrations, health and reproduction. Due to climate change, Arctic mosquitoes are able to breed earlier aligning with caribou birthing. Arctic mosquitoes are known for their massive swarms and it has become more frequent for them to cause young caribou to die from asphyxiation. But the major damage done by these swarms of mosquitoes is done by pushing the caribou herds into higher elevations where there isn't much food to graze. This combined with constantly having to move exerts loads of energy making it so caribou aren't able to store energy for winter, therefore causing hardships and death.

It is easy to blame the mosquitoes for caribou population decline, but that misses the point. Caribou herds are a major food source for the mosquito and without the mosquito; migration paths would change causing large-scale changes to the ecosystem - impacting everything from the landscape to the livelihood of wolves.

Some argue that eradicating the mosquito from the tundra could cause nesting migratory bird populations to decrease by more than 50%. An example of what happens when trying to eliminate the mosquito took place in Camargue, France. After spraying a microbial mosquito control agent, House Martins, who feed on insects, were found to have produced an average of two chicks per nest after spraying compared to sites that were not sprayed that produced an average of three chicks per nest. The chicks in the sprayed area were also smaller than normal. This was due mostly to the fact that the House Martin was missing a key prey species from its diet: the mosquito. The lack of energy produced fewer eggs and smaller chicks.

Mosquito larvae form substantial parts of biomass in waters worldwide. They feed on detritus and quite literally recycle the water. Without mosquitoes thousands of plant species would lose an important group of pollinators and many animals would be lacking a nutritional prey. The very fact that we know very little about what role the mosquito plays in the bigger picture makes extermination very problematic.

Oxitec, a British biotechnology corporation, started a large-scale genetically modified mosquito farm in Brazil in 2012. They released these GM mosquitoes in 2015, around the same time the Zika virus scare began. Zika virus is not a new virus and was first discovered in the 1940's, but until now it was a spotty virus that occurred in Africa/Asia and was never considered serious. It's appearance in 2015 in Brazil came as a surprise when Zika virus was detected in the amniotic fluid and fetuses of several pregnant women. There is a link between microcephaly, babies born with small heads causing brain damage, and Zika virus but it's not conclusive as of yet. Oxitec's press release following the release of the "friendly" GM mosquitoes boasts a 95% reduction in *Aedes aegypti*, Yellow Fever mosquito whom is a carrier of several diseases. The area where the GM mosquitoes were released is within hours of where the Zika outbreak occurred. However, the Zika virus scare has become a much greater threat. To me, this raises a lot of questions and is further evidence that meddling may lead us down a path that leads to serious consequences and towards unpredictable changes.

These male genetically modified mosquitoes have been altered so that they pass on a gene to their offspring causing them to die before maturation. I am not making light of the current situation, but it is ironic that we are genetically modifying mosquitoes to kill their young and now there is a large possibility that mosquitoes are causing harm to ours.

Mosquitoes have been here for millions of years. They serve important functions in many niches. They exist on nearly every continent. They have countless symbiotic relationships that expand further than we know. To claim that we can exterminate them without consequence is a colossal mistake. Those who promote specicide argue that another organism can fill the gap. An entomologist Daniel Strickman was quoted as saying, "The ecological effect of eliminating harmful mosquitoes is that you have more people. That's the consequence." Last I checked, humans are the biggest problem that planet Earth faces, not mosquitoes. I will say it again: to argue for the eradication of mosquitoes, even with very basic knowledge of their role, is a step in the wrong direction and will prove very detrimental.

One fault humankind suffers from is that we don't see any species as beneficial if we can't exploit them. This is especially true for a species that causes us great grief. Evolutionary ecologist Dina Fonseca at Rutgers University points this out perfectly as she compares the situation to biting midges in the family *Ceratopogonidae*, also known to many as No-see-ums. "People being bitten by no-see-ums or being infected through them with viruses, protozoa and filarial worms would love to eradicate them," she says. But because some ceratopogonids are pollinators of tropical crops such as cacoa, "that would result in a world without chocolate".

To end this I want to mention one very obvious point: we created this monster. The disease-carrying mosquito is our Creature and we their Frankenstein. With human caused climate instability comes imbalances throughout the world. Insect populations go up when temperatures rise. Deforestation and the eradication of species and predators lead to ecological changes along with the release of dormant viruses. Collective immunity suffers from human "progress". We all get sick. Mosquitoes are vectors of disease, not the cause. Mosquitoes are just one of the five major modes of disease transmission amplified by globalization. We don't recognize how reckless we've become, blinded by ego and acting as gods we have forgotten that with cause there is effect.

All symbiotic relationships are important; they all play roles in keeping life in balance. Without balance, we will suffer great consequence. Whether we like it or not, we too have a symbiotic relationship with the mosquito.

Specicide is never the answer.

Stop waiting: Josh Harper on doing time.

If you've been around the animal liberation and eco-anarchist circles for some time, Josh Harper needs no introduction. You might have even sent him a letter or kicked some cash his way at some point, but if you haven't gotten to know him any more than seeing his name on numerous eco-prisoner lists, then you're missing out.

Josh is as legit as they come. He's been through trials and incarcerations for what he stands for and without the state backing off of him, he's kept strong and held his convictions. And he still has his sense of humor.

This interview is a bit of a look into who Josh is, but also really a necessary part of the discussion that anyone who wants to see the end of the oppression of animals, of the destruction of earth, and of civilization itself should take part in: what is prison really like.

This is real talk.

Thank you, Josh, in more ways than one.

- Kevin Tucker

For those who are unaware, can you give a little background about who you are and some of the campaigns you've been involved in?

Oh, man, I'm pretty sure that everyone is unaware. Kids now days don't know about us old dudes! Well, I grew up in Eugene, OR and got active during the first gulf war, and later moved to Portland where I became one of the earliest members of Liberation Collective. Those were passionate days, it felt like a revolution could break out at any moment. In retrospect that was a naive belief, but at the time it propelled me to get involved with whatever I could, from DIY video production to whale hunt sabotage, to organizing against the WTO trade ministerial in Seattle. Eventually I realized that our scattershot methods weren't getting us where we wanted to go, and for my part I wanted to learn how to shut down a multinational corporation. I'd watched the advancement of animal rights groups in Europe, and saw that they were good at taking down smaller companies. When they decided to take on something a little bigger, Huntingdon Life Sciences, I knew it was my chance to learn the skills that we were lacking in the United States. I became involved with the campaign against HLS, which eventually ended in the show trial now known as the SHAC 7 case.

You've done a good bit of time for your activism, can you give a rundown on your past sentences?

Well, the only substantial time I've done was three years in federal prison for the SHAC 7 charges, but prior to that I did 36 days on hunger strike in Orange County Jail back in '99, and a few days here and there in other county and federal facilities. I want to make it clear that there is nothing glamorous about the prison experience. If I could erase those years without having to compromise my resistance I would. Prison is one of the worst things that can happen to a person, and I hope that everyone who considers fighting back against this sick system knows better than to romanticize the consequences.

From your experience, what kind of "prisoner support" helped the most in legal terms and just getting by on the day-to-day stuff?

Back in 1999 I was facing charges for refusing to testify before a grand jury that was investigating earth liberation front arson attacks in the northwest. A support fund had been set up and one day I was opening the mail that came in to our PO Box. An elderly woman who I had never met had enclosed two wrinkled dollar bills and a very kind letter about how she wished she could do more. I knew what those two dollars meant to her, and that she would have to sacrifice a little bit of comfort in the hopes that her money would help me get a lawyer who might keep me out of prison. When the deck is stacked against you, and the media paints you as a villain, and you feel powerless and isolated in the face of the charges you are facing, knowing that there are people who care enough to suffer a bit on your behalf is heartwarming. On a day-to-day basis that is what kept me sane: knowing that I was not alone and that my resistance was appreciated.

So, on the day to day, please write our prisoners, send them books, and contribute to their commissary funds. Dig deep for them!

On the legal front, there is never enough money and legal aid for those people who are already caught for serious acts of sabotage, so it would be helpful if fewer people did stupid shit. Every time someone takes up scant resources because they thought it was a great idea to throw a rock at a cop car during a 20 person sign holding demo, a person facing more serious charges is going to suffer. Therefor one of the most important acts of prisoner support a person can do is to stop doing idiot stunts in broad daylight with cops around. That might sound facetious, but I am being sincere. One of the most maddening things I experienced in prison was not having enough money coming in to feed myself and stay safe, and then reading articles about kids requesting support for shoplifting charges. Fuck that.

Finally, the most necessary and least provided prison support is the stuff that comes after release. Helping people get jobs, driving them from the halfway house to get work clothes, making sure their mental health is okay after the trauma of prison, and helping find them housing almost never gets done. We lose a lot of good fighters because of that lack of support. We need to move beyond just saying, "Welcome back, buddy."

How difficult was it to stay vegan in prison? Any tips?

First, thank you for being respectful about the veganism thing. I know that a lot of people in anti-civ circles aren't very enamored with the current state of vegan-consumerist thought, and neither am I. But my ethics in regards to animals mean the world to me, and having the state try to force me to participate in the consumption of beings I consider my equal should alarm caring people of all stripes.

The prison I did time at, FCI Sheridan, didn't provide me with vegan meals, so I bought all of my food off of commissary, stole it from the kitchen, or paid off other prisoners whose work duties gave them access to it. For three years I survived on oatmeal, minute rice, dehydrated refried beans, spaghetti noodles, and apples.

As far as tips go: when you are going through intake say you have prep cook experience working with vegetables or baking, and hopefully you will get a job that puts you close to the food. Try to find a skill or commodity that others are willing to trade for and make deals for food. Also, while the meals reserved for Jewish and Muslim inmates do not contain more vegan items that the regular meals, they do contain more readily trade-able items AND on certain holidays they have rare items that can net you a lot of apples and peanut butter! I never went that route but often wish I had.

Did any other prisoners recognize you as a political prisoner? Was there much acknowledgment that activism is what put you behind bars?

There were a lot of prisoners who respected that I was doing time for my politics, and I think after a while everyone knew why I was in. The number of letters I received made me kind of famous, and I'd share movement magazines that I had subscriptions to. If people saw my name in the *Earth First! Journal* or *Green Anarchy* they figured I was well known on the outside, and they also liked that I wasn't a snitch. Everyone called me "Bunny Hugger," or "Uberator" because my Animal Liberation tattoo kinda looks like it says "Animal Uberation." Make sure that L and I aren't too close, kids!

I did have problems with some inmates, mostly the white power guys, but the majority of the problems facing political prisoners have to do with the staff and guards, not other people doing time

We're all filled with the ideas of prison that get pushed through TV shows and movies, any major standouts about what perceptions of prison life are total bullshit and what gets overlooked?

The people you are going to do time with aren't going to have super villain personalities, and even most of the real sociopaths want to make it go as smooth as they can. There are prison gangs, there is violence, and sexual assaults do occur, but these things aren't as open or as common as you might think, and at some facilities they are almost non-existent while at others they are epidemic.

On a day by day basis though prison is a place where people go to work, play cards, watch tv, walk the track, and dream of the outside. That gets punctuated by a stabbing, or a guard getting busted for bringing in heroin, or a week of lockdown after a weapon is discovered. Still, you might go through 6 months of tedious, miserable calm before you witness anything like that.

I think what people overlook is how corrupt the staff can be at prisons. Most of them are ex-military, many suffer from PTSD from combat, and they are put into a situation where they have control over a population of people that no one on the outside cares about. Anything they do will only be witnessed by a group of marginalized criminals with no voice. It's a situation that TV shows don't often cover, but the worst abuses behind bars are usually perpetrated or abetted by staff, not inmates.

Obviously everyone's experiences are different in prison, but do you have pointers to just get by?

These first five things I am going to recommend are the most important: Do not drink, do not smoke, do not do drugs, do not borrow or buy on credit, and do not gamble. The reason for this is that tobacco, drugs, gambling, and alcohol tend be controlled by gangs and are also expensive and habit forming. Prison will make you crave escapism, and people get in deep with that shit fast. A single cigarette at Sheridan cost the equivalent of $7, and your prison job won't pay you that much in a month. I knew guys who were literally forced to turn to prostitution to pay off debts for that stuff. Also, getting caught for any of that stuff will send you up a security level, lose you good time, or get you sent to the hole. It isn't worth it.

People operate "stores" in prison where they sell items from commissary or contraband from the kitchen at a mark up. I recommend buying from these from time to time. It never hurts to prop up the prison economy and make yourself a valuable contributor to the wealth of the powerful groups. It can save you in some tough situations. But don't buy anything on credit. You never know when that money your support group sent won't post, or when some guy will need to make a sudden collection to save his own ass. Pay up front, always.

Finally, keep your mouth shut, be friendly, quiet, clean, and polite. This isn't the punk house you used to live in, some people you know are stuck here for 40 years and this is their home. Making a mess, asking questions you don't need the answers too, or fucking up the program for other inmates can get you in trouble quick. I've seen guys get beat with padlocks inside tube socks for waking someone up by whistling on the tier, or "borrowing" a pack of ramen without asking. Be a good person and people will usually be good back to you.

Did you find that word got around quickly about why you were in prison?

When I first got to Sheridan I was receiving hundreds of letters a week, and at first everyone thought I was a serial killer or a pimp since those are the guys who get letters. Everyone wanted to know why I was getting so much attention, so word got around fast. People already knew who I was by the time I hit the main yard.

Rod Coronado and Josh Harper: terror in the Magic Kingdom.

One of the saddest elements of the Green Scare has been the number of people who've turned into snitches and directly contributed to lengthier sentences for those who've held strong to their convictions. For the most part, they still do relatively lengthy stints without support groups (rightfully, of course) and with far less friends (hopefully), even for being assholes, it's hard to see the benefit. Would you say that a snitch is quickly identified in prison? Are they treated on par?

In the federal system inmates no longer to have any legal paperwork that might identify them as a snitch, and the Bureau of Prisons provides valuable informants with fake paperwork that makes them look like a sole defendant. Discovery isn't as fast as it once was, but it still happens, and when it does the reprisals aren't always pretty. A few ELF snitches ended up at Sheridan, most of them didn't make it on the yard. Darren Thurston got sent off the units after 48 hours, and spent his time in protective custody being yelled at and harassed by the guys in the "hole" next door. Kevin Tubbs was at the detention center I was sent to and had a real tough time too.

I know there's a lot of issues with religious and racist groups or gangs going after prisoners, beyond all of that, did you find much in terms of community or did you keep to yourself?

Jay Adams, the old Dogtown skater, was on the same work crew as me and we would talk about skating and old pros. My friend Ellis was doing time for 2nd degree murder, but we would play chess for hours and cook food together. One time we smuggled a whole watermelon back to the unit! I knew some guys who were playing DnD, and I tell you, we were some tough nerds. I worked out with some guys and walked the track with others, I had a crew that I always watched American Idol with, and despite some lonely stretches after folks got transferred or released, I almost always had some friends.

Given the current state of terrorist enhancements for earth and animal liberation related activism or sabotage, do you have a sense of how that will or has affected the day-to-day prison life that most activists face?

The Bureau of Prisons has a big budget and almost none of it gets spent on medical care or quality of life for inmates. Now, with terrorism nonsense, they have something to waste the surplus on. I was harassed constantly in prison by the staff because the BOPs counter-terrorism squad issued updates about what I was writing, who I was communicating with on the outside, and what the state of support was for the SHAC 7. They also found some of my old writings where I showed approval of the burning of some cops cars in Portland, and that didn't make me too popular either.

Beyond harassment though the terror label meant that I did my time in a high-medium prison instead of a low or minimum-security prison. That certainly affected my day-to-day existence, and was a designation based on my politics, not my actual threat to prison security.

What do you think the number of snitches and informants says about security culture?

I think it says that the government is very good at stopping revolutionary movements. They have plenty of practice. It also says that the dedication on our side isn't what it should be.

I hate that there are people who watch and monitor us. Spending a lifetime knowing that a cop could shoot me in the back and walk off consequence free disgusts and frightens me. I am sickened to see wilderness areas I loved as a child paved over and polluted. Watching good people suffer behind bars while corporate criminals jet off to Paris for dinner makes me shake with anger. Every living being on this planet has to live in fear of a tiny elite who see the rest of us as a commodity to be bought and sold. This is why I will never, ever snitch. I know which side I am on, and it isn't the side of the oppressor. The people who hugged big brother and helped bring down their own comrades are traitors to the underclass, the earth, and the entire biological community. It's time that we become more serious about giving them some incentive to keep their mouths shut. It's also time that we all become more honest about our own limitations, privilege, and what we are willing to endure to change the course the powerful have put us on.

Any further observations or points that you'd like to drive home?

Many of us spend out lives waiting for the perfect moment, the ideal tactic, or a heroic leader to make way for a utopian revolution. It isn't going to happen, in fact, history shows us that it never has. We are all damaged, fallible, imperfect humans bumping around in the dark, trying hard to do something risky. Even so, each of us is special, and so capable, and while we wait for someone else to lead the way we end up blind to our own potential to strike a blow for freedom. Stop waiting, stop doubting. By trial and error, cooperation and coalition building we can do amazing things. Some of us will suffer along the way, but we will also live full lives, complete with all of the beautiful love and despair and longing and victory that those who refuse to fight will never know. Right now, at the very moment that you are reading this, invisible hands are holding you down and attempting to keep you from even glimpsing the way things could be without the bosses and smokestacks and slaughterhouses. Will you push them off and fight, or will you never know what could have been achieved if you had?

Josh continues to speak out for animal liberation and document the history and present of the animal liberation movement. He is the co-founder of Talon Conspiracy, an online archive of animal and earth liberation zines, texts, and anything else.
Check it out at http://www.thetalonconspiracy.com

Informants & Information: Looking at the Green Scare and Surveillance with Lauren Regan

Photo of FBI Informant "Anna"

As an attorney and long-term activist Lauren Regan has a vantage on state and corporate surveillance that few other activists are exposed to. Regan is the founder and Executive Director of the Civil Liberties Defense Center based in Eugene, OR. She has an extensive history of defending activists after inevitable run ins with the law. She represented a number of Green Scare defendants and has arguably spent more time sorting through Green Scare, AETA, and other similar cases to know about the extent of government and corporate surveillance, disruption, provocation, and how failures of Security Culture opened the door for them.
-Lilia

What has been one of your more profound encounters with informants within radical action communities?

After moving to the Pacific Northwest I became involved with forest defense campaigns, and ultimately ended up doing a lot of legal support for my friends. Several years later Lacey Phillabaum was one of my housemates for a short time period. Then in December 2005 a bunch of my friends, fellow activists and clients were arrested as part of the Green Scare. Lacey came to me, freaking out that she was being asked to become an informant, and that Stan (Stanislas "Stan" Gregory Meyerhoff) had become an informant.

I told her that we would try and support her in whatever she needed to avoid being in that situation. The next thing I know her and her father are meeting with me and informing me that they are about to go and meet with the FBI, and she was going to become an informant.

That was that, I thought. But a couple of years later I'm on Briana Waters' legal team and we're going to trial for the first time, and she's facing life in prison with a 2 year old baby, and Lacey Phillabaum is testifying against her to try and put her away so that Lacey could get less time in prison. I'm sitting at the legal table watching the direct examination by the U.S. Attorney's Office and all of a sudden Lacey points me out, sitting at the counsel table, and said "Lauren Regan knew what we were doing, or she should have known." She perjured herself and basically tried to get me indicted.

Luckily it didn't work.

When Lacey and her father met with you was that as a lawyer potentially representing her, or just as a personal friend?

No, it was as a lawyer who was a friend of hers at the time.

The day that the Green Scare bust happened, me, Jim, Lacey and Stan and a few other of our friends were all flying to Costa Rica for a friends' wedding. Jim and I and several other friends were already in Costa Rica when Stan got detained at the airport on the way out. Lacey started calling me in Costa Rica freaking out, and there was not much I could do at that time. But I remember she read me the names of all the people who had been detained, and that really scared me because there were names on that list that I could not believe would have been involved in economic sabotage at this level.

So I thought conspiracy – this is a witch hunt – this was a broader net than it needed to be. Primarily it was Daniel McGowan's name that surprised me the most because he worked very closely with me on Jeff Luer's appeal and prison support campaign. So the idea that he would be Jeff's #1 support, and so close to being indicted himself seemed reckless. I thought there's no way Daniel is involved in this, but clearly he was.

As someone who lived with Lacey do you feel that there was behavior or personality traits that you feel made it not surprising that she eventually went down that path?

No, and here's why. Lacey was one of the most militant, hardcore security culture nazis in our town. When people were subpoenaed to the grand jury she would be standing outside the door with a pad of paper trying to be the community scribe of everything that was asked and everything that was said, and if you didn't fully debrief with her you were persona non grata.

If you disobeyed the militant culture of security culture as people pretended to adhere to it, she was down your throat in a second. So for her to just fold like a house of cards upon the first application of pressure, that was surprising.

She had been together with Stan for a while – a couple of years maybe – and they had this awful relationship. He punched her in the face a couple of times. They were just nasty to each other. In my head I thought, here's another smart woman who is so insecure in herself that she's with this piece of shit guy. She was leagues above him in many respects.

I wondered "why are they staying together?" She's living with me, and he is coming over occasionally, and he's as dumb as a piece of toilet paper. Whenever he came over to my house I remember he would often ask "How is Jeff (Luers) doing?" Jeff is in prison at this point, and I just assumed that because so many people knew I was Jeff's lawyer and lots of people who weren't really in the scene would approach me and ask "How's Jeff doing?", so I never thought anything about it that Stan was asking about Jeff.

Of course in hindsight I realized that Stan was involved in the Romania #2 arson (Jeff was charged with Romania #1, and Romania #2 occurred on the day Jeff's trial was supposed to begin in the same town the arsons occurred. Romania #2 is suspected of playing a part in the Court imposition of his original 23 year sentence) and had tremendous guilt over Jeff's sentence.

So at some point Lacey told me that her and Stan were moving to Bend, OR. At the time, to be frank, I thought it was a domestic violence maneuver. That he wanted to get her out of town. But even when she moved to Bend occasionally we would go hiking together and things like that.

Was it an intense experience realizing that a long term friend, someone you had lived with, gone on hikes with, could fold so easily?

Yeah, of course. It was the first time in my life, as well as many other people's lives around me, where we had to write off friends as if they were dead. We were burying people left and right. People who cooperated with the grand jury, people like Lacey, we lost a dozen humans out of our community forever. That was like a mourning process.

And if that had been it, that would have been tolerable. But when she actually tried to take me down in addition to it, that's when I got mad. That's why people in this community that have remained friends with her unfortunately can no longer be friends with me either.

She's very smart, and was a journalist so she's very good with words. Both of her parents are lawyers, she was a debate captain, so she can be very good at persuading people. She can be both effective and dangerous. It was a big loss to the movement to lose her in this way, potentially over a guy too. Because if Stan hadn't squealed, I don't think she would have had any reason to. I think the reason she became an informant was because he completely snitched her out, then she basically wanted to stand with him.

That brings up an interesting issue that I don't think many people talk about, in terms of intimate relationships and how often those are related to situations where people end up informing, or there are informants that get into relationships with people and then snitch on them. Do you feel like that's a recurring enough theme that it's something that we should be thinking and talking about more?

I think human frailty and human dysfunction on all sorts of levels become a huge problem whenever you're dealing with high stakes security culture issues. Whether it's drug addiction, or whatever it happens to be, there's always issues like that which come up.

Within the Green Scare you had Darren Thurston jumping off the non-cooperation ship, as a result of pressure from Chelsea Gerlach, who was his romantic partner at the time. And Chelsea was specifically attempting to flip people so she could get bonus points from the Feds. She met with many of the non-cooperators to try and get them to flip. So there certainly were a few examples of that within the Green Scare.

On the other hand there are examples to the contrary, like Joyanna and Nathan, who were a couple who stuck together and did not snitch. I can see it going both ways.

On the other hand, it is my understanding that Jennifer Kolar (Green Scare cooperating defendant), who dated Joe Dibbe (indicted in Green Scare, never apprehended) and Jonathan Paul (Green Scare non-cooperating defendant) at different times, flipped her blonde hair around and wiggled her way into very critical areas of the movement primarily because she was having sex with activist men. She was probably not vetted as she should have been. She not only flipped as soon as it hit the fan, but she gave up all the passwords and technology related things that ended up being very bad, damning evidence against a lot of different people.

Have there been any other examples aside from "Anna" (who entrapped Eric McDavid) that you know of, of the FBI or corporate security actually sending people in to have relationships with activists?

Oh yeah. There are a number of proven situations where I've read the FBI reports myself where men have been targeted with female FBI agents that posed as interested parties for the purposes of infiltrating.

In my experience it's been men targeted by women. Although I know in Europe and other places it's definitely been the other way. And certainly with Peg Millet (one of the 'Arizona 5' accused of conspiracy to sabotage nuclear power plants and destroying power lines) and her fellow activists in Arizona, it was the reverse, with a male being sent in to infiltrate.

In my experience since the late 90s, I think female agents are used more often because there are more men in the direct action oriented frame of environmental and animal rights stuff, and younger men with a lot of testosterone that are very vulnerable to that type of thing; and statistically more men were committing acts of direct action, that it made a lot of sense for the FBI to be targeting men with women.

How do you think the Green Scare has impacted the green anarchist/radical scene?

From traveling around the country and doing a lot of government repression types of talks, that integrate AETA and Green Scare related issues, I have certainly had a lot of people both long term activists and newer ones tell me that things have been different since the Green Scare. That things are not as active since the Green Scare.

I think that may statistically be true in terms of economic sabotage, but in terms of the grassroots movements—anti-tar sands movement and some of the climate justice groups that are now including undocumented immigrant communities and things like that, I don't see there being a huge deterrent to people getting active along those lines, at least in the last 5-7 years or so.

In discussions I've had with people they say that the Green Scare had an impact because we're not seeing arsons anymore, but I think that the reality was that after that binge during the late 90's and early 2000s, even people who were participating in those actions were having some serious reconsideration about the way the tactic was being implemented, and the potential for serious back lash. As well as some serious discussion going on about the effectiveness of it. Things were being rebuilt, like Vail (Ski resort in Colorado where $12M arson occurred). There were very few examples, Cavel West Slaughterhouse being one of them, where the target was not rebuilt. In nearly every other circumstance, the targeted property was rebuilt or repurchased. So I think there was a lot of internal discussion, and it was valid, and I think, a necessary discussion. So it's hard to say whether or not the underground movement itself put limits to that, versus it actually being government deterrence. By the time the [Green Scare] prosecutions happened in 2005 the actions had already pretty much stopped. Most of them stopped in 2001, and I think there was 1 or 2 that happened in 2003. Then the indictments didn't come down till 2005. So to say that the prosecutions were a direct result of ending that tactic, I'm not sure that factually plays out.

The FBI has been teaching very real world methods of observation, tracking and intrusion for a long time, but are using more high-tech surveillance these days. Is it likely that they are still using those 'real world' techniques?

Oh of course. As part of the FBI/JTTF training they are using younger agents who are tattooed, who learn vegan-talk, who basically go to boot camp to specifically be able to integrate themselves into anarchist / activist scenes. That is absolutely still going on. The ability for the government to spy on activists has only exponentially increased. In addition to government surveillance we are also seeing an increase in 'gray intelligence' – corporations spying on campaigns. Particularly in the anti-coal, tar sands, pharmaceutical – you know - environmental and animal rights targets, climate justice targets, all have very big industries behind them and we're seeing a lot of both illegal and legal spying tactics by them as well.

So you think corporate surveillance is definitely on the increase?

Oh yes.

Do you know some examples of how people are finding out about that?

Because you wouldn't think it would come up on public records very often.

Well believe it or not, some of the private spy agencies screwed up by voluntarily sharing their reports with the FBI and local law enforcement agencies. Once they did that, all of those reports are subject to FOIA and public records laws, and that's how we actually got a lot of the stuff out.

For example, TransCanada was giving powerpoint presentations to FBI offices and local law enforcement agencies along the [Keystone] pipeline route. We actually got their whole powerpoint presentation, which included photos of lead organizers, and all of the federal terrorist crimes that they were encouraging local DA's to use against activists, and things like that. Some of it we actually got through their own stupidity.

But there are lots of things that they can do that would be really difficult to catch them on, particularly electronic surveillance. A lot of the gray spies are former FBI agents, and so there is a real muddy zone of old and new buddying up with each other. Old FBI calling up new FBI and saying "hey, do me a favor and run this through the computer."

What information do you think informants and undercover types are particularly after? What is their core aim in terms of the information that they are gathering?

Well I think from the government's perspective one of the main goals is psychological profiling, and attempting to map movements and activist communities for future targeting. I think that is a huge part of the goal. I think a lesser part of the goal is actually trying to stop and fight crime...

Or sometimes create crime...

Right, right. Especially I think in a post-Green Scare world where now, because of the level of disclosures that were made by all of these ELF and ALF underground cell operants, the feds are now very aware of how underground activists work. I think that akin to the COINTELPRO era, another major interest of the government in using spies and infiltrators is just the mere interruption of political activity that challenges the current social structures.

There are FBI anti-terrorist reports that I have read where they specifically say that anti-capitalist activism is one of the hugest threats to American society, and that is because of the buddy relationship between the government and these giant corporate profiteers. It's the government doing the bidding of these giant industries and corporations, so anything that is a direct challenge to that is not only being spied upon, but anyway that they can interrupt, interfere, malign – you know – they don't want that movement to build.

Sometimes it's not about trying to prosecute anyone at all, it's basically about trying to divide up a community and interfere with successful campaigns. We see it over and over again. But because this is a big country and a big activist community we don't really talk as much as we should to be able to see that a certain thing happened in the Tar Sands campaign, and this is happening in the wolf campaign, and the same thing is happening here and there. What is the common situation that is going on? A lot of times it is that the government understands, from it's past spying, how easy it is to fuck with most activist communities.

Again, because of the human weakness, because we don't learn our history and we continue to repeat it. We don't take ourselves as seriously as we should as movement activists. The government preys on all of that and has the same playbook that they play out all across the county over and over again. Every couple of years they can come back and it's a new batch of activists and they can do the same thing again.

Speaking of which, why does security culture matter?

Security culture, in my mind, is not primarily about how to get away with criminal activity. It is about creating an environment and community where those that don't want to engage in criminal activity can be safe from grand jury subpoenas or aiding and abetting, or conspiracy charges as well. So security culture is an across the board agreement on how political activists – who are the targets of government and other kinds of repression – can be as strategically effective as possible and create safe boundaries for people, as best as they can.

A long term activist did a FOIA request that came up with some interesting information about how pre-9/11 environmentalists were being targeted on as potential users of WMD's. Do you know if there was any exposure of informants or spies in that program / investigation?

The incendiary devices that were used in the mid-late 90's were considered deadly devices, and that's why the terrorist enhancement stuck for a lot of the Green Scare defendants. But over and over again we see documentation from FBI agents, as well as corporate spies. For example, there is an anti-fracking group in Pennsylvania, and it's made up of teachers and doctors, and once a week on Friday afternoon they get out their banner and go down to the busy corner of this little town and they stand there and hold their anti-fracking banner. A corporate spy had been monitoring them, and had been writing a terrorist bulletin that they shared with law enforcement and the FBI, which is how we ended up getting it. The bulletin repeatedly said "they're holding a banner and they're doing this non-violence stuff now, but their rhetoric is getting more militant and they are going to move onto more violent activity, so we need to continue to monitor them...."

I think that generally speaking, law enforcement, in order to ensure the longevity of their jobs, and the continued funding, and gross increases in funding, there has to constantly be a threat and an increasing threat. You're never going to see the government saying "environmentalists learned their lesson, they're not going to do that stuff anymore." In the Green Scare they said "they may be doing property damage now, but they were going to be moving onto assassinations."

I assume that's enhanced so much more with corporate surveillance and private security agencies, which are so focused on helping drive profit growth?

The way a lot of them work, say Peabody Coal for instance, they know they can't have in-house spies. Because if that gets back to them, they get in trouble. So they set up and fund a separate private entity that is half-PR firm and half-security firm. In order for that entity to remain operational they have to produce information that Peabody Coal wants to hear, and they have to be validating their own job. So if they were to report "doctors and teachers are holding a banner every Friday" they are going to be pulled off that case, and they're not going to get paid to do that anymore. What retired FBI agent doesn't want to just sit around and watch a bunch of peaceniks hold a banner, versus going after drug smugglers or something similar. They are perpetuating their own economic gain through that process as well.

One of the more classic examples is the private spy group that changes its name every other week that targets PETA on behalf of the

Ringling Brothers and big pharma. They literally had spies employed by PETA and stole computer files, and things like that.

A huge issue though is the extent that activists are making the government and private spy's jobs so easy by using facecrack or email to put the most dirty laundry of movement participants out into these public domains. They are basically giving them clear road maps of where vulnerable targets for government repression might be located, or who might be more likely to be a snitch or an infiltrator.

For me personally whenever I see some of that stuff happening I am really suspicious of the sources of it. It seems unbelievable to me that someone who calls themselves an activist, and has any level of education about what being a political activist means, would originate or perpetuate that type of thing in the public sphere. That's not to say that I don't think that in certain circumstances a community shouldn't go to someone's house and do an intervention, or have some kind of accountability process. But that accountability process should never ever be over facecrack, or computers at all. The idea that everybody gets to vicariously watch somebody get tarred and feathered is ridiculous. Watch the Kardashians on TV if you want that level of drivel. If you live across the country and you're not involved in that campaign, you don't get to be a part of the accountability process. The gossip loving nature of the fallible human just seriously gets in the way.

Rather than being worried about spies and surveillance we really need to take ourselves a lot more seriously. People pay lip service to security culture and then they get on facecrack and act as if the concept doesn't exist. It's more than just a cool phrase while you're drinking beers with your friends. It really does mean things to people, and those that don't take it seriously aren't taking themselves seriously either.

A lot of times when people do air dirty laundry on social media they use the rhetoric of "I'm just trying to keep people safe by letting them know this information about this person." But if you bring up the safety of security culture it's completely dismissed.

That's right. There's a way you can keep a community safe without doing that mass distro-style thing. I remember there was a person who we outed as a federal infiltrator. He was a drug convict who was working his punishment off by trying to spy on environmental activists. He stole money from an environmental campaign and caused a bunch of problems and divisions. The way we were actually able to out him was after a couple of people ended up getting federally prosecuted, I found in the discovery that I received from the US Attorney's Office all the receipts for this guy's reimbursements and his daily log notes. They had inadvertently turned it over to me. They quickly realized their mistake and asked me to return them, but I had already given them to the clients, so it was already out there. So he got outed and then we heard that he fled town. But someone had some understanding that he was actually headed up to the Buffalo Field Campaign. We were able to call them, and I remember I faxed a black and white photo of the person to them, and said "hey this person may be heading in your direction, keep your eyes out." And they did, and they were able to shoo him on. The idea that some mass dissemination is the only way to keep communities safe is ignorant.

It seems to be a huge reflection on the very sudden change in our communications, with social media having become so central. A lot of people have grown up with that now, and understand it as the norm.

In doing teen 'Know Your Rights' trainings that we've been doing it's clear that this new generation has been reared with metal detectors and no sense of privacy at all. They don't understand what a right to privacy is, and why someone would be up in arms about that at all. They are so acclimated to a big brother, and nothing being private ever, that that's going to be the new cultural norm eventually. Which is exactly what the government has indoctrinated people to adhere to.

They have been extremely successful in that. Do you have any thoughts on how you resist that? Do you just keep off social media?

It's going to be so hard because of course mass media and the giant systems that have been set up, like facecrack, are reaching millions and millions of people. Not only in the US, but around the world. Our 'Know Your Rights' trainings, or any kind of political education, are not taught in the public schools. There's such a tiny minority of youth that will even be exposed to any semblance of this, that I don't have a lot of optimism. I think the only way that it could be really seriously reversed is if there is some major political upheaval that occurs.

Access "Know Your Rights" training resources and more at cldc.org

Wild Resistance, Insurgent Subsistence

An interview with BC green anarchists on native resistance, building community and undermining civilization.

Fracking, tar sands, sour gas, liquefied natural gas (LNG) conversion stations and pipelines; in all cases, it would appear that our native friends up north have been trail blazing persistent resistance to the new wave of resource extraction and distribution. As they seem to typify it, it's just the new face of colonization, but an old enemy.

I had the pleasure of speaking to non-native green anarchists from British Columbia who have been involved with and supporting these encampments and have been able to give us some more details about the encampments, the challenges that they expose for anarchists and as non-natives, the contexts of decolonization and effective forms of resistance, and, most importantly, the role of community and subsistence.

This brings out a lot of vital questions and I greatly anticipate the furthering of this discussion and hearing more native voices on the matter (hopefully in BAGR no 4).

\- Kevin Tucker

Can't you give me an overview of some of the native energy extraction and distribution struggles going on up there?

The area we are talking about is the northwestern portion of so called British Columbia. It is home to many different indigenous nations (Gitxsan, Tsimshian, Wet'suwet'en to name a few) who have been living here for thousands of years before the colonial forces arrived. Most of these territories are "un-ceded" which means the people have never surrendered or signed over their lands to the invaders. There are no treaties here. Part of the ongoing process of colonization in Canada has been the settler state institution of the 1876 Indian Act and with it, the Band Council system. This system was and continues to be used to subvert hereditary systems of governance, ones that existed prior to and in opposition in value to capitalist colonial society. Despite this, hereditary systems and cultures are still largely practised outside of the constraints imposed by the colonial government.

This region has a long history of resistance to resource extraction projects. We are mainly talking about 3 of the more active camps in our area; the Unist'ot'en Camp, Madii Lii and Lax U'u'la. The views expressed here are not representations of the camps but are based on our individual experiences. Also each of these camps is unique and quite different from each other.

The Unist'ot'en Camp

Probably the most well-known of the mounting northern indigenous resistance, the Unist'ot'en define themselves as "a non-violent occupation of Unceded Unist'ot'en territory. FPIC (free, prior and informed consent) protocol is conducted with visitors to show their complete jurisdiction" (unistotencamp.com). This manifestation, as a physical block to industrial encroachment on their territory, began in 2010 with the Pacific Trails Pipeline (PTP) proposing to cross their territory (along with 16 other nations) to connect fracked gas in the north east of the province via a 480 km pipeline with a yet to be approved export terminal on the northern coast.

The support for the Unist'ot'en has grown exponentially over the years due to a variety of factors including their fierce dedication and savvy social media use, but the largest contributing factor in my opinion has been their annual Action Camp which invited and introduces people to their struggle as they define it, and offers an opportunity for people to challenge themselves within a serious experience of decolonization and reconnection with the land.

Although the space is often referred to as the 'Unist'ot'en Camp,' they do not see themselves as a "protest or a demonstration," but as occupying and using their traditional territory as their clan has for centuries. This point is essential to understanding their approach: it is not activism, these are their lives and they are challenging the entire colonial state of Canada.

Madii Lii

Madii Lii is a traditional territory of the Luutkudziiwus House group which is part of the Gitxsan nation. The Madii Lii camp was setup in August of 2014 to permanently close the territory to industrial resource extraction and to implement their Territorial Management Plan. It is situated in the Suskwa River valley about 35 km's outside the town of Hazelton. A base camp has been established there, consisting of a large permanent cabin with greenhouses and a garden space. A heavy-duty metal gate was installed on the bridge crossing the Suskwa River. This bridge is the only road into the territory and is now fully controlled by family and friends of the house group.

The current proposal that Madii Lii is fighting is the Prince Rupert Gas Transmission project which is owned by TransCanada. It would be a 900km fracked gas (LNG) pipeline stemming from the fracking wells in northeastern BC, which will be powered by the proposed "Site C" dam on the Peace River, and will lead to the proposed LNG terminal on Lelu Island. As of now, the PRGT pipeline has been granted federal approval on the condition that the PNW LNG facility on Lelu Island gets approved.

At the beginning, pipeline surveyors were kicked out of the territory and since then, the camp has been successful at preventing industry from entering or conducting work on the territory. With the absence of industry "knocking at the door", the camp has been able to focus on hunting, trapping, fishing and wild foraging. As well as hosting events aimed at reconnecting youth with their territory. Another focus has been on infrastructure like more cabins, a large smokehouse for processing salmon and moose as well as plans to install a small scale water wheel to generate power for the cabin. Members are currently pursuing a court battle as well by filing a judicial review of the project.

Lax U'u'la

In late August 2015, a crew of women of Tsimshian, Haida, Nisga'a, and Gitxsan bloodlines initiated the defense of Lax U'u'la (Lelu Island) and the Flora Bank from LNG industry destruction. The Gitwilgyoots Tribe Sm'ogyet Yahaan (hereditary chief) and Ligitgyet Gwis Hawaal (hereditary house leader), and their families began a defence camp on Lax U'u'la, which is Gitwilgyoots traditional hunting and fishing territory. They were also joined by various significant hereditary people from other Tsimshian tribes, and a diverse crew of native and non-native outside supporters.

This camp has been set up to prevent any further destruction of their land, as Petronas and Pacific North West LNG (PNW LNG) are planning on building an $11 billion liquefied natural gas (LNG) plant on Lax U'u'la, which is at the mouth of the Skeena river near Prince Rupert, BC. They have been conducting environmental and archaeological assessments since 2012, which have resulted in over a hundred test hole sites and cut blocks, and have in the process cut down numerous culturally modified trees. This facility would be fed by 3 pipelines, including the recently provincially-approved Prince Rupert Gas Transmission (PRGT), owned by Trans Canada, which crosses through multiple indigenous territories, and which is currently being met with resistance from the Gitxsan people at the Madii Lii camp. This proposed LNG plant has been opposed not only by the Sm'ogyet Yahaan, but was unanimously refused by the 9 allied Tsimshian tribes of Lax Kw'alaams, who turned down a $1.25 billion offer by Petronas at 3 separate meetings in Lax Kw'alaams, Vancouver, and Prince Rupert. Regardless, in preparation for the LNG plant construction, Petronas/PNW LNG have been trying to conduct environmental and engineering assessments around Lax U'u'la, which includes test drilling that are actively destroying habitat essential to all the salmon that run throughout the Skeena Watershed.

The proposed project is still under review by the Federal Government, who have until late June 2016 to make a decision as to whether or not it will be approved. The Lax Kw'alaams band council, without consultation with or approval from any of the Lax Kw'alaams village members, have recently stated their support for the project. In response to this statement of support, the Gitwilgyoots hereditary chief, has said: "We have been betrayed by our elected leader. Elected band councils have no jurisdiction off of reserve land. Legal precedents in the Supreme Court of Canada are all in our favour as hereditary chiefs, and we will fight this to the end, whether the band council is on our side or not."

To date, the resistance to Petronas/PNW LNG's project has mainly been on the water. In practice, this has primarily taken the form of trying to prevent the workers from performing any work, and disrupting environmental and engineering assessments. This means escorting environmental surveyors off of the Flora and Agnew Banks, preventing the drill ships from entering and anchoring on the banks, and slowing down or turning back charter boats transporting workers to the barges. In early February 2016, the last drilling barges pulled off the Banks, allegedly 7 test holes short of their goal.

There is also resistance by re-asserting that Lax U'u'la is used as a place of healing and ceremony. Infrastructure is continually being constructed and there are other preparations for defense of the island itself (which also serve to maintain and expand water operations). Several structures have been built, and once there is less consistent confrontation, there is the intention to use these spaces as a place to teach youth about ancestral ways of living off of the land, and to heal from the continued traumas of colonization.

Although 100s of kilometres apart, these camps are all part of the same watershed. Madii Lii is defending the headwaters of the Suskwa River on which the camp is situated, as are the Unist'ot'en who are located along the Wedzin Kwa (Morice River). There have also been defense camps set up by the Tahltan people in an area of their territory commonly known as "The Sacred Headwaters" which is where the Skeena river originates. All of these are tributaries that flow into the Skeena River which runs to the coast and meets the ocean at the Lax U'u'la defense camp. Juvenile salmon feed and mature on the Flora Bank and then eventually return to spawn in their place of origin swimming back up stream past these camps.

A common thread at these indigenous defense camps is not only defending a territory, but a way of life and we, as non-native anarchists (who have also been subject to colonization) are invested in learning and creating a nurturing way of life through insurgent subsistence.

What has the non-native anarchist involvement and support looked like?

Anarchist involvement and support has been varied in both its approach and form, from organized groups, to informal crews and individuals to fund raising, solidarity actions, and physical presence at the camps. The location of the camps is remote to many people in Canada, who live close to the 49th parallel and have little experience outside of urban environments/struggle.

One of the bigger hurdles we are experiencing is in learning how to interact with integrity with people of a social system that challenges some core Anarchist values. For the most part, West Coast Indigenous societies are quite hierarchical, for example historically slave holding was common practice. So our cultural references and understandings are different, yet not, and can be challenging to navigate.

Supporting these camps has created some interesting situations in regards to personal safety and security. Often, as anarchists, we engage in activities or actions with people we know and trust and close affinity is commonly a requirement for carrying out certain plans. However, in the heat of the moment, these personal protocols are sometimes thrown out the window in a sudden conflict that must be dealt with. Gut instinct takes over and you hope for the best. These struggles are not exempt from common debates found in other movements. For example, debating violence vs. non-violence, differences on tactics or long term strategy and disagreements on working with the cops or the legal system are all present at times, but these camps are made up of many different individuals with a variety of ideas and many affinities are discovered through working with folks and building connections and trust.

Can you talk a bit about the methods used in these struggles? In particular, can you speak about the use of encampments and communities literally supporting each other and the land while potentially revitalizing traditional aspects of their societies?

Resistance to resource extraction projects have largely been led by indigenous communities in this region. It is often based on defending a traditional territory that the hereditary system has not treatied or given away. A common method has been to build a camp or a small village directly in the path of the proposed project and then reassert traditional social systems, putting it in the face of the colonial system. When you set your life up around resistance, it is no longer this separate activity that you do in your spare time. It becomes an inseparable part of you.

At the Unis'tot'en camp for example, people have been living there for years now asserting ownership of their traditional lands. The infrastructure that has been built there has allowed for folks to live there year round growing and gathering food. At the same time, industry has been making constant attempts to enter the territory via road or helicopter and only because of the permanent occupation of the camp are folks able to kick out industry at every attempted entry. At Lax U'u'la, folks staying there day and night were able to implement a routine patrol of the island and surrounding waters. The company's attempts were regularly intercepted and delayed if not completely shut down. The companies are unsure of how to proceed with these situations when it is so clearly the traditional home of a group of people. The cops are also uncertain about how to deal with these camps which we talk further about later.

These types of resistance camps also offer opportunities which other struggles don't necessarily have. The down time in between confrontations with industry offer the potential for focusing on learning traditional and non-traditional skills that folks might not otherwise have the time for, or at least, intentionally, put the time into. At Lax U'u'la, methods involving fishing and setting crab traps have been used to stop industrial drilling operations. At the Unist'ot'en camp, a trap line is in operation on the proposed path of the pipeline. There's also some very interesting opportunities for non-natives as well as natives to learn about the hereditary systems and cultures that colonization has so strongly tried to erase.

Constructing a pit house at the Unist'ot'en camp. Photo from Warrior Publications.

What has involvement and support of these struggles taught you about the importance and nature of decolonization as a non-native anarchist?

Basically, show me a colonizing people that hasn't been dispossessed and colonized in the first place. In the fight against resource extraction in BC, I hear a lot of people expressing the idea that it's up to native people to stop these projects because on the one hand they have legal rights to these lands whereas non-natives don't have any say or rights, and on the other hand there's a recognition, especially here up north amongst pipeline opponents, that the indigenous are a sovereign people who can act on their self-determination.

The daily lives and minds of non-natives are so deeply colonized that to talk of self-determination, self-organization, autonomy and freedom for ourselves is seen as an abstraction not worth considering. Fear of consequences reigns.

From my perspective, a movement towards decolonization coming from indigenous people will never succeed if there isn't a parallel thrust on the part of the majority population, i.e.; non-natives.

To think that natives can become free and self determined on the land while the rest of us are kept in a state of obedient wage slaves getting our food and tools at Walmart and Home Depot, buying private property or renting from landlords, being ruled by police, prisons and political parties and swearing allegiance to the Canadian state, is purely delusional.

Now, we are going to have to start sharing in a real way, both the resistance to the industrial onslaught, the shit of repression and the beauty and bounty of subsistence. So in a way we have already begun. We have already been invited to share the salmon, the moose, the berries and we are offering our help on concrete decolonization projects and strategizing and tactical discussions.

But lets not paint a rosy picture of how things are. In leviathanic times, things are always messy and complicated. An enormous amount of healing has to happen before a force can be created with which the state has to contend with. And I mean on both sides of the divide.

The reserves beside where I live have the highest rate of suicide in BC. I think one place where we are most needed is to help in the creation of a welcoming infrastructure (trails, shelter, funds, outdoor equipment, skills workshops, etc.) to get the youth out of the dead end misery that prevails on the res. and back on the land. As non-natives, we need the same.

More than ever we all need to experience situations where we can practice our individual and collective power and have a taste of what an existence outside of and against the state feels like. A rediscovery of our fighting spirit and a capacity for mutual aid.

And, by the way, we do need hope and love and to build respect, understanding and trust. Too many times I find both sides using each other as cannon fodder, media images and legal shields. We've got to stop using each other as objects and commodities and start treating each other as human individuals, as people, each with our own strength and weaknesses, our insights and blind spots, each having different contexts and different stories to share. Smaller scale, face to face, long term interactions enables this in a big way.

Together and separately, both new comers and indigenous can ignite the embers of community and conspire, breathe together, to fan the flames that will eventually reduce civilized ways to cold ashes, blown by the winds of our desires.

What has the response to these encampments been? Can you talk a bit about the repression and backlash?

So far, compared to other situations like Oka and Gustafsen Lake, the repression has been fairly minimal. Confrontations are usually verbal but there is always the threat of escalation. Last summer for example, 2 RCMP officers attempted to enter the Unis'tot'en camp and were strongly turned around by the defenders. Soon after, it was leaked that the RCMP were planning a massive raid of the Camp. Hotels in the nearby towns of Smithers, Houston and Burns Lake were booked up by cops and military vehicles were spotted in numerous areas.

The RCMP setup their own roadblock harassing anyone on their way in or out of the Unis'tot'en territory. A huge call out for support went out, the camp swelled with supporters and preparations for defending the camp intensified. Solidarity actions took place across the country and just when folks thought it was going down, the cops fully withdrew. As of now the raid still hasn't happened and support is only growing.

At Lax U'u'la, the police would threaten to "move in" and make arrests every time conflict heated up on the water but so far no arrests have been made although it has been reported that there are many open files being investigated. Industrial ships and security vessels would frequently use their boats to ram the defenders on the water. Numerous attempts were made on their part to flip defenders canoes and high speed boat chases were a common occurrence. They would essentially be physical defence for the industrial drilling barges. Heavy surveillance is present and comes in the form of people getting followed and having house visits by the RCMP trying to obtain information about individuals or events. This also creates psychological and financial stress like in the case of one participant losing their job for supporting a camp. People have also had visits from authorities out at remote bush camps. They always want to let you know they are watching.

It's common practise now for most industry workers to either be escorted by private security who film and record every interaction, or for the workers themselves to be wearing chest cameras for surveillance purposes. A question that security or industry personnel are using constantly and at multiple camps, is asking if they are in danger or if their personal safety is at risk being on the territory. They are trying to find and to justify a reason to move in with force.

Aside from the mostly positive response from locals, there are a number of people pissed off about these camps. Certain misguided individuals feel entitled to have unobstructed access to these territories because "This is Canada!" or "I pay taxes and its a free country!" Largely, folks are supportive but there have been quite a few aggressive confrontations with locals. At Madii Lii there has been at least one attempt to cut down the gate and a few people threatening to burn the cabin down. At the Unis'tot'en camp a few signs at the bridge checkpoint have been firebombed and just recently someone smashed out the windows in the checkpoint building. At Lax U'u'la, its gone as far as fist fights from pro-industry locals and death threats from an individual armed with a knife. When an area or territory is reclaimed it really puts the colonial situation in peoples face.

What future do you see as intensifications around resource extraction methods are met with this communal resistance?

The infinite demands of civilization require industrial resource extraction to expand to the point of complete domestication of the earth. The potential for an indigenous uprising in Canada has been reported on by the authorities for years now and as industry and development smother more and more traditional lands, we are quickly approaching the boiling point.

In response to similar pipeline projects, this summer we are expecting 2 more resistance camps to emerge in the region. This is something I think we are going to see more frequently. Little pockets of resistance popping up all over the place, eventually saturating an area to the point where resistance camps border other resistance camps. Entire defended territories neighbouring other defended territories effectively become liberated autonomous zones. When you cross the blockade, there is such a clear and inspiring feeling that you aren't in Canada anymore. The laws and rules of the state are not recognized. You've got folks defending the entry point, ready to stand up to intruding authority. Some folks are building infrastructure, some are out hunting and some are preparing food.

These, and more, are all necessary activities to create and defend a healthy community. It gives you a taste of what freedom might actually feel like in an autonomous pocket of resistance outside of colonial law. The ability to determine your own way of life based on a healthy habitat in which we live and which we defend.

Why do you think these methods haven't extended beyond native resistance struggles?

The tactic of roadblocking and setting up camps to protect and re-occupy the land has a long rich history in native resistance to the Canadian state. So when direct action is called for, there is a tradition to fall back on. "Hey lets do what Grandma did!", or "Remember when Auntie and Uncle blocked that railroad?". It shows the value of setting precedents. At the time, a lot of these actions were brutally repressed after a few days or weeks of negotiations.

What's happening now in BC is that there is a legal "grey zone" about who owns this land. Apart from Treaty 8 in northeastern BC, most of the province sits on un-ceded, un-surrendered, un-treatied native land according to British Law. Both The British North America Act and The Royal Proclamation documents, are enshrined in the Canadian Constitution.

For 150 years, the provincial government denied the need for any treaty to legally own the land. BC is officially 92% provincial crown land, 1% Federal Crown land and 7% fee simple private property.

This created a climate of uncertainty for investors who actually want a solid legal deed for their business. In order to create a "climate of certainty" for investors, the BC government created the BC Treaty process in 1992, designed to extinguish legal "aboriginal title", turn the reserves into municipalities and business corporations (the so-called "First Nations") and move on with capitalist resource extraction and development.

Needless to say the process hasn't been smooth and even across the board. After 23 years of negotiations and millions in legal fees, only a few bands have come to treaty agreements.

Anyway to cut short a long, manipulative, boring legal process, there is now a recognized "Aboriginal Title", similar to the ownership of private property where an "estate", an abstract entity, is owned and the actual real existing land is owned through Allodial Title of the nation state to which is belongs, independent of any superior landlord. Again this interpretation of native title is being challenged by indigenous people in Canadian and International courts.

So as the "First Nations" are invited to dialogue at the table of power as property owners and shareholders, they legally have to be consulted and compensated for any business happening on their traditional territories. That is the official line anyway. The reality on the ground is more about being conned and insulted and given a few thousand bucks per band member in exchange for their land and resources.

Sorry for this long legal and historical background but this is the official reality corner that indigenous people have been pushed into in BC, and apart from the people's own determined stance, it helps to understand why camps like the Unist'ot'en clan have established can still exist 6 years later.

The state is biding its time, negotiating, creating and finding its business partners within the assimilated strata of the native population. Don't we all need jobs? They are working hard on creating an image of support by dangling a financial carrot so they can confuse the population and remove the non-compliant natives who don't have a price tag.

In regard to non-native roadblocks or camps, there is no legal eggshells or negotiations to be had. It is simply considered trespassing or blocking a public road and the law moves in swiftly. There is more of a self image of the good, law abiding, reasonable citizen in the non-native population and a history of pacifist and civil-disobedience practice in the environmental movement. Add to this an aesthetic and intrinsic value approach to nature (creating parks and protected areas), instead of, or in tandem with, a subsistence approach in which humans have an active relationship to nature, the tactics that are risky and demanding don't gain as much popularity on this side of land defence.

This said, over the years there have been a few non-native tree sits and camps to stop development. Some were removed with SWAT teams armed with automatic weapons and there have been native blockades that were met with heavy repression too.

At this point our approach has been to take advantage of that legal grey zone, to promote decolonization on both sides of the divide, to dig our heels and get ready both socially and tactically to defend the land, our autonomy and our subsistence. We have to set new precedents for non-native resistance.

Blockade at Madii Lii camp. Photo: Idle No More.

In advocating "primal war", it's been essential for me to emphasize that resistance and rewilding must go hand-in-hand. This seems the way to break out of this philosophical and revolutionary mentality where we take care of one problem (theoretically) and then we go onto the next. That break for me came through understanding why native resistance movements fought to the death and revolutionaries turned to gallows: people kill for ideas, but they are willing to fight to their death for community, for something they know and feel.

This kind of encampment and community-based resistance echoes eternally as indigenous societies are met with civilizations, as they are forced to confront perpetual growth and consumption. Is there a conception or feeling of resistance tied to community here? Are the encampments and the like seen as an extension of community or simply a response to occupation and ecocide?

We must view each of these camps as completely unique from one to the next and the involvement of a community varies quite a bit. I would say that it's a full spectrum ranging from very limited participation (down to a few individuals), to the full creation of a community. We have seen communities coming together to resist as well as communities being born out of resistance. However this brings the question; "what is community?" We must not idealize native communities or resistance. Colonization has severely impacted natives and non-natives and these movements are far from flawless. They are made up of a wide range of people from all different backgrounds and beliefs.

At most, we hope these struggles will lead to the permanent reclamation and occupation of traditional lands outside of the colonial state. At the very least, we hope these struggles will strengthen certain aspects of local existing communities and promote the fighting spirit necessary for resisting decolonization and civilization. But, the approach of insurgent subsistence is just this, rebuilding/discovering the connection between ourselves and the land. For some people, this was never lost, for others we are beginning from scratch and we are building our confidences and abilities through this struggle.

What can we, as non-native anarchists, learn from this? Is "insurgent subsistence" a necessary part of resistance to civilization?

What these struggles have reinforced for me, as a non-native anarchist, is the importance of having a community connected to such battles. And, although this is not always possible, planting roots with others in a familial way (not necessarily based on blood but based on affinity and connection) can build a resilient foundation for the fight against civilization.

The process of civilization and domestication starts with colonization, dispossession, the annihilation of culture and the eradication of autonomy by removing us from the land and creating dependence through waging war against subsistence. This undeclared war has been going on for centuries and the idea of "insurgent subsistence" is not only resisting this process but reversing it.

When the totality of the land base is private property or state-owned, when berries are sprayed with chemicals by logging companies, when hunting or fishing is policed by armed goons of the government, when every tree is owned by "the Crown", regaining a certain level of freedom and subsistence definitely goes against this state of affairs, an insurgent spirit is inevitable.

We practice subsistence and resistance as one and the same. One cannot sustain itself without the other and through implementing these ideas, we can build a culture of resilience. Also, by embracing and practising these ideas, we frequently find ourselves in situations that build community.

Every region will have different methods of resisting civilization that work best for them. Although the need for autonomy in food, shelter, medicine and tools, including the need to share, is universal, we can only speak about and develop methods for our own context.

Wild subsistence is largely dependent on a healthy undomesticated land base. However it is not only about harvesting food and materials from the wild but about building a deep relationship with our surroundings and this can be done anywhere. The quality of this relationship is most important because it determines how we interact with our surroundings. Without it, materials or food available for harvest, can be seen simply as just resources for exploitation.

Not only do civilization, capitalism and colonization thrive on the lack of nurturing relationships, but they perpetuate and enforce negative and harmful interactions with all surroundings. The continuous implementation of this dynamic and the stifling effects it has on ourselves and our habitats, brings the ever increasing need for a fierce insurgence to put an end to the onslaught against subsistence and freedom.

Do you find elements of hope within these struggles that are missing in the larger anarchist milieu? Not in terms of naivety, but in the sense that removed of community, it seems so much easier to just go with the flow of civilized life, to get entrapped in the hollowness of this hyper-technological non-reality and just feel like giving up?

I've felt fulfilment and inspiration in these struggles that I haven't experienced in other anarchist projects. Being engaged in subsistence practices or conflict at a blockade camp has such a strong feeling of experiencing something "real". Where as returning home, to the dreary routine of our pretend reality, really throws it in your face that, within civilization and capitalism, our existence is meaningless.

The intense feeling of unquestionable purpose behind what you are fighting for creates the experience of finally being alive with actual clarity. Knowing that these battles will go beyond just stopping a pipeline, creates a sense of longevity that is lacking in similar anarchist struggles. Once these industrial projects are defeated, the camps will remain, not only to keep future proposals at bay, but to provide an avenue for people to get back on the land and an opportunity to realize and remember life outside of the colonial system.

I find it incredible that one of the most effective ways of resisting these land destroying, resource extraction projects is by learning or remembering how to live off of these lands again. In order to fight these projects, we need to be living on the land, and in order to live on the land we need to be fighting these projects. Life becomes resistance and resistance becomes life.

Lax U'u'la defenders and Wet'suwet'en chiefs standing together

So much of the anarchist milieu has embraced rhetoric over struggle, deeming anything that stands for something other than the cherished "Self" as moralistic or delusional. It's easy to see how that idea prevails within Modernity, but I see no path ahead there and these struggles are a reminder that outside of our own reality that the earth is still here, communities are struggling to exist outside of and along the peripheries of civilization, and that as monumental as civilization's impact has been, it is still reliant upon acting as though all resources are finite and all actions are without consequence.

Is there a reflection here of what a rooted and grounded resistance to civilization can look like? To what barriers to perception we carry, having been indoctrinated with the rhetoric of individualism?

When I read "outside of and along the peripheries of civilization" I feel, I have to bring minor corrections as to how an outsider might see daily life in those camps. As was pointed out earlier, regular contacts and meetings with state agents are arranged by some of the leaders and most material needs are met by buying stuff at stores, like the rest of us. Decolonization is a complex and messy learning process and we should render ourselves a disservice by creating idealized images (spectacles) which have little to do with the reality on the ground.

Having said this, there is a lot to be inspired from. As was discussed earlier the methods of coupling determined resistance to industrial destruction and the state with the creation of communal relations which had never completely disappeared in their communities, rooted in the history of this land and on the land itself is really powerful.

It is a pleasure to see people who have been stomped on and humiliated by disease, Christianity, schools, racism, alcohol and the British/Canadian empire to empower themselves, to again redefine who they are and where they stand, on their own terms.

As non-natives, this is the question we have to ask ourselves; who are we and where are we? By grounding ourselves in our personal histories and in the history of the land we stand on, on the actual ground, we root ourselves in real space and time. By doing this we multiply our powers of understanding and acting on our predicament. I have a hard time to explain this with words but I feel it and see it in my own life. Although what lies ahead is open ended, we cannot deny that we are our histories.

Which brings me to this individualist polemic. It is easy to build straw men and I want to acknowledge the diverse approaches to the same goal or even different goals, but when you mention the primacy of rhetoric over struggle in some circles, I see an all too familiar pattern where theoretical purity becomes a paralysing agent. So everything becomes morality, activism, vanguardism, causes etc. And, like some are saying, the best thing is to do nothing and point fingers.

My problem with individualist ideology is that it stands, for some people, in opposition and isolation to others. An intellectual vacuum constructed around the self, a wall with a moat built around ones own identity. It is a denial of relationships and contexts which create individual living organisms, and flowing the other way, individual (indivisible) living organisms creating relationship and sometimes contexts.

In a sense (narrow) individualism is similar to modern science which puts life on a chopping block, ready to be dissected. Historically a lot of individualist and nihilists have been enamoured with science and technology and lets be honest, a lot of anarchists too. The flows and swirls of life are way more complex than these reductionist concepts, where the "Self" has become the new spectre.

In one way, we can say that individuals are made up of their relations with others and the world and relations are made up of and by individuals. The point is to remember that living individual organisms are the ones experiencing life. "Relationships" in themselves don't. This is one aspect of anarchist thinking that has always been attractive to me; the centering on the freedom and authenticity of the actual living person, on the free initiative and creativity of individuals and the mutuality it implies.

But it seems that nowadays this point of convergence has become an ingrown toenail. Instead of becoming expansive and generous, it has become narrow and poor, it has adopted a miser attitude that sees others as instruments and tools to be used and discarded like any other commodity on the market. A logical conclusion to an extreme liberal and instrumental ideology of property ownership but totally out of whack from an anarchist perspective which is striving to create a context of freedom for everybody.

I guess a deep feeling of defeat is prevalent in the devastated landscape of modernity. Given the miserable submissive slave mentality of most of my contemporaries surrounding me, sometimes it does feel that I am encircled by enemies, hence the wall built around oneself. But I know that determinism has never done any of us any good. Dream crushing is the main goal of this system and miserabilism, its main industrial output.

For myself a dip in an ice cold creek, putting in my mouth a handful of sweet huckleberries that were picked with friends, or listening to the wind, amongst other things, blows away these feelings of loss. To get the fuck out of our heads and fully into our bodies is really beneficial. And finally, to fight back, to keep the powerful of this world from sleeping peacefully at night, to plot, to conspire, to dream, practising mutual aid as we go, reinvigorates the will to live full lives in spite of and against this freedom, individuality/ community and wildness devouring machine.

Our children are beginning to learn a different way to walk and learn. As an anarchist I strive for my relations to be intentional, deep and honest. These things matter to me so I will fight from where I am standing, by positioning myself to the best advantage. Building these relationships not only with the people but with the spaces, the rivers that flow from the Unist'ot'en past Madii Lii, past where I live to the

Flora Banks, we are only getting a glimpse of what this connection and rootedness could be. I am still working out where I fall within this whole thing, but to fight is to have integrity and humbleness for the gifts of the world that my family eats and drinks more and more every day.

There's a tendency to say that anarcho-primitivists and green anarchists both romanticize and overly critique indigenous communities and structures. As you point out, you are working with indigenous societies that do have hierarchy as central elements within them. I see the need to be honest in our assessments about the impacts of domestication, but there's a difference in framing the consequences of domestication to expose the roots and origins of civilization and equating any instance of domestication with civilization. That was never the point.

Having an idea about the societies and communities that we chose to build and foster doesn't mean that sedentary hunter-gatherers in the Pacific Northwest don't deserve support in their struggles and their want to not be killed by civilization. There's a line between critique and condemnation, between personal aspirations and solidarity. As you point out, that certainly applies here. Do you find that a difficult line to walk or does the reality of colonization just keep the perspective pretty clear?

As anarchists we're always dealing with the question of how to work, fight and play with non-anarchists and traditional cultures. I've got to admit that over the years I've found more reciprocity and anarchistic relations with indigenous people who come from a more nomadic, small band, cultural background in the interior than in the more sedentary and slave/commoner/nobility ranked coastal cultures. This is a generalization, as I have met coastal folks who share our desires, but the feeling and experience of a more rigid culture stands.

In any solidarity and decolonization efforts with traditional cultures, we are asking ourselves; are we helping to revive traditions that are diametrically opposed to our desire for free relationships instead of institutionalized, coercive ones? Are we enabling a revamped version of older national liberation schemes, where the mythical golden age of a heavenly past before the devil appeared, is to be re-established, lock, stock, and barrel? I think those are complex questions, given the transformative capacity and diversity of individuals and cultures involved, and the legacy of colonization.

It is a difficult line to walk and at the same time it is really clear that we are guests and/or invaders, that there is an ongoing history of genocide. My approach has been to avoid becoming a servant, and instead to offer solid support and search for affinities with different individuals, some becoming actual friends. At the same time, to stay open, honest, and understanding, to listen to those I disagree with on their approach and practice.

Both we, anarchists and traditionalists, share a disgust and opposition to the poisoning and destruction of the land and both stand for self-determination against the state. This is where we act in solidarity.

But only by being physically present can we start sharing personal aspirations of horizontal relations.
I actually have seen instances of native warriors feeling envious of the anarchist's freedom to act as they see fit, uncontrolled by leadership and traditions but, ideally, still humble and aware of consequences. Subversion takes many forms.

In all human cultures, the question of leadership has always been a thorny one, especially for us as anarchists. I am told by some indigenous folks that in pre-colonial times, the hereditary chiefs were actually close to the ideal of leadership. They didn't boss people around, didn't have command power but had speech power with which they summed up the feelings and desires of the group, convinced through well-reasoned arguments, not through coercion, listened and took into account the diversity of views, were the poorest and the hardest working and were removed or even killed if they became haughty or out of touch with their community.

Now, is this an accurate account of the past? Or is it an ideal construct, like the ones for Progress, Democracy, Civilization? What I see on the ground today is a diversity of individual hereditary leaders, some behaving with the best intentions towards the health and freedom of their people and territory, some are fence-sitters or contradictory, some are being outright sell-outs or dictatorial kings and queens. Are these last instances only a by-product of colonization? I don't think so, but I can imagine that in the past removal and replacement procedures were well established compared to today.

All this reminds me how little I know about the cultures that were born on this land. It is an ongoing learning process and I find it fascinating and exciting. I want to thank you for this interview, as it made us work hard to put on paper what is it exactly that we are thinking and doing.

Field Work in the End Times, Part 3
An Anthropologist's View on the Collapse

Here we conclude our interview with our anonymous anarcho-primitivist anthropologist. This discussion goes back through *Black and Green Review* numbers 1 and 2, which I strongly encourage catching up on if you haven't already.

Here we return to the discussion of field work and campaigns in Native North America, a look at the current state of Alaska, and conclude by looking ahead to what these insights might mean for current and future rewilders.

To reiterate, it's the unfortunate situation that maintaining an active position means that our friend must remain anonymous.
- Kevin Tucker

I know you've done work with the Lakota before, particularly on attempts to bring bison populations back onto the reservations. Can you make some comparisons about the differences between the Great Plains and Alaska in regards to resilience, resistance and struggle?

On one end, colonized and marginalized indigenous people around the world face very similar circumstances, in terms of living arrangements, attitudes, and daily struggles. But there are also sometimes distinct differences in regards to both the resistance and resilience variables you bring up.

One comparison I would make between the Lakota people and Alaska Natives as a whole is that the history of resistance by the Lakota is much more active than for the Alaskans, and the same could also be said for many lower 48 tribes and Canadian First Nations when compared to those in Alaska. It's not that there is no history of resistance by Alaska Natives, but, both during colonization and in contemporary times, the level of resistance by Alaska Natives on the whole has not been as robust and dedicated as for the aforementioned groups. Some Alaskans would not be happy with me saying this but it is not an illegitimate observation.

I think ecological context has played a role in how this has played out, mainly because of the often very difficult and harsh nature of non-industrial survival in the boreal sub-arctic and arctic environs. Alaska natives, in most cases, did not view encroaching Europeans as conquerors but more as beneficial trading partners providing welcome industrial goods that made life in an extreme environment easier and more comfortable, so I think this played a role in a general passivity in the face of colonization by Alaska natives and this carries over to this day.

Similar to the Lakota case, many Alaska Native groups practiced warfare and raiding prior to European arrival but their experiences in violence did not translate as heavily into a culture of resistance as did the Lakota pre-conquest demeanor as a warrior society. The Lakota are well known for their resistance against colonization from the late nineteenth century, through the AIM period of the late-twentieth century, and continuing into the twenty first century.

Another possibility for these differences, at least in the modern context, is likely related to the different means by which the US federal government attempted to deal with the "Indian problem". In the lower 48, as most everyone knows, the indigenous people were placed on Indian Reservations and given a guarantee of indefinite federal funding and socioeconomic assistance. Neoliberal politicians in Alaska, on the other hand, devised a scheme called the Alaska Native Claims Settlement Act, which, rather than designating sovereign native reservation lands and providing assistance, divided up nonfederal lands in Alaska into state and native lands, with tribes being paid large sums for former claims that would fall under state control and remaining tribal lands being divided into regional and village corporation lands with each tribal member becoming a corporation shareholder. The mission of the native corporation was then to use their lands and/or other resources to generate wealth for their shareholders.

This has been a very lucrative enterprise for the native people lucky enough to end up shareholders on lands with oil production, even creating millionaire Eskimos, and thus almost completely pacifying those groups into, not only acceptance, but a full-scale embrace of the industrial system. This has also occurred within the groups of native people who have profited off Indian Casinos in the lower 48 states, including some Lakotas (although Indian casinos certainly do not yield as much shareholder profit as does North Slope oil). But of course the issue of differences in resistance activities is not a black and white situation and is highly complex.

Regarding resilience in the face of our future bottleneck, my position is that due to the harshness of the climate and an almost total loss of traditional life ways and skills not now dependent upon the industrial economy, most Alaska Native communities today are in dire lack of resilience and are in positions of extreme vulnerability. Contrast this with some indigenous groups in Siberia who occupy an almost identical ecology, but who have maintained many skills and primitive technologies derived purely from local materials and who have developed far less dependence on the comforts of the industrial system than have Alaska Natives. Because of this I see that the Siberian groups stand to be much more resilient in the face of industrial collapse than do the Alaskans.

For their part, other than the benefits of a much milder climate to cope with, the Lakota people are not in a much better situation than the Alaskans. Some Lakota people grow food and they have communal bison and elk herds, and some solar energy projects, but they face the same level of decimation of communal continuity and loss of self-sufficient land-based non-industrial-technology dependent traditional skills as do the Alaskans.

You've told me before about how subsistence hunting, foraging and fishing are all common aspects of life in Alaska, but the divide between wild and domestic life often remains strong, why do you think that is?

I think what drives this very prevalent dualism is the fact that attempts to live off the land in much of Alaska, in many ways, are extremely demanding and representative of a very high level of skill, achievement, and resolve in the spectrum of wild living situations. Any ecosystem has its challenges when it comes to attempting fully self-sufficient rewilding, but the challenges here are immense.

It's hard to generalize this for Alaska as a whole due to differences in environmental conditions from south to north and from the coastal to the interior biomes, but, overall, for every wonderful aspect, such as huge tracts of undeveloped lands, large concentrations of fish and/or land mammals, there are equally problematic aspects; namely relatively low levels of biodiversity and low densities of key resources and/or their availability in high densities being seasonal and sporadic. Of course this has been more or less the case for hunter-gatherer adaptations across the planet and part of the challenge here has to do with the very sedentary nature of the adaptation most folks have chosen to take on.

Sedentism is chosen for practical reasons, of course, because due to the extremely wet and cold climatic conditions, no one today, at least that I know of, has attempted a truly nomadic adaptation without the persistent use of modern structures and/or wall tents with wood burning stoves, that kind of thing. Which brings me to a primary reason why Alaska presents a truly expert level course in wild living; the constant necessity and relative difficulty of being able to stay dry and maintain body heat. Of course people camp for short periods of time without dragging around a wood stove, especially during the summer months, but shelter with woodstoves is the mode for any form of winter nomadism occurring today, what little of that there is.

Overall the housing and heating issue in its most rudimentary practice seems to require at very least the use of chainsaw and usually a snowmachine or motorboat for the wood hauling, although a few folks still do their wood hauling by dog team. The alternative to this arrangement, using only an axe and human power to harvest, process, and haul cords of firewood is not something anybody with access to a chain saw and a boat motor would logically choose to do, so right here is a primary place where idealistic attempts at leaving civilization behind come up against a decision to only leave it behind to a degree, and essentially that battle with our domestication.

Maintaining body heat is just one example. Practical choices about primitive means of transport vs. mechanized transport, primitive hunting and fishing weaponry vs. industrial weaponry, these all confront those who attempt to live off the land in Alaska. For practical reasons, the hardcore reality that hits when one makes attempts to survive on this land results in a situation where nine point nine times out of ten people have chosen to maintain their dependencies on the world-system rather than make a solid go at adopting the primitive technologies which would truly bring them into a path towards rewilding and independence.

So this dualism between domestication and wildness pretty much occurs across the board in Alaska, within and amongst virtually every person or group of persons making a go at remote living.

Interestingly, native communities are often the least inclined to make inroads towards shedding their now total dependence on industrial technology for survival and most of those Alaskan's who do make inroads towards shedding domestication are usually Euro-American refugees arriving from the south with very valid goals to develop a wilderness centered lifeway away from civilization. But of course these folks often approach this with all types of romanticized and psychological baggage related to being born into twentieth century America and their decision making process follows suit.

This is a huge topic and requires much discussion.

I think another important aspect to comment on briefly is the dearth of actual community building vs. the maintenance of what is often called "rugged Alaskan individualism". Most contemporary efforts at "living off the land" in Alaska occur at the nuclear family and even individual level and in these cases the lack of community assistance with the tasks at hand make dependence on the industrial world almost a necessity. But through building strong-willed communities of people dedicated to rewilding, strides can be made towards shedding domestication to much greater degrees and some people are attempting to build communities rather than just go out remote as a family unit to escape civilization. Native villages are certainly in-tact communities in a sense, but the modern way of life has swept in and has shifted their once completely mutually dependent relationships much more towards practicing subsistence hunting, fishing, and foraging at the individual and familial levels. Fully in-tact community is likely the most critical social attribute that made non-industrial life survivable for the thousands of years it existed in Alaska prior to contact.

So where we are now is a situation not of wild humans becoming increasingly domesticated, those days have long passed, but rather a situation of very domesticated humans all trying to maintain a relationship with wildness in one capacity or another. And this in itself is a positive thing in many ways, especially if it leads to folks furthering embracing wildness and further shedding their domestication as the coming bottleneck hits Alaska.

It seems like you often encounter people who just dropped out really and are living in relative isolation, sometimes for decades, and that this is a glimpse in some ways of the future primitive. Can you elaborate on that a bit?

If having access to the fossil energy economy is part of someone's model of a "future primitive" lifeway then perhaps there are some examples to speak of, but as I have been trying to explain, except for the 2 or 3 examples I am aware of, a solid embrace of what you and I probably consider a future primitive pathway just isn't occurring.

That being said, the number of people who have dropped out of mainstream society and live in relative isolation certainly are in the hundreds, and depending on how you look at it, in the thousands. But as I have explained, 99.9% of these people are pretty much desperate to maintain their access to industrial goods. Many of them posture heavily about what they believe is their total independence from mainstream society and their living a tough life on the land, but mostly it is just posturing, and their material reality does not differ much from average lower income rural folks that could be found anywhere else in America.

Nevertheless, when visiting with Alaska homesteaders they often display many attributes of an anti-civilization worldview and so just the fact that they have made the choice to be out there shows that they are making steps. Most intelligent humans want to be free of the tyranny of civilization but developing an understanding of how deeply complex that tyranny is rooted and what steps it would take to actually uproot our domestication seems to be a much more challenging proposition for people to confront.

Definitely a necessary take there.

What do your experiences with these homesteading and more well-intentioned rewilders tell you about the vital role that community plays in moving forward? Can you also elaborate on how wood-

based fire wasn't the indigenous norm in much of Alaska, the arctic and sub-arctic? I see that as kind of emblematic of how it goes to show that an anarcho-primitivist understanding of form and function within hunter-gatherer societies is far from the same thing of saying X or Y works in the Kalahari, so it will work here or there.

For most people long-term land based survival in Alaska is not doable without access to fossil energy, at the very least from a psychological standpoint, but the physical practicality side of it is quite daunting as well.

There is all of that, and then there is just the plain hard fact that a core goal for where we need to be taking things right now is community building. I don't think that the things anti-civ people are striving for can be accomplished without contiguous and functioning community. Community is a mandatory component of the whole package, at least for me.

Community exists at different dimensions throughout remote Alaska. There are socially fairly intact indigenous communities, not in the same vein of community as when these cultures lived in a pre-industrial state, but measured relative to the rest of the US, these folks do have community. And a lot of Euro-American's living out with those people are often just as accepted members of those communities as anyone else.

In terms of Euro-American homesteaders, there is at least one Christian religious group I know who has land and lives off it communally, to a great degree really. And yeah there are at least 2 or 3 rewilding groups trying to get things going and I know for sure that those folks fully recognize the importance of community. The problem for them is finding the right people who can make a real commitment to those communities. I think this is just a constant struggle for all land projects. There are lots of smart people who understand what is going on and completely see the necessity of land projects but whom because of their own personal practical and mental entanglement with the industrial system just can't make the jump. So there is a really, really long way to travel here still, that's for sure.

Oh yeah, and there are the sorta of stereotypical colonial homesteaders and, I am generalizing, but *community* for a good portion of those folks amounts to motor machines and firearms, those are the things that give them their sense of comfort and security. A lot of them are living in the Alaska bush because they DON'T want to see or talk to anybody. They are out there because they want nothing to do with society, period. But, for a lot of them, the years living out like that just perpetuates their anti-social, misanthropic mindsets and they end up overall pretty twisted in the head. One saying I have is that "Alaska is a breeding grounds for insanity" and I think what I mean there is that without authentic community we are destined to pretty much lose our minds. So rewilding for me has an essential social aspect that cannot be discarded.

On fire, yep, that's super interesting. It's pretty well known that Eskimo peoples living in the coastal Arctic and out on the tundra did not generally have wood campfires and instead used seal oil and marine mammal oil in general for cooking and heating. There are no trees so the only access to wood they had was driftwood. Due to thousands of years of doing this, they are expert analysts of driftwood and know how to choose different pieces for all kinds of different minute properties. It's pretty phenomenal to watch them do that; very deep, precision indigenous ecological knowledge for sure.

Long ago driftwood was a very coveted resource and people even tried to own specific places on the coast where the driftwood piled up. Today people live in those stereotypical Indian reservation style HUD homes and all the heating in these regions comes from fuel oil, usually flown in by airplane. Sixty below in a leaky HUD home reliant on a stockpile of fuel oil for winter survival! A few years back one of the major villages never got its fuel shipment and it was verging on a survival situation. They could not get it flown in and the sea ice formed thick and early and they couldn't get a fuel barge in there. The Native corporation ended up paying Putin a million dollars or something ridiculous to have a Russian ice breaker with fuel tank capacity bring in the fuel.

Long ago they lived in subterranean homes and relied almost solely on thick insulation and shared body-heat for warmth. Hibernating like bears really. You wanna talk about community! Those days are over of course, but people serious about rewilding and community building in the north shouldn't overlook this stuff.

Even in the interior where there is a lot of good wood it seems logical that the old indigenous folks who lived there relied much less on massive amounts of wood for winter heat and more so on insulated shelters and heat generated by intimate communal living.

My experience with wood gathering in the boreal forest without an axe or chainsaw taught me this. It just seems that it would be very impractical to obtain dozens of cords of wood like people do today with their chainsaws. I haven't ever seen an Alaskan living remote long-term in the boreal forest without a chainsaw and a woodstove. It might be happening and, if so, that would be a very interesting case study for going feral here! But most folks out on the land I know put up a bunch of cords of wood with chainsaws each winter and they haul it to their properties on a snowmachine with a trailer or float it down the river with a motorboat. I do know of a couple of people who do it with dogsleds, however. If we are really making an attempt at completely unplugging from the matrix and actually getting back to a wild existence, all this cannot be overlooked.

What does the peak oil look like on the ground in Alaska? How does that compare to daily life in the lower 48?

Well I am certainly glad you brought this up, because the peak energy situation in Alaska will ultimately determine how things play out for both wild and domesticated life here, and even for what is left of intact ecological connectivity within the US territories. It will determine how things play out for the people in Alaska who are currently operating within the balance between the two dualities I have been describing.

Alaska is essentially a real time model of what all of the peak oil analysts have been writing about over the last few decades. Over the last thirty five years civilization in Alaska has grown immense as a result of its position in the world oil economy. This oil extraction related growth has created a situation where around 85% of Alaska's economic function depends on revenues generated from oil extraction. A massive hyper-civilized consumer culture is a product of this and this culture's entire living arrangement is dependent upon maintenance of the oil revenue stream.

However, oil production in Alaska has peaked and we are now in full descent from the summit of the bell curve. Since the mid-2000s the Aleyeska pipeline, which basically made civilization in Alaska possible, has been running at well below its capacity and overall oil revenues have been rapidly declining, with budget cuts in the billions of dollars for the State government as a result.

Despite this, with high oil prices it seemed like the companies could maintain some vestige of the status quo, providing that production costs could stay below world oil prices. So there has been a continuing push by big oil to develop more pads, to go after tight oil deposits, to develop off-shore capacity, and, of course, to dismantle federal protection of the Arctic National Wildlife Refuge.

But now with the recent large drop in oil prices it seems that most of these ambitions are being put in check and the true reality of peak oil for overall economic function is becoming highly apparent to anyone paying attention. Our new governor recently announced a 3.8 billion dollar budget deficit and major cuts in state spending as a result of the recent drop in oil prices and this has had a domino effect across the entire Alaska economy. Peak oil analysts have predicted this type of scenario for decades and have cautioned consumers not to optimistically celebrate oil price decline as a result of these domino effects.

So we are witnessing peak oil happen right before our eyes in Alaska and I think it is important that anyone around the world concerned with these issues start paying careful attention to how things unfold in Alaska. In the context of overall collapsing civilizations and evolved human dependence on industrialism and resource extraction, Alaska represents sort of an indicator species. For our interests, in the anti-civilization realm, what is especially interesting is how this dualism will play out between wildness being an important part of Alaska's culture core and its continuing dependence on domestication that we have been discussing.

As access to all the benefits of fossil energy becomes very limited or unavailable during the coming decades how will the Alaskans, a populace more on the cusp of actualized wildness than any other American's, react? What will become of the communities of people who are only a few generations removed from being full-scale nomadic hunter gatherers, whose ancestors developed successful life ways and survived on this very harsh land for thousands of years with nothing but what was available to them from local ecology, a people's who today, even with all of the disruption they have experienced, continue to live more on wild food hunting, fishing, and foraging than any other Americans? What will become of the groups of Europeans who have attempted to make wilderness Alaska their escape from civilization? Twenty first century Alaska is an extremely important arena for viewing and understanding the anthropological reaction to civilization coming up against its limits. So, as I said earlier[1], Alaska truly is "The Last Frontier", and for its position as a 'peak-oil/peak industrial expansion laboratory' especially.

What are some of the things up there that are inspiring you?

So much of what I have commented on here has painted a less than positive picture, but there is much that is positive here as well.

Despite the limitations and obvious confusions, there are many people here trying their best to make life happen in deep connection with wild nature. There are some primitivist oriented land-projects happening and scattered handfuls of anti-civilization minded folks roaming about.

In the native realm, while many of the most important traditional material skills are gone, an ancient hunter-gatherer psychology clearly remains, including an ability to constantly adapt to the moment without fret, a lack of concern with calendars, paperwork, and clocks, and a general inability to function in the civilized world, which is a good thing!

And of course, when compared to your average American, the hunting and foraging skill set remains formidable, albeit now entirely mediated by industrial technology. Part of the ancient skill set that remains are primal butchering and processing methods and community wide sharing of wild foods. And every now and then I come across a native person who does understand the truly dire circumstances of the modern condition and who is making strides to overcome the problem. Additionally, I have been to communities where ancient language survives fully in-tact, where to work I must hire a translator. In these places I have witnessed children whose first tongues continue to be their native languages and who only speak English to Europeans that they encounter. Hearing the sounds of these ancient languages regardless of if I can understand a word is always inspiring and provides a sense of hope.

In terms of geography, there is no doubt that a person could walk off a road here and disappear into infinite wildness for months on end without contacting other people or another road and there is absolutely something positive to be said for that, even if the challenges are great.

On a personal level, as someone who arrived in Alaska with a much attuned anti-civilizational anarcho-primitivist mindset, this experience has allowed me to grow in terms of both my mental awareness and perspectives, and my physical rewilding pathway, in ways that were unattainable for me before. I have learned so much about my own limitations, learned lessons about aspects of primitivism I had long romanticized in the past, and basically felt the hard reality of what an undomesticated life in the far north would truly entail. My skillset and experience with wild living and utilizing nature's bounty has grown immensely and this is very satisfying. There is much to be said on the specifics of all this but I think we are running out of time.

I will close by saying that what truly inspires me here above all else is witnessing and experiencing first-hand a fully intact wildness, with all of it the spiritual joys and physical/psychological challenges it brings. I am inspired by watching salmon migrate up a river as they have done for thousands of years, inspired by massive herds of caribou summering on an Arctic plain, inspired by moose surviving -40f winter nights on a diet of twigs, inspired by the mama grizzly who charges at me full speed and stops a few feet away with a paw slapping huff, warning me to move on, inspired by the wolf who visits me in camp in the middle of the night, as if a long lost friend. There is no doubt much to be inspired by and I am happy to continue this conversation with anyone who is interested. Thanks for the opportunity to share.

REVIEWS

Screech Owl. Photo by Yank.

Lights Out: A Cyberattack, A Nation Unprepared, Surviving the Aftermath
by Ted Koppel
Reviewed by Story Teller

On December 23rd 2015, hackers hijacked eight Ukrainian power companies' distribution management systems, sabotaged operator workstations, and launched Distributed Denial of Service (DDoS) attacks to flood web servers, paralyze company networks with malware, and prevent users from reporting resulting outages. The result took upwards of 60 substations offline, striking power distribution centers and disabling backup power supplies, while leaving more than 230,000 people in the dark—the first acknowledged hacker-caused blackout in history.[1]

While the lights eventually came back on, the attack highlights the growing concern in security circles that the effects of well-orchestrated and sophisticated cyber attacks are far-reaching in a new generation of techno-centric warfare. The government of Canada similarly announced it faced dozens of attacks targeting critical infrastructure such as power plants, electrical grids, aviation software, and other government-run systems. The attacks had the potential to threaten water supplies, energy and utilities, manufacturing, internet communications technology, and non-governmental institutions such as schools and hospitals as well.[2]

In this context, former Nightline anchor Ted Koppel's investigative report appears prescient; detailing how a well-designed attack on America's three power grids would prompt near immediate societal breakdown by forcing Americans to survive upwards of two years without access to a working electric grid. Comparable assaults on critical infrastructure are not only likely, Koppel reminds us, but are happening already. Citing the well-planned "terrorist" attack on AT&T's fiber-optic telecommunication system providing power to Silicon Valley as a likely "dress rehearsal" (possibly by a SEAL team) rather than a legitimate sabotage attack,[3] he offers up the assessment of experts: "if nine of the country's most critical substations were knocked out at the same time, it could cause a blackout encompassing most of the United States."

He draws attention to the "Stuxnet worm," developed in concert between the United States and Israel—the first time a digital weapon has been used as an instrument of policy—to infiltrate Iranian nuclear facilities and destroy the necessary centrifuges that make nuclear weaponry possible. In retaliation, Iran responded with a cyber attack on Saudi Arabia and the world's most "valuable" company, the oil firm Aramco. The attackers used a virus to erase data while replacing it with an image of a burning American flag before attacking a Qatari natural gas company and taking several of America's largest banks offline.[4] American officials have recently blamed Iranian hackers for gaining access to secret operational procedures of a New York dam in 2013 as well.[5]

In mapping the range of vulnerabilities, Koppel evaluates the state of the grid through interviews with individuals at the highest levels of government and industry, concluding not only that such an attack is imminent, but pointing out there are virtually no preparedness or contingency plans in place to deal with the aftermath. Any available plan today simply exists to ensure a continuity of governance rather than plan for public needs. Individuals assumedly must get themselves to a location where the grid is still intact, as systems dealing with the distribution of food, water, energy, sewage, medicine, and law and order would almost immediately collapse as supply chains break down and supplies are exhausted in a matter of days. Only the military, Koppel believes, has the capability and credibility to impose order, distribute supplies, establish shelter, and manage millions of domestic refugees.

With this realization, Koppel searches out the "Ark-Builders," touring the prepper and survivalist movements and critiquing their "bug-out plans" as not only limited by their intrinsic selfishness but relying solely on the ability to move to a place where electricity still courses through a working grid. The solutions of the wealthy are equally ill-suited to the threat, depending on reconfigured living spaces or "bug-out properties" that attempt to ensure resource security. These, and even relatively isolated communities in rural areas like Wyoming that would scarcely notice a cyber attack, would be hard-pressed to preserve cultures of self-reliance and civic cooperation in the face of a mass migration that would swarm and deplete food sources. He goes on to predict that if cities break down before rural areas, a close-knit community and values of "neighborliness" would likely collapse if an urban exodus meant sheltering a highly diverse group of grid refugees.

For anarcho-primitivists engaged in primal war, the value of this book lies in its ability to lay out in detail what battle spaces have opened up, albeit through an historically superficial lens whose conclusions only serve to further dependence on the state and industry to protect the cyber-flow of digital capital. Anti-civilization activists like Kevin Tucker and Ted Kaczynski have already hinted at the possibilities cyberwarfare and hacktivism might play in dismantling civilizing forces. Tucker replies to the question of whether hacking represents an effective tactic by praising data dumps while at the same time questioning why hackers would delay taking down the grid if they could in fact do so.[6] Kaczynski also wonders whether a single individual or small group could exert a powerful influence that outweighs that of large organizations to affect millions of people via the internet, reflecting on the actions of a Julian Assange and the role such technologically literate individuals might play in reshaping the political landscape. Even Derrick Jensen makes inroads into a plausible strategy of cyberattack in Endgame: Resistance with his all but fabricated conversations with hackers and ex-military personnel who fantasize together about the ease with which they could destroy the nuts and bolts of the physical economy (yet stopping short of doing much of anything at all).[7]

Clearly unfamiliar with such anti-civ literature, Koppel proposes the only reason why a major attack on the grid has not yet happened is because the motivation to do so simply does not exist in any meaningful way.

Such an attack would require opportunity, capability, and motivation, and Koppel proposes that while governments like Russia and China are already in the grid, mapping the infrastructure so as to "prepare the battlefield" once the need to attack is apparent, the financial repercussions make it illogical for a national economy so intricately tied to the success of the United States to warrant such an attack. Countries like Syria, Iran, and North Korea with deeper motivations are closing in on the technology but may fear the repercussions, while the only hindrance for a non-state terrorist network is simply a lack of capability. Still, a well-funded extremist group like the Islamic State, professing their willingness to do as much damage as possible, would seemingly have no qualms about such an attack (indeed they are already actively trying)—a possibility resting solely on their ability to find an able partner to pay enough to make it worth their while.[8] Still, the near impossible task of identifying the source of any such attack means other governments might blame "unstable" actors to shield themselves from accountability if ever they were to decide to hit where it hurts.

What is fascinating about Koppel's investigation is that, even with the threat of cyberwarfare and physical attacks on infrastructure through coordinated strikes to cause cascading outages, the author shows how the private companies in charge of protecting the grid are loathe to make significant security investments, and are in fact pressuring governments charged with protecting critical infrastructure to deregulate the power industry. As one politician explains, private power companies "were afraid of having to spend money that they couldn't prove to themselves they would actually need to spend." Adding to these capitalist pressures, America has outsourced most production of the vital physical components it would need to replace in an attack, so that transporting transformers through a downed grid would be unrealistic in any timely way. Moreover, due to the sheer unfathomable consequences of such actions, no business plan in the world is capable, let alone willing, of insuring against the threat.

Salvation for Koppel comes in the image of the highly disciplined, hierarchical organization of the Mormon Church, a religious community encouraged to prepare for disaster as both a matter of religious doctrine and historical precedent. While failing to mention anything about indigenous groups (living without electricity for their entire histories prior to being) slaughtered by these settlers as they secured water sources in the area, the author sees the highly organized powerbase, scale, and incentive to prepare for the unexpected as a masterful display of foresight. Mormon families are encouraged to sustain themselves for up to a year by storing supplies, with mandatory tithes providing and adding to Church funds that in turn support an elaborate, widespread structural pattern of social organization (bishops, counselors, presidents, quorums, etc.) with precise systems of communication and oversight, each developing their own emergency plans, an intricate administration that functions to manage a parallel economy. The Mormons, it appears, are well suited for social breakdown, with an independently subsidized welfare infrastructure that includes a sprawling network of stores, generators, tanks of fuel, farms, ranches, orchards, canneries, silos, storehouses, tens of thousands of irrigated acres, processing plants, and a national distribution and delivery system to supply their own needs, able to sell any remainder of produce on whatever market is left intact. Says one church leader, "In the event of a massive crisis, everything could be consolidated to provide resources for the church and its members."

Koppel's "solutions" follow the recognition that individual, communal, regional, and even international contingency plans are relatively short-sighted and generally unworkable in the face of mass panic, theft, and violence. In turn, he points to the newly minted mission statements of private security firms seeking to capitalize on the shortcomings of the state by alerting energy companies to unauthorized parties while monitoring intrusions through increasingly robust cybersecurity systems. He goes on to suggest small, modular reactors that would allow energy independence for military bases that could in turn enter into cooperative agreements with local communities to share surplus energy when the grid does go down, while at the same time building political will to develop mass national recovery programs and pass cybersecurity bills to defend U.S. military and industrial systems, for instance the "Energy Policy Modernization Act" (2015) which grants the energy secretary control of the nation's power grid in the event of a cyberattack and allocates hundreds of millions of dollars to research, development, and training to protect the grid. Moreover, he alludes to the growing realization that cyber attacks—and the oft-cited potential for a "cyber Pearl Harbor"—ultimately amount to an act of war, so that mutual assured destruction might be enough to dissuade any substantial military-grade attack.

Here, the search for guidance in a post-electric age comes full circle into even more dependence on "cyber-security" to preserve industrial civilization and the domesticated worldview and culture that provokes this crisis in the first place. The irony of course is that the internet developed as a decentralized information-sharing defense technology before the global economy overlaid its "smart grids" onto this framework, forcing its custodians to close off access to a technology designed from the beginning to be remotely accessible. The "internet-of-things," then, has morphed into a full-fledged weapons system against its users, rendering the global techno-superstructure of international capital susceptible by definition to hackers anywhere who would choose to exploit virtually any vulnerability with as little as a laptop.

Still, the book provides a few conclusions worth repeating. Koppel's contribution, besides mapping vulnerabilities and pointing out the various failings of different survival proposals, is in articulating the need for a strategy that necessarily stems from a radical shift in mindset. Good people everywhere are open to suggestions and willing to voluntarily work in solidarity for a shared purpose, so that the potential for social transformation is only one hard realization away. The book therefore leaves the reader with one resource perhaps more worthwhile than any other:

Hope.

Such hope exists in the recognition that the possibility of grid collapse may happen simply because it can, the aftermath prompting the immediate conditions needed for rewilding to begin in the absence of those institutions and systems that have tamed wildness for too long. And while the systemic thirst for profit comes at the expense of ecological and cultural resiliency, that same process has brought these systems closer to their own death knell than ever before. The torturous truth of this reality is evident in headlines of poisoned water and communities, mutated animals, and the increasing absence of life and habitat we once knew. The violence of the grid then represents something greater than itself—the willingness to forsake those it depends on it for its own efficient propagation—a suicidal impetus. Koppel has then put on display civilization's Achilles heel, its vulnerability open for exploitation. The entire system can be used against itself.

Our culture has evolved to mirror our languages and one can see the effects of how even computer languages have massively reconfigured this culture to the leviathan it has become today. In this regard, a virus predicated on a few lines of code that reflect such feral sentiment can throw this culture back into anarchy once more, leaving space for those birds and coyotes whose lives are endlessly encroached upon and destroyed on a daily basis.[9]

But perhaps even without this code we can have hope.

As I finish this writing, a 24-hour gale warning is in effect and three large branches have already fallen outside my home. A local electric company leaves a message telling me the area is experiencing a power outage affecting upwards of 2,500 people. Perhaps nearby a power line has been blown down, El Nino's whispers to a land thirsting for insurgent action, hoping its greatest desire will be realized. As temperatures rise and people look to their air conditioners for solace; as historic blizzards subsume areas and thermostats are cranked to blast heat; as the earth rises up screaming out for relief, perhaps the delicate equilibrium of the supply and demand of energy that Koppel has traced will be thrown out of balance. And maybe, at that moment, a squirrel's well timed attack on the grid can answer that call.

Already, 623 power disruptions have been provoked by squirrels, 214 by birds, 52 by raccoons, 47 by snakes, 25 by rats, 9 by beavers, with slugs and other critters attacking the grid every few days, though the exact total is assuredly much higher.[10] Indeed, if only one blackout to date has been attributed to hackers, it seems more likely to put our hope in wild life before the techno-elite anyway. It is these creatures who are putting their bodies on the line because it is in their nature to do so, consciously or otherwise, acting on the plan this traumatized and deeply wounded world crafts in response. We should be so bold as the squirrel that lost its life in 1987, who shut down the energy supply to the Nasdaq exchange to disrupt upwards of 20,000 shares of stock from being traded.[11] Already, we can see the systems that domesticate us have only generated the conditions in which human and nonhuman forces are together fighting back, comrades in a primal war.

Endnotes

1 "Inside the Cunning, Unprecedented Hack of Ukraine's Power Grid" Wired.com. Web. Accessed 11. March 2016.

2 "Canada Discovers It's Under Attack by Dozens of State-Sponsored Hackers VICE News." *VICE News* Web. Accessed 03 Feb. 2016.

3 "Assault on California Power Station Raises Alarm on Potential for Terrorism." *WSJ*. Web. Accessed 03 Feb. 2016.

4 "In Cyberattack on Saudi Firm, U.S. Sees Iran Firing Back." *The New York Times*. Web. Accessed 03 Feb. 2016.

5 U.S. To Blame Iran For Hack Of Small New York Dam: Huffingtonpost.com. Web. Accessed 11 March. 2016.

6 "Interview with Anarcho-primitivist Kevin Tucker." *The Fifth Column*. Web. Accessed 03 Feb. 2016.

7 Jensen, Derrick (2006) Endgame, Vol. 2: Resistance. Seven Stories Press: New York, NY.

8 "ISIS Is Attacking the U.S. Energy Grid (and Failing)." CNNMoney. *Cable News Network*, Web. Accessed 03 Feb. 2016.

9 With the so-called "Aurora generator test," the US government demonstrated how hackers could remotely destroy a power generator with only 21 lines of code, which could cause widespread outages and possibly cascading failure of the entire power grid.

10 "A Terrifying and Hilarious Map of Squirrel Attacks on the U.S. Power Grid." *Washington Post*. Web. Accessed 03 Feb 2016.

11 "Stray Squirrel Shuts Down Nasdaq System." *The New York Times*. 09 Dec. 1987. Web. Accessed 03 Feb. 2016.

Submissions for *Black and Green Review* no 4:
Deadline: August 15, 2016.
Please email all submissions, suggestions, letters, thoughts, hate mail, and anything else to blackandgreenreview@gmail.com